DEC _ 1 2010ๅ

"David Lynch's book is an amazing story of rampaging greed, dirty doings and even adulterous sex . . . Old Mother Ireland doffs her peasant's garb and emerges as a provocative siren, infecting the Irish with diseased materialism. Along with a concise history of Ireland, Lynch makes even economics funny and fascinating."

—Malachy McCourt

"A brilliant set of insights into the true and completely general nature of 'crony capitalism'. Close connections between politicians, bankers, and property developers brought Ireland great apparent prosperity—while really creating the conditions for a huge and horrible crash. Lynch is optimistic that Ireland can rise again and find a more robust model for growth. Let's hope he is right."

—Simon Johnson, Professor, MIT Sloan School of Management and author of 13 Bankers: The Wall Street Takeover and the Next Financial Meltdown

"David Lynch's book will enrage, enlighten, and sadden you. His superbly written account of what really happened in Ireland during the boom of the Celtic Tiger and the ensuing bust is, to be sure, a story about Ireland. But it is also a cautionary tale for all of us. The next time somebody tells you that the market can only go up, run away and re-read this book!"

—Terry Golway, columnist, The Irish Echo *and author of* So Others Might Live

"Lynch marvelously weaves together politics, history, and religion to explain the incredible economic and social transformation that has swept Ireland over the past three decades and the deep financial crisis that Ireland is grappling with today."

—Kenneth S. Rogoff, Professor of Economics, Harvard University and coauthor of This Time Is Different: Eight Centuries of Financial Folly

"David Lynch has produced a terrific read—a hair-raising gallop through the hills and valleys of modern day finance. After reading this book, you'll never think about Ireland—or global financial markets—in quite the same way."

—David M. Smick, author of The World Is Curved:
Hidden Dangers to the Global Economy

"A tour de force of reportage and analysis. As much social anthropology as economic forensics, it is a cautionary tale of post-colonial success and excess. As cold as the eye he casts upon the land of his forebears is, Lynch retains an unmistakable affection for Ireland and a confidence that it can change, change utterly, for the better."

—Kevin Cullen, columnist and former
Dublin bureau chief, The Boston Globe

WHEN THE LUCK *of* THE IRISH RAN OUT

THE WORLD'S MOST RESILIENT COUNTRY
AND ITS STRUGGLE TO RISE AGAIN

DAVID J. LYNCH

palgrave
macmillan

First published in 2010 by PALGRAVE MACMILLAN® in the United States–a division of St. Martin's Press LLC, 175 Fifth Avenue, New York, NY 10010.

Where this book is distributed in the UK, Europe and the rest of the world, this is by Palgrave Macmillan, a division of Macmillan Publishers Limited, registered in England, company number 785998, of Houndmills, Basingstoke, Hampshire RG21 6XS.

Palgrave Macmillan is the global academic imprint of the above companies and has companies and representatives throughout the world.

Palgrave® and Macmillan® are registered trademarks in the United States, the United Kingdom, Europe and other countries.

ISBN 978–0–230–10273–6

Library of Congress Cataloging-in-Publication Data

Lynch, David (David J.)
   When the luck of the Irish ran out : the world's most resilient country and its struggle to rise again / by David J. Lynch.
      p.   cm.
   Includes bibliographical references.
   ISBN 978–0–230–10273–6 (hbk.)
   1. Ireland—Economic conditions—1949– 2. Ireland—Economic conditions—21st century.   3. Social change—Ireland—History—20th century. 4. Social change—Ireland—History—21st century.   5. Recessions—Ireland—History—21st century.   6. Ireland—Social conditions—1973– I. Title.
HC260.5.L96   2010
330.9417—dc22

                                                                    2010019489

A catalogue record of the book is available from the British Library.

Design by Letra Libre, Inc.

First edition: November 2010

10 9 8 7 6 5 4 3 2 1

Printed in the United States of America.

For my parents,

Jack and Connie,

With profound love and thanks

CONTENTS

INTRODUCTION

"THE BOOM TIMES ARE GETTING MORE BOOMER"

*I*F THERE WAS A PLACE AND TIME THAT SHOWCASED Ireland in all its prosperous Celtic Tiger glory, it was the Galway Races in the summer of 2006. That year, as every year, tens of thousands of people flocked to the horse track outside the city for an annual celebration of thoroughbreds, fashion, and what the Irish call good *craic,* or fun. The extravagant hats worn by female racegoers alone were reason enough to attend the week-long festival: from foot-high, black mesh discs to outlandish feathered golden bows, the annual "most elegant hat" contest was almost as fiercely fought as the action on the turf.

But there also was more serious business conducted amid the festivities, much of it beneath what was perhaps the country's most controversial piece of canvas: the hospitality tent of Ireland's governing party, Fianna Fáil. Entrée could be had for €400 (roughly $500 at then-current exchange rates); tables for 10 went for €4,000. It was a steep cover charge, but the business executives, bankers, and property developers who paid considered it money well spent. For along with enjoying tables groaning beneath plates of salmon and three-layered mousse, they got a chance for a quiet word with Prime Minister Bertie Ahern and members of his cabinet.

Ahern was an enthusiastic sports fan, though his tastes ran more to European football than to the ponies. The 57-year-old politician was at the top of his political game in the summer of 2006, just three months removed from becoming Ireland's second-longest-serving prime minister or *taoiseach* (pronounced *tee-shuck*). Only the legendary Eamon de Valera had served longer. Over three decades, Ahern had risen through the Fianna Fáil ranks as a loyal ally of former prime minister Charles Haughey, earning the nickname "the Teflon Taoiseach" for his ability to float above recurrent questions about his personal finances. Ahern's rise to the summit of Irish politics had even survived a marital separation and the quite public affair he conducted with his long-time partner, Celia Larkin. Such an open dalliance was unheard of in Ireland, where the Catholic Church had long called the shots on public mores. Ahern's success owed something to his talents as an ideological chameleon; he was a politician who proudly called himself a "socialist" while enthusiastically working hand-in-glove with the richest members of the business community. Ahern's unbroken record of political accomplishment had left him dismissive of critics who accused him of holding court in Galway like an Arabian prince. Of the annual fundraising spectacle, he said unapologetically: "We can't run the party without it."[1]

For the common folk, the people Ahern called "average Joe Soaps," the Galway Races may have been about long shots thundering to the finish line. But for those inside the tent, the event was all about the sure thing. Get the nod from the right public official with the power to change some irksome tax or zoning regulation, and your profits would be pretty much guaranteed. What had begun in the 1990s as a genuine export-led economic boom had degenerated in the first years of the new century into a mammoth property bubble, orchestrated by politicians and their allies in the business world. The brazen crony capitalism that now defined Irish commerce was on display at Ballybrit race track. Gathered inside the tent were some of the country's best-known commercial figures, many bearing the stain of controversy: businessman David McKenna, among those later found to have given thousands of dollars to Ahern during the latter's tenure as finance minister; the Bailey brothers, Michael and Tom, already exposed as tax cheats to the tune of $28 million. Even the most prominent jockey in attendance, Kieran Fallon, was facing trial in Britain on charges of conspiring to fix races.[2]

Many of the developers seeking shelter from the bright July sun had something else in common: they shared a genial banker, Sean Fitzpatrick, who had built tiny Anglo Irish Bank into the nation's third-largest counting house, with operations across the water in both the United Kingdom and the United States. As chairman of the board, Fitzpatrick that year was presiding over breakneck growth at Anglo Irish; 2006 ultimately would see record profits for the twenty-first consecutive year and an extraordinary annual increase of almost 50 percent in the bank's lending. Under Fitzpatrick, who'd been chief executive until the end of 2004, the bank grew rapidly by emphasizing what it called a "relationship-based" approach to finance. Anyone who knew the glad-handing, green-eyed Irishman would understand why. His pink silk ties and tailored double-breasted suits betrayed a well-honed appreciation for the good life. As Anglo Irish became synonymous with the Celtic Tiger prosperity, "Seanie" had grown perhaps a touch overly enamored of his own wisdom, publicly opining on government policy with the habitual certitude of the wealthy. Still, even to his critics, Fitzpatrick remained immensely likable, whether on the golf course where he spent so much time or in the corporate boardrooms of Ireland Inc.

As the business and political elite mixed easily that day, sipping chilled wine and pints of black, creamy Guinness, they could be forgiven for a feeling of some satisfaction. Contemporary Ireland was nothing like the nation they had grown up in, the one *The Economist* magazine had memorably lampooned as "in hock, out of work." Now, private helicopters shuttled above the race grounds, bringing the high rollers from the city airport. Once the poor colonial subjects of Her Majesty's empire, the Irish were now richer on a per capita basis than the British. The violence and instability of Northern Ireland, until just a few years ago as permanent a fact of life as the soft summer rain, had been left behind by a historic, U.S.-brokered peace accord. Yes, these truly were good times.

LIVES OF APPALLING POVERTY

It was hard to believe that the well-heeled people mixing in the Fianna Fáil tent were descendants of the cursed race whom Oscar Wilde had cheerfully indicted as "brilliant failures." Indeed, it was only by considering the country's sorry history that the true extent of contemporary Ireland's achievement could be appreciated. For eight hundred years, Ireland's story had been one of almost unbroken impoverishment and national impotence. For eight long centuries, the dirt-poor Irish had been on the losing end of history while other nations rose in turn. The country's lack of industry and wealth was exceeded only by its record of failed nationalist uprisings and bad governance. Forever, or so it seemed, Ireland had been poor, Catholic, and troubled.

At the heart of Ireland's woes was always one thing: land. From the beginning of the British domination of the island, English settlers had seized the property of the Irish, rich and poor alike, consigning many of them to lives of squalor and hardship. In the early 1600s, the British Crown introduced Protestant colonists into the province of Ulster, igniting a national and religious conflict that would smolder for centuries. Under absentee British landlords, Irish tenant farmers throughout the island held no title to their tiny plots of land and could be evicted with little notice. Generations of native Catholics were barred by British law from owning the land they worked.

Even before the potato famine of 1845–1847, "the Great Hunger" that starved or forced into exile 2.5 million people, many of the conquered Irish endured lives of appalling poverty. In the west, more than half the population lived in windowless one-room mud cabins. The inhabitants of these foul shacks usually owned little or no furniture and slept on the floor within feet of their livestock. They farmed tiny, inefficient plots of less than an acre and spent their lives in what one historian called a "desperate competition for land."[3]

That changed in the late nineteenth century after a long period of political agitation and unrest known as the Land War, which gradually led to ownership of farms by the people who worked them. Though by 1910 Ireland still trailed the richest European nations, it produced more per capita than Italy, Sweden, or Finland.[4] Early in the next decade, Irish patriots carved out an independent Free State in the 26 counties of the south. Partition and the resulting civil war did huge damage to the new nation's economy, savaging vital rail links and leaving the island's major factories and shipyards sequestered in the British-ruled north. The government in Dublin, however, concentrated its energies on molding a nationalist identity, not on developing an economy. Newly sovereign Ireland sought self-sufficiency in a largely agricultural economy eventually girded by high tariff walls. Priority was given to reviving the Irish language, not Irish industry. The father of the state, Eamon de Valera, famously defended this approach against claims that it would inevitably lead to a lower standard of living: "You say 'lower' when you ought to say a less costly standard of living. I think it quite possible that a less costly standard of living is desirable and that it would prove, in fact, to be a higher standard of living. I am not satisfied that the standard of living and the mode of living in Western Europe is a right or proper one."[5]

As a rationale for poverty, there could be few more straightforward statements. The results were as predictable as they were dreary. T. K. Whitaker, the legendary civil servant who was born just a few months after the 1916

Easter Rising and lived to see Ireland grow rich, remembers the poverty he glimpsed on childhood visits to his grandmother's home in rural County Clare. "We didn't have running water. We didn't have electricity," he recalled. "It was the oil lamp lit in the evening and there was a special grace [said] for light."[6] Later, even as the ruined economies of war-ravaged Europe rebuilt and modernized, Ireland stagnated.

There was an abortive boom in the 1960s. But long after the British could no longer legitimately be blamed, home-grown errors of mismanagement and profligacy conspired to hold Ireland back. As late as the 1980s, Ireland lagged well behind the rest of Europe, with a staggering one-third of the population living below the poverty line. Incredibly, fewer people held jobs in 1987 than had been working in 1926. Each year, in a dispiriting ritual, the nation's best college graduates fled overseas for the opportunity they could not find at home. Ireland was long on charm and short on almost everything that mattered to a modern economy: roads, telephone lines, jobs. The culture was repressive, nearly theocratic, and chronic violence and instability in the North, which flared into sectarian bloodletting in 1969, only soured the atmosphere further. "We were a Third World country but people were too kind to say it to us," recalls historian Kevin Whelan.[7] Little, it seemed, had changed in a hundred years.

And then, over the span of a decade, everything did. A stagnant economy, freed by bold policies and ample investment imported from the United States, roared into a growth miracle dubbed the Celtic Tiger. The culture, too, long dormant under the censorious hand of the Catholic Church, erupted in a fountain of creativity, ushering onto the global stage the rock band U2, the Riverdance troupe, and the Nobel Prize–winning poet Seamus Heaney. Even the open wound of Northern Ireland healed, thanks to a peace midwived by American diplomats. Suddenly, the Irish, long on the periphery of global affairs, were at the center of everything. The scale of the transformation recalled Yeats's oft-quoted verdict on the Rising: "all changed, changed utterly."

A FORESHADOWING OF DOOM

By the July 2006 running of the Galway Races, prosperity was no longer an unfamiliar state of affairs. Indeed, it was taken for granted, regarded as the way things ought to be in a nation that was now hip, affluent, and quite satisfied with itself. True, there were occasional hints of unease beneath the surface calm. Inflation flared periodically, leading to one of Ahern's more memorable analyses: "It's because the boom times are getting more boomer." Even as the races got underway, the executive board of the International Monetary Fund (IMF) in Washington was putting the finishing touches on its annual assessment of the Irish economy. As usual, the IMF had plenty of praise for Ireland's performance, but this year's report would also warn that a "sharp correction" might lie ahead. No one seemed to take that statement, nor similar cautions from Dublin-based iconoclasts, terribly seriously. After all, earlier in the decade, when the United States sank into recession after the bursting of the Internet bubble and the attacks of September 11, the Irish economy nearly ground to a halt. The head of the Central Bank even said, "The Celtic Tiger phase is now over." But the government responded with new tax breaks that fueled an enormous increase in home building and breathed new life into the decade-old feline. In retrospect, this refusal to accept limits or make hard choices would define the era, suggesting that less had changed than Tiger cheerleaders maintained. Ireland gambled that it could marry an American-style economy with a European society, that somehow the tax rates of Texas would provide the safety net of Sweden. And as the decade wore on, and Ahern and his allies insisted they could pilot their out-of-control economic rocket to an ever less likely soft landing, only a few scolds said the stage was instead being set for catastrophe.

The scolds, it turned out, were correct. Far from being a symbol of Ireland transformed, the cozy dealings inside the Fianna Fáil tent represented a foreshadowing of approaching doom. The incestuous links among Ireland's top politicians, bankers, and property developers would ultimately prove to be a cancer on the Celtic Tiger. Much of the corruption underlying the economic rise occurred behind closed doors. But enough was known about the lavish payments to politicians and the regulatory forbearance they granted their businessmen cronies to have ignited public disapproval—if the public were inclined to disapprove. But while the good times rolled on, few were so inclined. Following disclosures that one prominent businessman had funneled tens of thousands of euros to Ahern during his tenure as finance minister, the taoiseach's public approval ratings had actually gone up. The Irish, it seemed, would always have a weakness for their rogues.

The giant canvas tent, well stocked with food and drink, was a visible symbol of hubris and rot. And within months, as the global economy trembled and Irish home prices began sinking, it became clear just how much had been undermined by allowing the rot to spread for so long. When the first aftershocks from a financial crisis in the United States hit Ireland in 2007, an already weakened economy quickly tumbled into recession. Ireland had prospered by aping American-style capitalism. Now its undoing was triggered by a financial crisis that bore an American pedigree.

Some had always known the good times wouldn't last forever. Others had been happy to pretend that they would. But the way the boom ended, in scandal and regret, bore an uncomfortable resemblance to the way so many mornings after in Ireland had felt. This time, though, people's losses were real, tangible enough to be felt in shrinking paychecks and property values. As the national hangover deepened, and the nation's discredited elites desperately sought to regain their magic touch, the Irish looked back in pride and anger and shame and resolve. Theirs had been an extraordinary quarter-century journey, and it had begun in a very different place from where it ended.

CHAPTER I

FRUGAL COMFORT

*T*HE IRISH, OVER MANY MISERABLE CENTURIES, had endured famine, deprivation, and the British. But by 1984, few contemporary irritations compared to the simple act of completing a telephone call. In Whitegate, a small town in the west, the telephones stopped working on weeknights at 10 p.m. On Sundays, the lines were silent save for a 90-minute window in the morning and two hours at night. A local man named Hugh Weir recalled the time a neighbor had died and two of the dead man's relatives, including a young woman clad only in her nightdress, were forced to run a mile into the night to get help at the local pub.[1]

Making a phone call in Ireland required time, patience, and a bit of luck. Fully one-quarter of the country's telephone exchanges were creaky manual museum pieces; one dated to the nineteenth century.[2] Calls routinely failed to connect or endlessly rang busy. And tens of thousands of Irish men and women could only dream of such frustrations. In Greater Dublin alone, the waiting list for a telephone held forty thousand names. Some residents had already been stewing for two or three years or, in rural areas, even longer.

The state's new telecommunications agency, Telecom Éireann, opened the new year with a splashy ad campaign vowing to clear the waiting list. But the agency's initial achievements seemed unexceptional; it boasted of filling new phone orders in "just eight weeks."[3] When Telecom Éireann's marketers promised that by 1988 Ireland would have the most modern telephone system of its kind anywhere in the world, the claim seemed to the *Irish Times* "rather beyond belief."

Still, the telephone network was positively futuristic compared to the roads. Highways in modern Ireland were all but unknown. The lack of bypass roads skirting town centers meant that motorists journeying between any two major cities—say, Dublin and Cork or Waterford and Galway—had to pick their way through interminable local traffic in dozens of small villages. To travel from a town in the midlands to the capital—a distance of perhaps 75 miles as the crow flies—consumed a soul-crushing four hours, puttering along narrow roads shared by passenger cars, intercity buses, farm tractors, and the occasional horse or sheep.[4] An association of engineers called for a national "rescue program" after finding that more than one-third of the nation's crumbling roads were in a state of structural collapse.[5] Yet even when officials tried to improve matters, they often stumbled. One proposed road designed to slice through the heart of Dublin was known as "the road to God knows where."[6]

During a parliamentary debate over road financing, lawmaker T. J. Fitzpatrick complained that he had traveled to the capital along the Kingscourt–Navan road, which was in "a bad state of repair with potholes and so on over an extensive length of it." Before leaving home, he'd tried to obtain some information from the transport ministry but had been stymied by an all-too-familiar problem. "Due to the breakdown in the telephone system, I was unable to contact the department," Fitzpatrick told the Dáil.[7]

Amid such constraints, it was a wonder the Irish accomplished anything at all. In truth, the woeful physical infrastructure was a visible symbol of a moribund society. Six decades of independence had left Ireland one of the poorest countries in Europe. An embryonic boom in the 1960s had fizzled after the politicians responded to the twin oil shocks of the following decade with an orgy of spending. In just one year, 1979, the government had increased the number of public sector workers by 5 percent and total government salaries by 29 percent. "It was a disaster," the then-taoiseach Garrett Fitzgerald later recalled.[8] In the most recent year alone, the national debt had increased by a staggering 23 percent.[9] Nearly one of every six workers was jobless, and almost one-third of the population was receiving some form of monthly welfare payment.[10] Inflation, which had topped 20 percent earlier in the decade, remained stubbornly in double digits.

As 1984 dawned, a pervasive gloom and lack of opportunity hung over Dublin like a wet blanket. "1983 will be seen to have been perhaps the worst year," Fitzgerald said hopefully, one day before news that the national jobless figure hit an all-time high.[11] It was more than just an inert economy that was responsible for the dreary atmosphere. Ireland was also hamstrung by a cultural stasis, caught between the traditional conservative influence of the Catholic Church and a long-gestating impulse toward modernization. And though it had been several years since terrorist bombers last struck Dublin, the specter of sectarian violence in the North cast a pall over the Republic. Two policemen had been killed before the new year in the rescue of Don Tidey, a supermarket executive who had been kidnapped and held for three weeks by ransom-seeking gunmen of the Irish Republican Army.

The torpor was especially profound in the stagnant rural communities that dotted the countryside. Banagher, a sleepy crossroads village on the banks of the river Shannon, had changed little in the years since independence. The local economy revolved around farming, as it ever had. Children were raised with modest ambitions, advised by their parents to seek out a "good pensionable job" in the traditional anchors of the flat-lining economy: teaching, government, or banking. Many young men survived by harvesting turf from local peat bogs during the summer before going on the dole for the remainder of the year.

Eamon de Valera, the first taoiseach and the father of modern Ireland, had famously recommended for his people a life of "frugal comfort."[12] Four decades later, beneath the tacit endorsement of such minimalism, members of a new generation were agitating for the nation to raise its sights. An urban politician was quietly making himself indispensable to his party's leadership while a schoolteacher nursed dreams of a writing career. A young woman who had recently earned a law degree bristled at the limits society imposed upon her gender. And an aggressive financier laid plans to invigorate a failing bank with a culture of drive and entrepreneurship. None would realize instant success, but all were sowing the seeds of a new Ireland.

FAMILY, FAITH, AND FARM

A farmer's son named Jack Byrne aimed to be among the relative handful to exceed the limits of the possible. In an age when many in rural Ireland took jobs in mills or factories rather than complete secondary school, Byrne had become one of the first from his parish of Lusmagh in 50 years to make it to university. He had studied agricultural science at University College Dublin since farming was all he knew. But it bored him and seemed to offer only the backbreaking life that had so worn down his mother and father. Almost on a lark, he switched to the still-young field of computer science.

Byrne found that he thrived on the detail and iron logic of computer programming. In 1983, he graduated with an honors degree and, at a time when good jobs were as scarce as snowflakes in July, landed a position working for an American software company in Cork. It was a good job, well-paid and offering interesting work. And it promised a more varied life than what he'd known as a boy. One of 13 children, Byrne had experienced a typical upbringing for the era. Life revolved around family, church, and helping on the farm three miles outside Banagher in County Offaly, smack in the middle of Ireland. At 150 acres, the Byrne farm was one of the larger operations in the area, raising beef and dairy cattle and growing cereal grains. Life was comfortable, if unadorned. "As a kid, I never went to Banagher. There was no such thing as going to the sweet shop. There was no such thing as buying candy or Cokes or Fanta or any of that stuff. It just wasn't done," he recalled.

With so many children in the house, birthdays passed without notice. But each child's First Communion and Confirmation were occasions for a family feast of goose or duck and plenty of apple pie. It was a simple life. "I'd knock on the door and say, 'Is my friend coming out?' And we'd go off skipping through the fields," he remembered years later. "Who'd know what we'd wind up doing and nobody would ever say, 'Where are you going?' or, 'What time will you be back?'"

Banagher was a great place to live, but a great place to leave, too. For anyone with intelligence, drive, and ambition, there was little opportunity. Somehow, without ever directly saying so, Byrne's mother imbued her children with the notion that it was necessary to leave to thrive. Eight of the 13 Byrnes would eventually go abroad. "We just grew up knowing we weren't going to stay there," said Byrne.

Among University College Dublin's two dozen computer science graduates in 1983, all but two had to leave Ireland to find work, a slight improvement over the previous year when the entire graduating class had been forced into occupational exile. During the spring recruitment season that year, no Irish companies even bothered to appear at the college. Byrne was one of the two graduates lucky enough to find good jobs at home, in his case writing software for an early forerunner of e-mail called "teletext." His employer, CPT Corporation of Minneapolis–St. Paul, was part of a burgeoning American high-tech colony in Ireland, which included better-known companies such as Apple Computer and Digital Equipment Corporation.

In October 1983, Byrne moved to Cork. After a bone-jarring six-hour journey in the family's Hillman Hunter sedan, he arrived in time to witness the fallout from the closure of an iconic Ford Motor Company assembly plant that had operated since 1917.[13] Romantics believed Henry Ford had chosen Cork for the plant in honor of his maternal grandfather, who had emigrated to the United States from West Cork. But the factory, which opened with the Model T and was once the world's largest tractor plant, owed its existence to the protectionist policies Ireland followed from the 1930s until it joined the European Economic Community in 1973.[14] Ireland's decision to embrace open trade ultimately doomed the Ford plant and its eight hundred workers.

Cork was Ireland's second city. But the economy there was no better than anywhere else, and the city's diversions were few. "When I moved to Cork, there was something like 17 percent unemployment. . . . And even when people were employed, you had nothing," Byrne says. "Nobody had a new car. Nobody had clothes like what we have now. Nobody went to restaurants." Stores closed at 5 p.m., except on Thursdays when they remained open until 8 p.m. Traditional pubs were the beginning and the end of the city's nightlife.

CPT was solidly profitable, but its revenues were slipping. In May 1986, after five years in Ireland, the company announced it was shuttering its 44,000-square-foot Cork plant and consolidating production at a facility outside Minneapolis. The decision would boost future profits, but at the cost of pink slips for 89 Irish employees.[15] Suddenly, Jack Byrne, like so many other Irish men of his generation, was unemployed.

FROG-MARCHED TO THE FRONT PEW

The Ireland of the 1980s was smack in the middle of its own great depression. Fewer people were working than in 1926 while the output of goods and services was running more than 15 percent below the economy's long-run potential.[16] Almost everywhere but Ireland, it seemed, prosperity reigned. The United States had recovered from the deep recession of the early 1980s and was enjoying a full-throated boom. Presiding over the resurgent super-power, Ronald Reagan would campaign for re-election in November on a slogan of "Morning Again in America." In the United Kingdom, Prime Minister Margaret Thatcher had breathed life into the remnants of empire with her uncompromising brand of capitalism. Europe, too, was growing. Among developed countries, Ireland seemed uniquely hobbled. In truth, the country had been an economic disappointment since the 1922 founding of the state. Where once the nation's problems could be blamed on colonial oppression, they now were squarely Ireland's own. Something fundamental seemed lacking in the Irish, hamstrung by what the cultural critic Declan Kiberd labeled a "psychology of self-doubt and dependency."[17]

Ireland's political class was proving itself singularly ill-suited to the challenge of righting the economic ship. Neither of the two main parties—Fianna Fáil and Fine Gael—could muster a popular consensus. Unlike a typical European state, Ireland's modern political lineup reflected the legacy of its civil war rather than traditional left-right differences. Fine Gael had accepted partition and the establishment of the Irish Free State while Fianna Fáil struck a more aggressively nationalist stance. The competing political camps were thus more like tribes than ideologically oriented political groupings. As governments rose and fell, beleaguered Irish voters endured three general elections in the space of 18 months. Amid such political turmoil, it was impossible to enact the reforms needed to get the country's runaway borrowing under control. By 1986, government debt had exploded to the banana republic level of 130 percent of GDP. High debt and a reluctance to cut social spending locked Ireland into a tax trap—the top income tax rate hit 65 percent and the standard corporate levy was 50 percent.[18] A toxic brew of taxes and debt was poisoning the economy.

For more than a century, those with ambition had relied upon a straight-forward solution to Ireland's lack of opportunity: They left. By 1911, one-third of all people born in Ireland lived outside the country.[19] In the nineteenth century, impoverished farmers fleeing famine and rapacious land-lords had made up the bulk of the exodus. But now, the country's best-educated sons and daughters were leaving, steadily hollowing out Ireland's future. In Boston alone, there were more than 70,000 Irish men and women under the age of 25.[20]

Among the exiles was Linda O'Shea, one of eight children raised by a pair of civil servants in Limerick. Linda's mother, Kathleen, was born in New York, the same month as the stock market crash of 1929. Kathleen was three years old when her parents moved the family back to Carrick-on-Suir in southeastern Tipperary, where Kathleen grew up. She married Gerard O'Shea in 1950, and both found good jobs with the Post and Telegraph Office in Limerick, a gritty unsentimental city. It was an era when the most mundane civil service position carried a patriotic gloss; working for the government was synonymous with building independent Ireland. But that all ended for Kathleen when she was still in her twenties: as a matter of law, she was required to quit the civil service upon marriage. It was not something the smart, outspoken woman ever forgot, nor let her five daughters forget.

Linda O'Shea grew up in an unusual household. At a time when most people in Ireland were orthodox Catholics and staunchly Fianna Fáil, her parents were neither. The O'Sheas encouraged their children to think for themselves and to question received wisdom, whether it originated with a priest or a politician. Gerard was a student of history and an enthusiastic reader, especially of the Bible. He would end each day on his knees in prayer, yet he enjoyed arguing with visiting priests about history and religion. In other homes, priests would be received as visiting royalty. At the O'Sheas', they were just another pugilist in an intellectual slugfest.

O'Shea's mother was a bit of a dreamer, entertaining vague notions in her youth of being a war correspondent. Fiercely independent, she was a religious believer, but was utterly unimpressed by the intricate, man-made rituals of the institutional church. Even the nuns' legendary knuckle-rapping power failed to intimidate her. Believing one sister had been too harsh on a classmate, she once hurled her Latin book at the nun, dislodging her veil and blackening an eye. As a grown woman, Kathleen saw contradictions in the catechism everywhere she looked. Catholic women were taught they had to accept all the children God gave them, for example, and that procreation was the purpose of sexual relations. Yet the act of giving birth somehow made them unclean. "Woman had to be 'churched' after they had children. . . . Once you gave birth you had to be cleansed. Of what sin, we're not sure. This is as a married woman, now!" said her daughter. "You had to be cleansed before you could receive communion again. This kind of stuff didn't really go down well with my mother."

Others saw the liberalizing reforms of Vatican II (1962–1965) as a welcome step toward drawing the church closer to the laity. But to Linda's mother, it seemed hypocritical for Rome to have amended strictures that it had always described as immutable divine laws. In her view, the church couldn't have it both ways. Either the priests were taking it upon themselves to rewrite God's rule book or it had all been a fraud from the beginning. Linda's father was less troubled. "He wasn't as affected; he was a man. The church usually messed around with women's rights more than anything to do with men," O'Shea said.

For years, O'Shea's mother swallowed her objections and took the family to Mass for the same reason many Catholics did: it was the respectable thing to do. Ireland had the highest percentage of routine Mass attendance in the developed world. But religious observance often was like much of Irish life, a societal conspiracy of pretense. Full pews didn't make the Irish more devout or less likely to sin than anyone else. After the controversial reforms of Vatican II, the herd instinct lost some of its force for the O'Sheas, and the family's attendance at Mass became less regular. "Some of us would go to Mass and some of us wouldn't. . . . But there was none of that being frog-marched up to the front pew," Linda says.

Education was the O'Sheas' priority. Linda's mother seemed to feel that her sons needed no special push, that as men they would do fine. But for the girls, she was determined to ensure the best possible intellectual grounding. Linda brought to the classroom her mother's questioning stance, once challenging the nuns on a fundamental church tenet. If prayer was to be encouraged as a direct conversation with God, she asked, then why was prayer the standard punishment or penance when one transgressed? "We were not standard-issue children. We came with lots of questions. They were awfully good questions, probably questions the nuns hadn't been asked and wouldn't be able to answer. But they seemed cheeky. Like we were causing trouble," she said.

As Linda prepared to take the qualifying examination required of all graduating high school students, her father suffered another in a series of heart attacks and died. "I was just so grief-stricken . . . it was a nightmare, a total nightmare," she says. Instead of studying law at the country's premier university, Trinity College in faraway Dublin, she transferred to University College Cork. After graduating, she qualified as an attorney and then, with little to hold her back, decided to head where the opportunities for women looked a bit brighter. In March 1985, O'Shea emigrated to the United States, joining her boyfriend, Brian Farren, and leaving behind a country stuck in neutral amid a fast-changing world.

DEAD BABIES, LIVING STATUES

If the economy was stagnating, society, too, seemed stuck. Reflecting the values of the Catholic Church, Irish law banned contraception and abortion and prescribed penal servitude for those convicted of homosexual acts. In 1984, reports that the government was drawing up legislation to allow the sale of condoms in supermarkets and newsstands ignited a furor. In January, Bishop Kevin McNamara of County Kerry warned of "gravely harmful consequences" if such a step were taken.[21] The longstanding prohibition on access to birth control devices considered routine elsewhere in Europe or the United States was more than theoretical. One month earlier, Dr. Andrew Rynne, a general practitioner in County Kildare, had been placed on probation after his arrest for "illegally supplying condoms to a patient."[22]

Forces of tradition and modernization were joined in silent combat. Memories were still fresh of the summer of 1979, when Pope John Paul II had visited Ireland in what seemed at the time to be a triumphant reaffirmation of the faith. More than 1.2 million people witnessed the pontiff celebrate Mass in the open air of Dublin's Phoenix Park beneath a cross that reached 120 feet into the sky; an additional 300,000 welcomed him at Galway's Ballybrit Raceway with an ovation that lasted for 14 minutes. It seemed a victory for old Ireland, where the church had enjoyed an iron grip on society. From the founding of the state, the bishops had controlled state-financed education, dictated social priorities, censored books and movies, and specified the boundaries beyond which no good Catholic—indeed, no respectable Irish person—could stray. Some of it, in retrospect, seemed ripe for parody: in the late 1940s, the powerful archbishop of Dublin, John Charles McQuaid, barred the sale of vaginal tampons, fearing their implications for Irish virgins.[23] Yet through the 1970s, the church maintained an unquestioned hold on Irish life. More than 90 percent of people attended Mass every Sunday and two-thirds of the Irish said they had no trouble at all with any church teaching.[24]

There were costs, of course, to such unquestioning devotion, even if few were yet prepared to discuss them openly. Society had not yet been compelled to confront the collateral damage from a culture caught between past and future—not until January 31, 1984, when a 15-year-old girl named Ann Lovett walked into the grotto behind St. Mary's Church in Granard, County Longford, lay down on the ground and went into labor. A student at Our Lady of Mercy convent school, she was alone, carrying only her red schoolbag and a pair of scissors. Her infant son was stillborn and lying beside her on the wet, cold earth when she was found unconscious a few hours later in the rain.

Later that night at the local hospital, she died of exposure and blood loss. Lovett was the oldest girl in her family and one of nine children. Some said she had managed to hide her increasing girth beneath loose-fitting blouses and oversized jackets. Others said people knew she was pregnant, but remained silent while her family ignored the obvious. Her death came just four months after Ireland had added a ban on abortion to the constitution using language critics said elevated the rights of the fetus above those of the mother.[25]

In the weeks after the story broke, Ann Lovett's death became a national sensation. Gay Byrne, the host of Ireland's most popular radio show, was inundated with thousands of letters from Irish women of all ages, describing their own secrets. Read aloud during an extraordinary two-hour program, they unleashed on listeners a veritable epidemic of rape, infanticide, hidden births, and clandestine burials.[26] The Lovett case might have left no lasting impact, however, were it not for the separate storm that broke three months later in the country's southwest. On April 15, Jack Griffin, a farmer in Caherciveen, County Kerry, was taking an evening jog along the beach when he spotted what he thought was a doll lying on the shore. Drawing closer, he discovered the body of an infant boy, wedged face down between two rocks. The baby's neck was broken, its body riddled with more than two dozen stab wounds.[27] Investigators later determined he had lived for perhaps a day before being murdered and dropped into the sea, possibly wrapped in a plastic bag found a few feet away. Sgt. Patrick Reidy, the policeman who came to the scene, baptized the infant before removing the body.[28]

Incredibly, at almost the same moment 50 miles to the northeast, another individual drama was unfolding in the village of Abbeydorney. Three days earlier, Joanne Hayes, 25, an unmarried mother who'd been having an affair with Jeremiah Locke, a married coworker, had given birth to a son. The baby died soon after birth, in disputed circumstances. What was not disputed, however, is that Hayes put her son's body into a plastic bag from O'Connell's Pharmacy, stepped outside the family home and walked about two hundred yards across a field. Reaching a gate, she placed the bag holding her infant's remains into a watery hole.[29]

This human tragedy was compounded by an inept official response that some critics said underscored the hypocrisies of a society that punished women, but not men, for violating traditional Catholic precepts. Detectives investigating the death of the unidentified Caherciveen baby fanned out across Kerry looking for women who betrayed evidence of having recently given birth, yet had no babies. Eventually, they came to the Hayes family. A medical exam showed that Joanne Hayes, despite her denials, had given birth. Under persistent and unusual interrogation—Hayes at one point was perched on a detective's knee—she eventually confessed to killing her baby and told detectives what she had done with its body. But the police, already in possession of the Caherciveen baby's corpse, did not believe her. When the Hayes baby's remains were later found, the authorities effectively had one more dead baby on their hands than they could explain. So they hit upon a fantastic theory: that Hayes had become pregnant with twins by two different fathers. Even after blood tests proved conclusively that neither Hayes nor Locke could have been the parents of the Caherciveen baby, the police persisted in their bizarre supposition. The prosecutor, taking a more sensible view of the evidence, dropped all charges in October.

By then, what was being called the "Kerry Babies" case had become a cause célèbre combining sex, murder, adultery, and society's treatment of women. Amid a public storm, the government established a tribunal of inquiry under Justice Kevin Lynch to investigate the police handling of the case. Following an official probe in which every participant save a laboratory technician was male, the tribunal turned into what was seen in some circles as a sexist witch hunt. The inquiry delved into Hayes's sex life, her use of contraception, and local morals while giving blatant police misconduct a pass.[30] "Our culture is still saturated with an anti-woman bias. The conduct of the Kerry Babies Tribunal illustrates this very well," wrote Vincent Browne, one of the nation's leading journalists. "It would be unthinkable for a man to have been put through the ordeal that Joanne Hayes was subjected to."[31] One of Hayes's coworkers, a cleaner named Peggy Houlihan, for example, was grilled about an evening drink she had with Locke at the local pub while waiting for her husband to arrive. "And you are a married woman??!!" the prosecutor exclaimed.[32] The tribunal's report, issued in October 1985, spent more time castigating the Hayes family as liars than addressing the failures of the investigators.

The twinned cases of Ann Lovett and the Kerry Babies reflected a society struggling to reconcile traditional norms with the reality that had always existed and was now forcing itself to the surface. For as long as there had been Catholics in Ireland, unmarried women had gotten pregnant, men had had affairs, and both had lied about their behavior. What was different now was the wider attention such activities were drawing along with a spreading refusal to engage in the customary pretense. Sociologist Tom Inglis concluded that the tribunal's treatment of Hayes represented a clash between a lingering tradition of repression and a less judgmental Ireland struggling to emerge. "Joanne Hayes was not the classic Irish single mother. She was different. She did not hide away or give up the baby for adoption," Inglis wrote. "She went public."[33]

But the Kerry Babies tribunal overlapped with another extraordinary episode that seemed to demonstrate just how unsettling were the forces buffeting society. On February 14, 1985, seven-year-old Elizabeth Flynn in the village of Asdee reported that a statue of the Sacred Heart in St. Mary's Church had beckoned to her while a figure of the Virgin Mary moved its eyes.[34] Soon, 30 children in the village claimed to have seen the statues in motion. Other sightings quickly followed. Children at the grotto of Our Lady of Boola near Mountmelleray in County Waterford reported that their statue of the Virgin had begun speaking. Her messages ranged from "reserve Sunday for prayer" to "God is angry with the world" and "people must improve and pray." At one point, the statue told some local boys that the world had only ten years to shape up before suffering God's wrath. Within days, the boys were using hand-held mikes to relay the messages to a crowd of thousands via a loudspeaker. Police directed traffic while Red Cross personnel tended to those overcome by emotion or exhaustion.[35]

Then, in mid-July two elderly women said the blue-and-white statue of the Immaculate Conception at a grotto outside tiny Ballinspittle in County Cork had moved. Soon, crowds of thousands descended upon the tiny village, desperate to see the five-foot-tall plaster figure with the electric halo and a tendency to sway, dip, bow, and shimmy. A three-day weekend in August drew thirty thousand visitors, much to the delight of local publicans and tradesmen. Public telephones and toilets were hastily installed to deal with the throngs. Ireland's public bus company began running special tours from Dublin and other cities.

Officially, the clergy took a cautious view. Church leaders were caught between Catholicism's rejection of idolatry and their flock's conviction that what they were seeing was divinely inspired. Scientists from a local university, meanwhile, said the visions were effectively an optical illusion, caused by staring at a stationary object too long in the darkness. Still, the pilgrims kept coming.[36] By the end of September, the grotto in Ballinspittle, which had been largely ignored for 30 years, had drawn a cumulative crowd of 500,000 people.[37] To secular observers, it seemed no accident, however, that the wave of sightings occurred at a time of profound challenges to the social, economic, and religious status quo. In these rural areas, the rainy weather that summer—one of the wettest periods in years—threatened to drown the crops that represented so many livelihoods.[38] Amid such profound stress, it was no surprise that people sought solace in traditional icons. "These things never happen except in poor places like Asdee and Knock," wrote Fintan O'Toole. "Our Lady never appeared in Dublin."[39]

Indeed, she did not. Throughout the year, the Virgin Mary swayed and winked, but only in anonymous, unremarkable hamlets like Ballinspittle and Courtmacsharry and Melleray. By September, the sightings had spread to 30 locations.[40] But the hysteria eventually degenerated into farce. In Ballydesmond on the border of Cork and Kerry, a couple of boys who were inadvertently locked inside a church began banging on the windows to attract passersby. The commotion inevitably ignited another mini-furor,with one witness claiming: "The statues are trying to get out the windows."[41]

Cultural traditionalists recorded a major political victory in a June 1986 referendum on a proposed constitutional amendment allowing divorce. Fine Gael's Garrett Fitzgerald had entered office in 1982, promising to remake Ireland as a pluralist republic that would be equally welcoming to non-Catholics and Catholics alike. A principal motivation involved hopes of an accommodation between the Republic of Ireland and Protestants in troubled Northern Ireland. The Catholic Church's uncompromising stance on mixed marriages, requiring all children resulting from such unions to be raised as Catholics, was seen as one of the major stumbling blocks to better relations between the two communities.[42] With the south becoming more urban and more secular, there was latent support for Fitzgerald's effort. In April, when the referendum plans were made public, the initial polls showed a solid 57 percent in favor of the change.[43] Further, the government's proposal was a conservative one. It would scrap the blanket constitutional ban on divorce in favor of allowing the dissolution of marriages that already had failed for five years, showed no hope of reconciliation, and in which provisions could be made for any children. The official statement from clerical spokesmen was that Catholics were free to vote their consciences. But the church distributed one million copies of a 15-page pastoral letter on marriage and the family while bishops thundered their opposition from the pulpits.[44] The archbishop of Dublin likened the impact of even limited divorce rights upon Irish society to that of the "Chernobyl disaster."[45]

Hard-line Catholics hammered away at the idea that divorce would inevitably lead to societal decay and would put women at risk of losing everything: their homes, pensions, and incomes. Posters proclaiming "You can be forced to divorce" sprang up in rural areas, inflaming fears among farmers' wives.[46] On polling day, four women who said they had been abandoned by their husbands chained themselves to the gates of Leinster House in protest.[47] Fitzgerald belatedly recognized the danger, running election eve ads warning women: "You are being misled."[48] But by then, it was too late. The referendum, once expected to be a signpost pointing the way toward a more inclusive Ireland, was an utter and comprehensive failure: 63 percent of voters reaffirmed the divorce prohibition, leaving countless miserable Irish men and women to ride out hard times in unhappy unions. "Twenty-five percent of people changed their minds because of clever propaganda by right-wing Catholic extremists who persuaded farmers that their wives would divorce them and have half the farm and the wives were persuaded the farmer would throw them out and leave them with nothing," Fitzgerald said. "I didn't handle it as well as I should have, I suppose."[49]

FROM STRENGTH TO STRENGTH TO STRENGTH

The church's role in shaping Irish attitudes also affected the country's economic development. Traditionally, the Irish had an ambiguous relationship with wealth, which was what their British Protestant rulers had and what they chronically lacked. In the seventeenth and eighteenth centuries, explicit discrimination prevented Catholics from holding property, engaging in business, and doing just about anything else that would be needed to prosper. Protestants also saw riches as a kind of immediate feedback from God as to how they were living their lives; Catholics, in contrast, eschewed "materialism [and] commercialism" in favor of a "preoccupation with the next world."[50] By the end of the nineteenth century, prominent voices were arguing that "Irish Catholics were not very good money makers and that there was something hostile to money making in the version of Christianity that had won out in Ireland."[51]

There were those, however, who seemed immune to the Irish curse. A young accountant named Sean Fitzpatrick emerged from Bray, a seaside community in County Wicklow, south of Dublin, and began in the 1980s to make a name for himself in the capital's modest financial services industry. Born on June 21, 1948, he was the son of Michael "Mick" Fitzpatrick of Shankill, County Wicklow, and Joanna Maher of Tipperary. His father operated a small dairy farm in Greystones during Fitzpatrick's youth. Mick Fitzpatrick was a hard-drinking, sociable man who liked sports. Johanna Fitzpatrick was "full of ambition for her family . . . the driving force" in her children's lives.[52]

In the 1950s and 1960s, the family resided in an unexceptional semi-detached house in a lower-middle-class part of Bray. The Fitzpatricks didn't own a car, so going to Dublin, 15 miles away, was a major trip. The family wasn't poor, but like many others of the time, enjoyed no luxuries. "There was no wealth. I didn't know anyone that was really, really rich [but] there was no huge poverty. . . . I never went on a family holiday as a child. We just didn't do that," Fitzpatrick says. "There was never any spare money around."[53]

Mick Fitzpatrick was a hard worker, but he fell into debt to a local bank and was unable to make his payments. From the age of 14, Sean earned his spending money working various jobs, starting as a water boy in a pub called the Silver Tassie. When he was 16, his mother organized a trip to France where he worked for two months washing glasses in French bars. He arrived in Paris the day before Bastille Day with no plans and just 10 Irish pounds, rang a local monastery, and was taken in for the night. When the money ran out, his mother mailed him four Irish pound notes carefully folded into a letter. Fitzpatrick's first experience with foreign exchange involved taking the notes to a local banker, who matched them against sample banknotes in a ledger before converting them into French francs.

Savvy rather than smart, Fitzpatrick was an unexceptional student, academically overshadowed by his sister Joyce. "I wasn't thick. I wasn't stupid but I certainly wasn't in the upper quartile," he said.[54] He had an unmistakable self-confidence, no doubt derived from his exploits on the rugby field, where he captained the school team. His sense of humor and conviviality mirrored his father's. During his final year at University College Dublin, various professionals visited to give the graduating seniors a sense of their career options. Fitzpatrick knew he'd found his niche after a simple sales pitch from the local chartered accountant who said: "If you want to make money, this is the place to go."[55] Still, he failed his first try at the exam to qualify as a chartered accountant, leaving Johanna Fitzpatrick to brood in silent disappointment. When he passed on the second try, the 24-year-old and his mother celebrated by attending 8 a.m. Mass.

After getting married in 1974, he and his wife, Triona, were turned down by their local building society when they applied for a mortgage. Shortly thereafter, Fitzpatrick saw a help-wanted ad placed by a merchant bank called the Irish Bank of Commerce (IBC), which was seeking an accountant. Along with the $8,800 salary came a home loan. "I said, Jesus, that's the job I want! So I went for the job and I got it," he said. "That's how I ended up in banking. That's the only reason why I ended up in banking."[56]

Irish Bank of Commerce was a tiny institution with perhaps two dozen employees. Its banking license was a legacy of a cooperative venture by Irish tea importers in the early 1950s, who pooled their deposits to circumvent trade quotas on imported tea from India and Pakistan. The bank was owned by a small retail lender, City of Dublin Bank, which specialized in consumer loans for televisions and automobiles. When a second consumer lender, Anglo Irish Bank, ran into financial trouble, Ireland's Central Bank midwifed an acquisition by City of Dublin.

Fitzpatrick's bosses tasked him with finding a new general manager for Anglo. After a cursory search, the young accountant recommended himself for the job. His boss wasn't convinced until Fitzpatrick made an impassioned appeal: "Look, at school I knew how to buy cigarettes off the guys. I knew how to get my money back from guys. I'm a smart kid, not academically bright, but I'm a smart guy. I could actually do that for you. I could relate to people; I could get business in, I know I could," he said, the words tumbling out.

Impressed, the boss said, "Ok, you're in."[57] And just like that, in 1980 at age 32, Fitzpatrick became general manager of tiny Anglo Irish Bank. It was a grand title, but not much of an empire: the bank had a balance sheet of just $2 million and was effectively bust. The first order of business was carving a path to profitability. Large-scale lending was the province of IBC. Consumer loans belonged to City of Dublin. If Fitzpatrick had any hopes of making something of his tiny fiefdom, he needed a niche. So he proposed having Anglo specialize in midmarket business lending, loans that would be too big for the City of Dublin's mom-and-pop operation and too small to be worth the time of the sophisticates at IBC.

In those early days, Fitzpatrick would drum up business by personally making the rounds of local building sites. He'd talk to contractors, finding out where they got their loans, what they paid for them, and whether they were interested in better terms. "The big thing that we brought into the whole game, and why we got customers, [was]—there was no shit," he said. "If you wanted a loan, you went into Anglo Irish Bank and if they were prepared to give it to you, you got it. And you were told there and then you were going to get it, or the next day. And if you weren't going to get it, you were told, 'no you're not going to get it.' So there was none of this hanging on for a week or two weeks or three weeks waiting. And that was the big thing people wanted: certainty."[58]

Operating from a nondescript basement office on St. Stephen's Green, Anglo in those early days was really just Fitzpatrick and his first major hire, lending officer Peter Killen. The bank's few accounts were kept in two old-fashioned red ledger books, marked A–L and M–Z. When borrowers could-n't or wouldn't pay, there was no bad-debt department to step in. "Collections" involved Fitzpatrick or Killen, sometimes both, hopping in the car and heading out for a visit. When the owner of a North Dublin fish-and-chips shop stopped making his payments, Fitzpatrick and Killen drove across town at midday and got in line. "We would have gotten in the queue until we got to the counter and then we'd say, 'How are you? Hey, listen you never give us any money, lad. We're from the bank.'"

"And we'd have all the people behind us and we'd say, lookit: we want some money. And the guy'd say, well, I have no money and [we'd say] well, for fuck's sake, we've seen nothing but notes goin' in there. We want the money!" Invariably, they'd come out with something, perhaps not the full amount owed, but enough to have established in the borrower's mind the principle that debts owed to Anglo Irish Bank need to be repaid.

By 1984, tiny Anglo was making more money than either IBC or City of Dublin, and Fitzpatrick was starting to wonder why he couldn't move up the ladder. He took his complaint to Gerry Murphy, chief executive of the parent City of Dublin. The next year, Murphy reluctantly agreed to Fitz-patrick's demand to be put on the board of directors, but then four months later withdrew his assent. As a consolation prize, Fitzpatrick got a spot on the board of a small U.K.-based outfit that the bank owned.

Still pushing, Fitzpatrick used the threat of taking another job to finally land a spot on the bank's board. The promotion gave Fitzpatrick his first look at the parent company's internal financials. And he was staggered by their ramshackle condition: "I said, fuckin' hell. This place is fucking, absolute shite, fucking wrecked." Over lunch with Murphy, Fitzpatrick—still the older man's subordinate—pushed for a complete makeover of the institution to include dumping the bank's U.K.-based chairman, Thomas Kenny. Murphy would move up as chairman, leaving the top operational slot for Fitzpatrick. "I was now getting cocky and I was an outsider and I was making money and I could fucking demand a bit more," he says.[59]

Fitzpatrick met with Kenny and laid out the bank's financial weakness. But Kenny balked at the plan, proposing instead to leave Murphy as chief executive with Fitzpatrick as managing director. After Fitzpatrick resisted, Kenny opted to elevate Murphy to the post of executive deputy chairman and promote Fitzpatrick to run a renamed institution called Anglo Irish Bankcorp. Fitzpatrick instantly brought a brashness and proprietarial culture to the staid, straight-laced world of Irish banking. On his watch, Anglo began galloping through the financial markets, raising new capital with seven rights issues over the next six years. "We just fucking murdered them all. Just went from strength to strength to strength," Fitzpatrick said.

The freshly minted bank boss also had some family business to pursue. Years before, his father, exhausted by the nonstop demands of a small dairy farm, had tried to get ahead by selling two acres of land and reinvesting the proceeds in labor-saving machinery: plows, tractors, combine harvesters. Then, he'd borrowed some additional money from a bank, which he failed to pay back. "He borrowed 70 or 80 quid and never paid it. They used to come out to the house every week to get a pound to pay it off," Fitzpatrick recalled.

Mick Fitzpatrick's son now ran that bank and, like most Irishmen, he had a long memory. Soon after becoming chief executive, he dug into the archives and retrieved the ledger card for his father's account. It was littered with derogatory handwritten notations from the collections department—

"He's a bastard. . . . He won't pay etc." Fitzpatrick had it framed alongside a newspaper account of his ascension to the corner office and presented it to his father. He was little more than 38 years old, and he already had managed both to fulfill his mother's rigorous expectations and to avenge his father's humiliation. It was a heady moment, but there was more to come, for both the young banker and his country.

CHAPTER 2

THE MOST IMPORTANT PUB IN IRELAND

UBLIN HAS PUBS THE WAY OTHER CITIES have manhole covers. But in a capital blanketed by watering holes, Doheny & Nesbitt stood apart. The Victorian establishment on Baggot Street was just around the corner from the Dáil, the taoiseach's office, and several government departments, ensuring a steady stream of politicians, journalists, and civil servants passing through its wooden doors. A pub had stood on the site since the 1840s, and when a pair of County Tipperary men, Ned Doheny and Tom Nesbitt, took it over more than a century later, they wisely left untouched the original chocolate-colored bar and nineteenth-century fittings. Others might modernize; Doheny & Nesbitt retained its cozy snugs, with their frosted glass partitions, and its intricate papier-mâché ceiling. By the 1980s, as Ireland sank into a seemingly bottomless abyss, the crowded pub emerged as more than just a place that poured a lovely pint. It became ground zero in a high-stakes debate over the country's future. On any given night, economists like Colm McCarthy, a blunt Dubliner with a reputation for suffering fools not at all; Paul Tansey, the economics editor of the *Irish Times;* and Sean Barrett of Trinity College could be found hoisting glasses of creamy dark Guinness while loudly expounding on the Irish economy's ills.

Wags dubbed them the "Doheny & Nesbitt School of Economics" and for years, while Irish governments spent as if the island's peat bogs held oil wells, their calls for fiscal discipline went largely unheard. In the late 1970s, runaway spending on social benefits drove the national debt to banana republic levels. Almost every dollar of revenue collected in income taxes was siphoned off by interest payments on that debt. Governments in the late 1970s and early 1980s had wrecked the public finances by their response to the twin oil shocks of 1973 and 1979, spending generously in a doomed bid to bolster growth even as soaring oil costs absorbed millions of dollars. The result was a deeply depressed economy: unemployment in 1986 topped 17 percent, and emigration, after a lull in the 1970s, returned with a vengeance. By mid-decade, the country was suffering a net annual loss of more than 31,000 people, the highest in 20 years.[1] And unlike in the nineteenth century, when it was the least skilled and least financially secure people who were driven abroad, Ireland now was losing its best-educated youth. Entire university classes were emigrating en masse, stripping the land of its hope for a better future. The bishop of Killala worried publicly that half of the nation's 15- to 29-year-olds might be forced to leave the country.[2] The departures were as sudden as death. One day, people were here; the next, they were gone without even the melancholy "American wakes" that their nineteenth-century predecessors had enjoyed. Kerry's popular Gaelic football team, for example, saw its chances in a critical match dim when goalkeeper Tom Lynch unexpectedly emigrated to Australia less than a week before kickoff.[3]

Circumstances were so dire there was talk that, if Ireland couldn't solve its own problems, the International Monetary Fund would impose a solution and thus make explicit what many were coming to suspect: Irish independence had failed. Worse, there was little expectation that the situation would improve. The eminent Irish historian Joseph Lee wrote that in the continued absence of sound policymaking, only a "sheer accident" might spark an economic transformation. "It is difficult to avoid the conclusion that Irish economic performance has been the least impressive in western Europe, perhaps in all Europe, in the twentieth century," he concluded soberly.[4]

Irish voters got an opportunity to pass judgment on this mess in February 1987, after the collapse of the four-year-old coalition government of Fine Gael and Labour. Predictably, the government fell when Labour balked at the public spending cuts planned by its coalition partner, preferring higher taxes instead. But with income tax rates already at 65 percent, that idea drew no support outside Labour Party circles. Over the ensuing four-week campaign, Fianna Fáil and its leader Charles Haughey lashed Fine Gael over the likely consequences of its spending reductions. Fianna Fáil billboards warned voters of the coming cataclysm, especially for the health service, if the government were returned to power: "Health cuts hurt the old, the poor and the handicapped." The financial chores that awaited a new Irish government were so confounding that visiting American correspondents wondered why anyone would want the job.[5]

In north Dublin, a young politician named Bertie Ahern was deep into his fifth general election campaign. Unlike the titans of the dynastic Fianna Fáil party, Ahern claimed no political lineage of note. His father wasn't a former minister or member of parliament, just the latest in a long line of farmers. With his tousled hair curling past the ears, and a slightly disheveled look, the likeable Ahern seemed to personify the common man. He had risen politically via community sports groups, which provided an outlet for his natural organizational and leadership skills. First elected to the Dáil in 1977, Ahern—known as "anorak man" for the hooded jacket that was his standard garb—quickly carved a career as a parliamentary fixer, becoming Haughey's chief whip during the Fianna Fáil government of 1981–1982. In opposition, he served as the party's spokesman on Labour issues. The assignment put him in line for a cabinet post whenever Haughey returned to government, and it afforded Ahern a chance to study mediation and labor policy in innovative countries such as Sweden and Austria. "Unemployment in the inner cities, in part of my area, 40–50%; nationally, 20%. . . . So it was a very bleak period. And there was that sense, by successive governments from 1980 on, that we were never going to get out of it," Ahern said.[6]

The morning after election day, voters awoke to headlines touting an apparent Fianna Fáil win, albeit one that would require the support of smaller parties to form a government. Haughey, the once and future taoiseach, was "disappointed" by his failure to secure an outright majority, especially in the wake of party operatives' confident projections of a "landslide" at the campaign's outset. But if Haughey, a crafty player who combined the leadership of a born politician with the ethics of a mob boss, was surprised, it was nothing compared with the voters' disbelief when Fianna Fáil unveiled its budget. On Tuesday, March 31, Ray MacSharry, the new finance minister, reading a text with key passages underlined in green ink, gave the new Dáil a blunt assessment. "People are dispirited because the economy has been on a downward path. There have been too many failures, too many missed opportunities and a prevailing lack of confidence in our ability to achieve progress. . . . It is evident that conditions are extremely difficult and that there is no room at all for soft options," said the new finance minister, his hands shaking slightly.[7]

It would have been difficult for anyone in the octagonal chamber to argue. The picture MacSharry sketched—of an economy producing fewer goods and services than it had in 1980 along with falling employment and investment—was familiar to all. But the remedy he recommended looked nothing like the sacrifice-free prescription his party had just campaigned on. Instead, it looked remarkably like Fine Gael's draconian belt-tightening, which he and his colleagues had just spent several weeks maligning, a fact that did not go unnoticed. "I have great pleasure today in welcoming Fianna Fáil's acceptance of the Fine Gael analysis of the problem and of the targets which we have set down. This is grand larceny of our policy as put before the electorate," said Fine Gael's Michael Noonan, the benches around him erupting with cries of "Hear! Hear!"[8]

MacSharry's budget, in fact, went beyond the cuts Fine Gael had planned. The previous year, the gap between the amount of revenue the government collected in taxes and its spending amounted to 13 percent of annual output—a distressing and unsustainable deficit. In January, before the coalition dissolved, Fitzgerald had proposed shrinking the gap to a still high 11.7 percent. Now, MacSharry said, the new government would go a full percentage point of output farther, to a deficit of 10.7 percent. The millions of pounds worth of cuts that would be required, especially in the health services, sparked howls from industry and trade unions alike over broken campaign promises. They also earned the new finance minister a moniker he bore happily: "Mac the Knife."[9]

In mid-1987, Colm McCarthy, a charter member of the Doheny & Nesbitt school, was appointed to a special expenditure review commission to scour the budget for savings. He marveled at Haughey's ability to pivot from campaigning as a spendthrift to governing as a miser. "In a wonderful piece of political theater, he went into the department of finance with the [television] cameras to inspect the books," McCarthy said. "Now, he knew perfectly well what was in the books. Everybody over the age of six knew. But he came out an hour later . . . and he announced that all of the money was gone and all bets are off. When there's a change of government you can do things like that."[10]

The swordplay over the public finances took place against a backdrop of genuine deprivation. In February, the European Economic Community began releasing its surplus stockpiles of milk, beef, cheese, and other food-stuffs, the legacy of agricultural subsidies that encouraged overproduction. In Ireland, the St. Vincent de Paul Society, which coordinated local distri-bution, initially estimated that perhaps 300,000 people might avail them-selves of the free food. Two weeks into the program, after lines hundreds long formed outside some distribution centers, that number jumped to 400,000.[11] By the time the program ended on March 31, 500,000 had re-ceived aid, giving Ireland the unenviable distinction of having a greater pro-portion of its population in need than any other country in Europe.[12]

The new government's program had an almost immediate market im-pact. Interest rates fell from 13.25 percent in March to 11.75 percent the fol-lowing month.[13] Despite the gripes and political jousting, voters' early reviews of MacSharry's budget were also largely positive. In an *Irish Times* poll one week after the speech, 57 percent said the program would be good for the country even as people anticipated a lower standard of living for themselves.[14] Still, it was one thing to lay out a roadmap. It was another to keep everyone moving in the same direction. The key to making the new economic program work lay in enforcing pay discipline with the unions. An early test of the government's claim that it couldn't afford pay increases for anyone came two weeks after MacSharry's dramatic budget speech. Work-ers at the state-owned Electricity Supply Board (ESB) rejected management's offer of a 3 percent pay increase and instead demanded a 12 percent jump. To enforce the demand, which would have eviscerated the new government's call for society-wide restraint, the utility's 12,000-worker union bruited the idea of a rolling series of 48-hour power cutoffs. As the May 5 deadline neared, ESB's chief executive forecast "a collapse of the electricity system," while farmers warned of catastrophic effects on food production.[15]

MacSharry had drawn the limelight in the government's first weeks. Now as the focus turned to potential worker unrest, the government's youngest cabinet officer, Minister for Labor Bertie Ahern, stepped to the fore. Ahern had been a loyal Haughey lieutenant as chief whip, marshalling the party's forces in the Dáil. He also was in his first year as Lord Mayor of Dublin, a largely ceremonial post, but one that offered visibility and executive experience along with a thick ceremonial chain to be worn around the neck. (Ahern had adopted a distinctively Irish approach to planning a promotional campaign for the city, centered on the idea of Dublin's 1,000th anniversary. "We had no idea when the date was. We'd made it up," he would later recall with a laugh. "We decided it was 988 Dublin had started. So we hyped it up [and] we had everyone celebrating a thousand years.")

The labor post carried little of the gravitas of the more senior cabinet positions, such as *tánaiste* (deputy prime minister) or finance. Some saw the job as a political sinkhole, where politicians would disappear into the endless series of industrial disputes that defined the era. Ahern, who would become the longest-serving labor minister in the Republic's history, wasn't one of the skeptics. "I took a different view; I saw it as my opportunity," he said.[16]

The young politician had spent much of the past year juggling a deteriorating marriage as well as responsibility for incubating a new relationship between Fianna Fáil and the Irish unions. Still only in his mid-thirties, Ahern had been married for 11 years. From the outset, his political career took precedence over his responsibilities to his wife, Miriam, and their young daughters. He typically left home at 6:30 a.m. and returned perhaps at midnight. What free time there was, he spent socializing with other politicians. It was a recipe for a failed marriage, precisely what it produced shortly after Ahern took up residence in the Mansion House, the Lord Mayor's city center dwelling.[17]

He had better luck with politics. While still in opposition, Haughey had decided to reach out to the trade unions. It was an unusual move. With the Labour Party then in power, the unions would have seemed to have no need for the opposition. But pragmatic, down-to-earth union leaders such as Billy Attley, general secretary of the Federated Workers

Union, were uncomfortable with the professorial Fitzgerald and his coalition partners in the Labour Party. Wits gibed that Fitzgerald, a professional economist, would muse, "It works in practice. But will it work in theory?" Unlike the British Labour Party, whose politicians rose from the mines and workplaces of industrial Britain, Irish Labourites bore university pedigrees and smooth hands. "The Labour Party had lost its leader, Frank Cluskey who had a big trade union background and who was replaced by Dick Spring who was a Trinity [College] boy. . . . We didn't have a very good working relationship," said Attley.[18]

The lack of chemistry between union and government leaders left an opening for Haughey, which widened as the likelihood of his returning to power rose. At the direction of "the Boss," Ahern, who had been a union member while working as an accountant at the Mater Hospital, began talking privately with union leaders. Meeting over pints at Fagan's pub, across the street from his constituency office in north Dublin, the rising pol and the street-savvy unionists would discuss the country's troubles. Ahern's calling card was an unaffected, man-of-the-people stance. "Call me Bertie," he'd say. Phil Flynn, general secretary of IMPACT, the public services union, said of him: "Here's someone we can relate to, right? Here's someone from whom we can get feedback. Here's someone if you engage with him, it's not one-way traffic and here's someone who clearly has influence where it counts."

Several months before the election, Haughey collected his brain trust and traipsed to the headquarters of the Irish Congress of Trade Unions (ICTU), the movement's governing body. It was a seminal moment, illustrating just how much was about to change. Fianna Fáil hadn't had an official meeting with ICTU for 35 years. "The unions were sending out signals they were willing to work out a national recovery program . . . and Haughey and Ahern picked up those signals fairly quickly," said Peter Cassells, the general secretary of ICTU.

Union leaders marveled at Ahern's ability to gather intelligence on labor disputes in any industry or part of the country by tapping into union members who were also active Fianna Fáil loyalists. "He has an incredible capacity to know people . . . when you met him to some extent he actually knew more about what was happening than some of the key people," said Cassells.

So when one of the country's most powerful unions staged a showdown, Ahern was well positioned to grapple with it. Early on, as ESB's unions threatened to shut off power, Ahern took a hard line, telling a radio interviewer: "They can be out 'til Christmas and we'll all be getting together in the dark, but it ain't going to change our policy."[19] Nonetheless, there were many who thought the new Irish government, like its predecessors, would cave in the face of a determined challenge. That sentiment only grew on May 5 when, after weeks of jousting, the union pulled the plug, kicking off a rolling series of 72-hour blackouts and threatening a complete shutdown on May 12 if no settlement were reached.[20]

Ahern's civil servants had warned him not to get personally tied to settlement efforts. The risk was too great, they said, of a climbdown tarnishing his political future. He ignored them, realizing that the new government's credibility was on the line. It was not much of an exaggeration to say that Fianna Fáil's hopes of instigating an economic recovery rested upon holding the line on the ESB matter. But when the lights blinked off on that Tuesday morning, the new government faced immediate pressure from the business community to compromise. At midday, Haughey called Ahern to an emergency meeting. "The employers have bottled it," the taoiseach growled. "They're saying we can't have ESB out, because industry will close down." An angry Ahern insisted on the need to stand firm. Haughey agreed, but the labor minister understood he would pay the price if the unflinching stance provoked disaster.[21]

Public sentiment was overwhelmingly against the workers, quasi-public employees seen as among labor's pampered elite, enjoying job and pension guarantees most workers—not to mention Ireland's army of jobless—could only envy. Union members manned skeleton crews in hospitals and other key sites. But traffic lights, cash machines, gas pumps—all were disrupted. When the power to Patrick Collins's milking shed near Tuam was shut off on the strike's second day, the 42-year-old farmer tried to rig his tractor to generate enough electricity to milk his cows. Something went wrong, and Collins's arm was severed at the elbow.[22] Those involved in the dispute felt the rising public heat. As Attley sat in one negotiating session with Ahern and ESB officials, his wife telephoned to say that the lights had gone out at their home, ten miles north of Dublin. If he wanted dinner, he was told, he had better bring something home. He drove to a part of town where the lights were on and found a fish-and-chips shop. As he took his place in the lengthy line, Attley realized that he was still wearing a tie bearing a union logo that signaled for everyone to see that he was among those responsible for inconveniencing them. "There was such hostility . . . that almost without thinking I put my hand over the tie," he said. He reached the counter and held out one hand for his order while covering the emblem with the other.[23]

During secret talks held at the National College of Industrial Relations, the skills that would eventually earn Ahern his reputation were on display. The young minister seemed to have a boundless capacity to listen to warring sides, absorbing abuse from combatants who needed to vent. "Ahern's strength was his timing. He had a tremendous network built up over many years and the reason that he usually appeared to be successful was because of that," said Phil Flynn. "He was able to time his interventions. He had it down to a fine art." Ahern's efforts to broker a deal were helped by the fact that national labor leaders privately opposed the ESB unions' walkout. Union heads such as Cassells, who had been involved in the bridge-building exercises with Haughey and Ahern, felt they had more to gain by preserving their credibility with the government than they did by securing a fatter paycheck for workers who already were earning one-third more than the average industrial wage.[24] Haughey had handed them a chance to be equal partners with business and the government in charting a national recovery plan. To make that work, Cassells needed to demonstrate that he could control his troops, that if he committed labor to an eventual deal, he could deliver. "Bertie Ahern and ourselves were involved, essentially, in just getting it resolved and killing it off," said Cassells. "From the broader union movement's point of view, the broader labor unions and the central body, getting that strike resolved was absolutely crucial to proving your credibility."[25]

Still, in the first 12 hours of mediation, the parties spent only five minutes in face-to-face talks.[26] The next round, which stretched through the strike's second night, was more productive, producing a face-saving deal for the union and a big win for the government. ESB workers didn't get the double-digit wage hike they were seeking. Instead, they received vouchers for discounted electricity worth a few hundred dollars. It was the same deal the union had rejected before launching the ill-fated strike. Ahern was widely praised for resolving the dispute, which had dominated the national news all week. Later, his verdict was matter-of-fact: "They pulled the plug and we faced them down."[27]

SEDUCING THE SOCIAL PARTNERS

Buoyed by its early success, the government began talks on a national recovery plan with union and business representatives. Ahern was among the government ministers involved, though Haughey was the driving force. There had been so-called national understandings on wages and benefits in the past, but they hadn't really worked. Unions treated the agreed wage levels as a floor that local bargaining units could build upon. The industrial peace the accords were meant to deliver remained a mirage. In 1979, for example, strikes occurred on average almost every other day and cost more than 1.4 million lost workdays.[28] The lack of industrial harmony was taking a toll on an already badly wounded economy. AT&T in 1983 opted to close its plant in Tallaght outside Dublin in part because the company feared the unions wouldn't cooperate with needed retooling.[29]

If union leaders required additional motivation to compromise, they needed only to gaze across the Irish Sea. In the United Kingdom, Conservative Prime Minister Margaret Thatcher had taken office in 1979, determined to tackle what she described as "the problem of trade union power . . . exploited by the communists and militants who had risen to key positions within the trade union movement."[30] In a series of bruising confrontations, Thatcher broke the British unions and imposed a program of market-friendly economic policies that consigned them to the political sidelines for a generation.

There were numerous differences between the Irish and British labor situations. But with the Irish economy in desperate straits, the rise of an "Irish Thatcher" couldn't be ruled out. Already in 1985, several leading politicians had split from Fianna Fáil to establish a new party, the Progressive Democrats, which favored free-market policies labor leaders derided as "Thatcherite." Under the leadership of Des O'Malley, the PDs had won 14 seats in the 1987 parliamentary elections, elbowing aside the Labour Party to become the third-largest force in Irish politics. "When you looked at what had happened in Britain, the labor movement actually had painted itself right into a corner where not just the political sort of conservative Thatcher reaction, but public opinion had clearly labeled them and seen them as part of the problem. So there would have been a strong sense here that that is somewhere you don't want to be," said Cassells.[31]

By October, negotiators had hammered out a tripartite deal. At a press conference at Dublin's Burlington Hotel, Haughey—entering to a musical rendering of Padraig Pearse's *Mise Éire* ("I Am Ireland")—unveiled a 32-page "Program for National Recovery," or PNR. The document bore the by-now familiar indictment of Irish economic performance: gross domestic product per person that was just 64 percent of the European average; unemployment at 18.5 percent, which would be higher still if not for record emigration; a national debt that had doubled in four years; and five years of flat-lining investment while the rest of Europe increased its spending for the future by a full one-fifth. "The situation was so serious. The central fact [was] everybody realized action was necessary. Decisions had to be made to reduce expenditure," says Padraig O'hUiginn, who had helmed a 1986 National Economic and Social Council study that paved the way for the accord.[32]

Reflecting a consensus born of deep crisis, the PNR offered something for each of the key players. Skeptical employers won promises of labor peace and wage stability over the agreement's three-year horizon. The government likewise could tackle the yawning gap in the public finances confident that the unions wouldn't bust the budget with demands for higher salaries for government workers. And the unions—of whom much was asked, including a no-strikes pledge—received modest annual wage gains of just 2.5 percent but could anticipate higher take-home pay thanks to promised tax relief.

The last element was critical. The Irish Congress of Trade Unions had negotiated a 71 percent increase in pay over the previous five years—yet because of the higher taxes needed to finance the government's endless borrowing, the average worker was actually taking home 7 percent less than he had at the beginning of the period. Union leaders appreciated the deal's logic, especially since it afforded them continuing access to government leaders of a type they had never enjoyed under Fine Gael. But among the rank and file, it was a harder sell. "While the leadership was in favor of doing what we were doing, the fellas in the trenches said, 'ah, feck them. We don't listen to this oul stuff,'" Ahern said.[33]

Still, after some vigorous debates, the individual unions endorsed the program in open votes. In the Dáil, opposition deputies questioned the principle behind the tripartite agreement. It seemed to some to undermine the institutions of democratic government; after all, Ireland already had a forum where competing interests could make their claims and argue their cases—parliament. But with interest rates falling and public support for the government rising, Haughey was unfazed by the complaints, instead toying with opponents such as Fine Gael's Michael Noonan:

> Noonan: "Would the Taoiseach agree that he seduced the social partners into acting against their own interests, their members' interests and the national interest? Does he now appreciate that they are squirming in his embrace?"
>
> [Interruptions.]
>
> Haughey: "I could suggest that the Deputy try to keep the party clean."[34]

But the process known as social partnership was now well and truly launched. Building both on the earlier unsuccessful tripartite negotiations in Ireland and on similar ventures elsewhere in Europe, the series of national agreements would provide a bedrock foundation for efforts to clear away the wreckage of Ireland's failed economic policies and build a more sustainable model. The economists nursing their pints at Doheny & Nesbitt might not think much of the strategy; Colm McCarthy would ultimately deride it as a way of divvying up societal spoils with the unions, a "corporatist circumnavigation of parliamentary democracy."[35] But when in coming years, the economy finally would grow, and grow at a pace that few had ever believed possible, Ahern would say flatly: "That is what turned the country—social partnership."[36]

I LOVE IRELAND

Even as the economy was struggling to evolve, there were signs of a new Ireland emerging in society. At Greendale Community School in a largely working-class suburb of Dublin called Kilbarrack, a young schoolteacher was trying to find his voice as a writer. Roderick Doyle had been hired several years earlier to teach English and geography at a school that itself marked a break with traditional patterns. The institution was a joint venture between the local government and the Jesuits; and Anton Carroll, the principal who launched the school in 1975 to serve a new public housing development, had distinctive ideas about its mission. Carroll envisioned the school as a mechanism for inculcating middle-class norms of hard work, deferred gratification, and achievement orientation in his young charges. "We were into active socialization," he said.

Greendale opened in an era of ferment in the previously stagnant backwater of Irish education. It had been less than a decade since the government had finally overcome conservative opposition to free secondary education, setting the country on precisely the type of path that rural traditionalists had feared. The Catholic Church, which ran most Irish schools, worried that any education beyond basic literacy might instill heretical thoughts in the minds of the laity. Greendale was also designed to revolutionize one corner of an educational system that was "grossly neglectful of the children of the poorer classes in society."[37]

Doyle, a graduate of University College Dublin, was a perfect fit for what Carroll had in mind. He was under 30 years old, a classroom novice who hadn't yet acquired the hard shell of cynicism that could doom efforts to build a distinctive Greendale culture. Doyle's résumé was selected from among 700 applications that answered Carroll's help-wanted ad. The new hire, just a few years senior to his oldest pupils, struggled at first. "[I] hated it for the first month . . . couldn't project my voice, hated it, really hated it. Felt very uncomfortable," he said.[38]

Doyle survived his initial difficulties and quickly established a bond with his students. He addressed them by their first names, something that wasn't customarily done in Irish schools at the time, and talked easily with them about shared passions such as soccer. In return, some called him "Punk Doyle," in recognition of the gold stud he'd worn in his left ear since the late 1970s. "Roddy was brilliant. Roddy was a natural," Caroll says. "He had a very easy-going manner. Never raised his voice. Almost spoke conversationally with the kids."[39]

Doyle had grown up not far from Greendale, in a bungalow on Kilbarrack Road with his father, Rory, a printer, and his mother, Ita. He had two brothers and two sisters. An older brother, the first Roderick, had died less than two days after birth. Doyle's writing reflected his teaching experiences as well as a genuine affection for the community and its people:

> Last October, I saw Christy on the corridor just outside my room.
> He was holding a magnifying glass to the crotch of his trousers and every time a girl walked past him he made it go bigger, smaller, bigger, smaller.
> I roared at him. Christy! Stop that.
> He grinned.
> Ah now, sir, he said. They'll have to learn about it sooner or later.
> I'm glad I come from the same place as Christy.[40]

Doyle had attended university, harboring no specific ambition. But he'd written for student publications, alongside others who would become fixtures in the future Irish literary scene, such as Fintan O'Toole and Colm Toibin. Beavering away in his cramped studio apartment or stealing a few moments in the teacher's lounge, he produced his first novel, an undisciplined satire called *Your Granny's A Hunger Striker*. The 317-page opus made the rounds of 30 publishers without drawing a nibble.[41]

Doyle's university friend Paul Mercier had joined the teaching staff at the same time and started a drama program. The two collaborated on a rewrite of *King Lear*, set in Kilbarrack, and with a cast of students, won the Dublin Shakespeare Society's scholastic competition. Caroll knew that

Doyle was attempting to write for publication, but he didn't take it too se-riously. His young teacher was cooperative and hard-working and getting the best from his kids. No one expected much beyond that.

In 1986, Doyle spent six months on his second novel, about a band of musicians from an area much like Kilbarrack who enjoy a modicum of suc-cess playing American soul. He wrote in longhand, sitting in his apartment in Clontarf. This time, Doyle didn't even bother shopping the manuscript to publishers. With a friend, John Sutton, he borrowed the equivalent of a few thousand dollars and self-published five thousand copies. *The Commit-ments* went on sale at Eason's in Dublin in March 1987; the *Irish Times* re-view foreshadowed the problems traditional critics would often have with Doyle's work. Fred Johnson called it an "urban novel . . . virtually unread-able outside the Pale . . . an elitist novel, to be read by the few and in Dublin."[42]

The novel ultimately drew a readership of the many, not the few, and from well beyond the city's boundaries. Doyle sent copies of the book and of more positive local reviews to all the British and Irish publishers; one copy landed in the London office of editor Dan Franklin at the William Heinemann publishing house. An assistant retrieved it from the "slush pile"; Franklin liked it and put out a proper edition. One line spoken by the book's main character, band manager Jimmy Rabbitte, almost immediately achieved iconic status. Explaining the relevance of American soul music for working-class Dubs, Rabbitte describes the Irish as "the niggers of Europe," an overstatement certainly, but one whose spirit nonetheless rang true.

Doyle and Sutton, meanwhile, called their publishing venture King Farouk Publishing and styled it as a direct counterpoint to the traditional focus of much of Irish literature. The idea was to publish new voices while avoiding "the following well-chewed Irish themes: the provincial upbringing of the protagonist, often the author in disguise, in the fifties or sixties; the ab-sence of love in the home, usually the fault of the father; the brutality of the

Christian Brothers education, or the more subtle brutality of the Holy nuns or the Jesuits; the suffocating influence of the Church; the smallness of provincial town life; and, of course, the various frustrations that torment sensitive young men growing up in the provincial towns in the fifties and sixties."[43]

Doyle was deliberately charting a new path. He was an avowed atheist in a still fervently Catholic country, telling one interviewer he wouldn't have accepted a teaching job at a "religious-run school."[44] And he sought to raise the literary profile of the working class in an arts scene that had deeply ingrained middle-class pretensions. His writing shone a light on a slice of Irish life—the nondescript but vital city suburbs—that was invisible to other artists. In the late '70s, "there wasn't much Irish literature and all seemed to be out of the same mould, they were writing about the same things. They thought that Ireland started ten miles after Dublin," Doyle said.[45]

Mercier, Sutton, and another young Dubliner, John Dunne, working on a parallel track, had set up a new theater company called Passion Machine to write and produce similarly focused plays. "Irish drama—both on the Irish stage on Irish TVs and in film as well—wasn't really reflecting the world as we saw it or as we were experiencing it. It was very much concerned with the past or a literary type of world. It always set its sights on 'elsewhere.' It always was looking to pander to London and more recently to pander to America, to play to those audiences," said Mercier. "There was a serious neglect of what theater should be doing, which was reflecting what was going on in the society that we were living in at the time and the way the consciousness was and the way the zeitgeist was."[46]

After their first few offerings, Mercier had invited Doyle to attend a November 1985 performance of his play, *Wasters,* about a group of shiftless young Dublin men. "For the first time in my life, I saw characters I recognized," Doyle later recalled.[47] Seven months later, Mercier asked Doyle to try his hand at playwriting. The result, first staged in September 1987, was

Brownbread. The title, a rhyming play on the expression "you're dead," featured three ne'er-do-well north Dubliners who kidnap a bishop and ultimately provoke Ronald Reagan into ordering a rescue by the U.S. Marines. The absurdist piece was a hit, earning Doyle positive reviews and an appearance on RTE's popular *Late, Late Show* (Ireland's answer to *The Tonight Show*). The *Irish Times* credited Doyle with "a quite astounding debut."

Brownbread, like all of Passion Machine's productions, was staged in an inner-city bingo hall called the St. Francis Xavier center. When it wasn't being used by the RTE Orchestra for rehearsals, the Jesuit-owned center—whose 1957 opening the pope had blessed by telegram—hosted concerts by bands such as The Clash. There, Mercier & Co. were deliberately seeking a new audience: young, often working-class people who never would have thought of attending a play. To lure them onto the padded steel chairs that lined the SFX, ticket prices were cut to just a few Irish pounds; wine was served at intermission in plastic cups. Roughly half of the twenty thousand patrons who saw *Brownbread* in 1987 paid special discount rates for students or the unemployed.[48] After a three-week run before "packed houses" at the SFX, *Brownbread* shifted to the mainstream Olympia Theatre, just down the road from the Central Bank on Dame Street.

Brownbread reflected its writers' disdain for middle-class mores. One of the play's least attractive characters is the mother of one of the kidnappers, whom Doyle's stage instructions describe as "an appalling, overpowering person. Everything about her should scream 'I am middle class and it is the right way to be.'"[49] Doyle's first play—like *The Commitments*—also displayed his affinity for American pop culture. References to Chevy Chase, *Star Trek,* Whitney Houston, and *M.A.S.H.* populate the text.

Doyle's success was emblematic of a broader cultural stirring. U2 became international superstars with their 1987 album *The Joshua Tree.* Director Jim Sheridan won two Oscars for his 1989 film *My Left Foot* and poet Seamus Heaney was elected professor of poetry at Oxford that same year.

From a global perspective, it appeared that Ireland was finally shaking off the conservative influence of the church and seeing a more vibrant artistic output assume its rightful place. This was certainly a different country from the Ireland where John McGahern had been fired from his teaching job on orders of the archbishop of Dublin after his 1965 novel *The Dark* was banned for indecency. The cultural flowering (which included Ireland's qualifying for the first time for the World Cup) was replacing the traditional Irish sense of inferiority and doom with a robust self-confidence. Watching televised coverage of one Ireland cup match in a crowded pub, "A middle-aged man roared it twice—'I love Ireland!' So did I," Doyle remembered. "I was glad I was Irish, proud of it. I'd never felt that way before; I'd have been embarrassed to. Not now, though. I was Irish and it was a fuckin' wonderful thing to be."[50]

A DIFFERENT LEAGUE ALTOGETHER

Self-confidence couldn't truly blossom in a country with no jobs. As 1989 dawned, Irish officials were in a desperate scramble to fill in another piece of the economic development puzzle. The Program for National Recovery seemed to be having the desired effect: growth was percolating at an annual rate of 5.6 percent versus almost nothing three years earlier. An August 1986 devaluation of the pound effectively cut the price of Irish goods on global markets, giving exporters a boost. Critically, interest rates were on the decline as well, making it easier for businesses to invest in new factories. But the job market remained becalmed: total employment in 1989 was no higher than it had been in 1974.[51]

To really create an adequate number of jobs, Ireland needed to attract the world's best companies to its shores. Irish officials had finally accepted that fact after fruitless decades wasted on a quest for self-sufficiency. The architect of the country's dramatic U-turn from three decades of protectionism to open trade was a brilliant civil servant named T. K. Whitaker. Under the direction of the future taoiseach Sean Lemass, Whitaker penned a landmark 1958 report called "Economic Development," which argued for a thoroughgoing revolution in Ireland's economic affairs. Deliberately provocative, Whitaker told his superiors in one sharp-tongued memo that if Ireland wasn't prepared to change, it should approach the British about rejoining the United Kingdom. "There was a sense that things were failing. . . . It looked very much to people like myself that, whatever about political independence, we had not by any means—weren't in sight of achieving—economic independence," Whitaker said. "We went through a very grim period. . . . It was a kind of dark night of the soul."[52] It was a mark of the pragmatism and utter absence of ideology at the heart of Irish politics that Fianna Fáil, architects of the failed protectionist "Little Ireland" model throughout the party's entire history, transformed itself into a fierce advocate of free trade with hardly an explanation or excuse.

By the late 1980s, foreign investment, especially from the United States, had brought manufacturers such as Fruit of the Loom, Bausch & Lomb, and Digital Computers to Ireland. But the country remained a minor-league economic player. Officials at the government agency responsible for luring overseas investors, the Industrial Development Agency (IDA), were determined to change that. As Europe moved inexorably toward the planned 1992 launch of a single market, some American corporations feared the emergence of a Fortress Europe that would leave them on the outside looking in. To circumvent that danger, many were establishing plants inside Europe's borders. In March 1989, IDA learned that Intel, one of the world's leading technology companies, was among those shopping for a European location. In Dublin, IDA boss Padraig White established a 15-man crisis team and put his organization on "red alert." The semiconductor maker was scouting sites in Scotland, Wales, France, Germany, Austria, the Netherlands, and Spain in addition to Ireland. Still better known for Guinness and golf, the Emerald Isle had made the list largely because of a years-long campaign by IDA officials based in Silicon Valley to build relationships with the fast-growing chip maker.

IDA had attracted other electronics companies. The agency's goal was to ultimately create a self-reinforcing cluster of high-tech companies building every significant component of the personal computer, everything from displays to the chips inside. Wooing Intel, however, represented a challenge beyond anything IDA had yet accomplished, and the courtship was likely to be both difficult and expensive. Ireland had no history of large-scale semiconductor manufacturing. Within the Irish government, IDA faced skepticism about the wisdom of even trying to attract a semiconductor maker. Ireland had already lost one such factory when the American company Mostek closed its 500-worker plant in 1985. And a planned 1,000-job investment by Intel rival Advanced Micro Devices in County Wicklow had been indefinitely deferred. Intel also wouldn't come cheap: White was offering a package worth $124 million, equivalent to 80 percent of the agency's entire grant budget for the year.[53]

If Intel officials wanted reasons to be wary of making a multibillion dollar investment on the island, they needed to look no further than Northern Ireland. The same month Intel announced it was seeking a European facility, in fact, there had been a dramatic reminder of how bloody and intractable the North's sectarian conflict remained. Michael Stone, a Protestant gunman, was sentenced to 30 years in prison for killing three Catholics in one of the most brazen attacks in memory. Stone, a married father of two, had launched a one-man armed assault upon mourners at a 1988 funeral for three Irish Republican Army members in Belfast's Milltown Cemetery. As Sinn Féin President Gerry Adams and other prominent Republicans stood at graveside, Stone infiltrated the crowd from the M1 motorway, hurling grenades and firing a handgun as he ran. People screamed and dove behind gravestones. Others, infuriated, charged the gunman, who was clad in blue jeans and a tweed cap. He was close enough to taunt his pursuers as he shot two in the head and neck. After his gun jammed, Stone fled down the adjacent motorway, where he was caught and beaten. Adams, who escaped injury, said: "Today is a symptom of the sick little colony we live in."[54] There would be further reminders in the years ahead.

In truth, though North and South were frequently conflated in the eyes of outsiders, the conflict had little direct impact on life in the Republic. Intel, for its part, was more concerned with the availability of skilled semiconductor labor than with turmoil in the six counties. That issue was put to rest by an IDA-commissioned survey of three hundred Irish expatriates with semiconductor experience; 80 percent said they would move home for a good job. Intel winnowed its list to potential sites in Scotland and Ireland. Then in October 1989, IDA got the word that the U.S. multinational had chosen a 55-acre site on a former stud farm in Leixlip, about 15 miles west of Dublin, for its new plant. The Silicon Valley giant was drawn to Ireland by its well-educated, English-speaking workforce, low corporate taxes, and generous state grants. The three-phase development promised 2,600 total jobs. Front-page coverage of the announcement in the *Irish Times* competed with news from Eastern Europe, where the Soviet bloc was in turmoil. Inside the paper, an ad from a local computer supplier promised that Intel 386 series processors would contain Irish-made components by mid-1990. In Leixlip, reaction "was ecstatic," said Colm Purcell, a county councilor. "We were very much now a modern town with prospects and a future."[55]

The decision gave Ireland a sort of globalization seal of approval, one that elevated a chronically ill economy into a place worth a second look. Padraig White and his IDA colleagues joined Intel executives for a celebration on the sixth floor of the agency's headquarters. "From the day that happened, it put us in a different league altogether," he said. "Other companies and other countries began to look differently at us. It made a statement about the country."[56]

CHAPTER 3

LIFTOFF

A T THE FOOT OF A KNOBBY HILL, stone houses sanded smooth by generations of east winds roaring in from the Irish Sea cluster in snug regiments along narrow streets. Tidy shops, well-used pubs warmed by turf fires, and a proud bronze memorial to the Easter Rising welcome visitors to Leixlip, as they have since before the birth of the Republic. From atop a lush emerald rise, Our Lady's Nativity Catholic Church watches over a picturesque landscape. This was the scene that greeted Jim O'Hara and his Intel colleagues as they inaugurated their new European facility in the early 1990s.

Among the executives helming the Leixlip venture, O'Hara bore the strongest links to the Ireland that was about to be eclipsed. He had grown up poor in a north Dublin neighborhood called Cabra West, the son of a laborer and a homemaker. His mother was raised as a Protestant but had been compelled to convert in order to marry O'Hara's father in the Catholic Church. One of 13 children, O'Hara was the only one to attend secondary school. He grew up at a time and in a place where most kids, including his siblings, went to work at age 14 or 15. Like most families, the

O'Haras knew no luxuries. "The one thing I remember most about it is queues, lines. You had to queue to get medicine. You had to queue, with my brothers, for the dole. You had to queue for the pawn office to pawn stuff and then redeem it. You had to queue for the turf depot where you got dockets to get free turf. And you had to queue for sweet tins, aluminum sweet tins . . . filled with stew and a dessert I always hated called semolina. Looks like frog spawn. I used to queue [for it] with my mother and the nuns used to serve it."[1]

To get work, most of the men in the neighborhood eventually emigrated. Jobs were scarce, and those lucky enough to get them held on tightly. O'Hara's father was using a jackhammer to break up roads well past his seventieth birthday. O'Hara, smart and unafraid of hard work, spent five years making Brunswick bowling alleys before landing a job with the U.S. computer maker Digital Equipment Corporation. Only in the United States, and only in the technology industry, O'Hara felt, could a foreigner who lacked a university degree do so well. "The culture of competing with the best, learning from the best and aggressively competing—that's an in-bred culture in the States," he said.

O'Hara, who was working in Boston for Digital at the time, was surprised when Intel announced its move into Ireland. The company's arrival was welcome news for Leixlip, which had been battered by the recent loss of more than a thousand jobs from the closure of the Irish Meat Packers plant. The Intel project's first phase was a comparatively straightforward, 155,000-square-foot microcomputer systems-manufacturing plant, which would employ four hundred workers.[2] The far more ambitious second step involved a state-of-the-art semiconductor-fabrication facility where integrated circuits would be etched onto thin silicon wafers. By settling in Leixlip, Intel was making a bold bet that a country with no history of semiconductor manufacturing could reliably produce almost half the global volumes of its top-of-the-line chip, the Pentium. "If this goes wrong, it's a major, major issue for Intel," said O'Hara, who was lured home with a chance to join the start-up team.

Construction began in 1991. For two years, O'Hara shuttled among facilities in Ireland, the United States, and Israel, assembling and organizing the new workforce. He targeted Irish émigrés in Europe, reasoning that they would be the most likely to stick with what was even then regarded as a long-term venture. By the spring of 1993, the new fabrication site was producing its first chips. But some of the silicon layers in the initial batches displayed a disturbing tendency to peel away from the wafer. Known as "via delamination," it was a familiar headache in the industry, but one with catastrophic implications and limitless potential causes. "It was a huge problem and it took tremendous energy and focus and stopped us in our tracks," O'Hara said.

From the start, Andy Grove, the company's legendary founder, had impressed O'Hara with his insatiable drive for improvement. ("It's very hard to get Andy to say 'I am satisfied.' In fact, I don't think I've ever heard him say that," O'Hara says admiringly.) Now, as U.S.-based executives and their Irish counterparts puzzled over what was wrong, O'Hara saw the company's commitment to systematic, fact-based decision making in action. Compared with the more hierarchical approach that Irish companies had inherited from the British, one aspect of the ultimately successful effort stood out: the person who led the way was almost never the manager in charge. Instead, it was the individual with the best technical experience. The industrial detective work involved in isolating and fixing the subtle production fault was a good illustration of how foreign investment helped spread world-class management skills to Ireland.

With the Intel facility serving as an example of Ireland's attractiveness as an investment location, a second important component of the country's economic makeover was in place. And indeed, in Intel's wake followed Hewlett-Packard, which moved into the former Irish Meat Packers site, and a score of other multinationals. Employment in foreign-owned factories was a rare bright spot in the Irish labor market, with payrolls from 1990 to 1994 rising 9 percent, to top 100,000, even as Irish-owned companies were shedding workers.[3] "Americans started coming out of our ears," said Bertie Ahern, whom Haughey had named finance minister in 1991. But Irish officials had little time to celebrate. The economic brightening was muted by grumbling over a "jobless recovery."[4] Plus, a massive European monetary crisis was brewing, one that would test Ahern's mastery of globalized finance.

For Ireland's new finance minister, 1992 was proving a year of change and challenge. On January 30, Haughey announced his resignation as taoiseach, setting off a scramble to replace him. The decision capped an extraordinary career that had spanned five decades, with equal parts controversy and accomplishment. In or out of office, Haughey's heavy-lidded visage dominated Irish politics. He was a larger than life figure, the rare Irish politician gifted with the charisma of a caesar. But he'd never been one to let the letter of the law stand in his way, somehow accumulating over the course of a government career the wealth to afford custom-tailored shirts from Charvet in Paris, an eighteenth-century mansion north of Dublin, and even a private island off the country's west coast. After a tumultuous reign, Haughey finally fell to a scandal over the wiretapping of several journalists in the 1980s. Confirmation of his long-rumored involvement ignited a furor that drove him from office, though it would be years before the full extent of his transgressions was known.

Before stepping down, Haughey handed Ahern the finance portfolio, the customary springboard to the prime minister's office. But his mentor's abrupt departure just two months later came too soon for Ahern, who opted not to challenge Albert Reynolds for the party leadership. While speculation over his intentions swelled, Ahern took the opportunity to address a sensitive issue. It was no secret in political circles that Ahern's 17-year marriage had not been healthy for years and that he had developed a romantic relationship with an aide, Celia Larkin. In this still deeply Catholic nation, Ahern's messy personal life could potentially cripple his career. Ahern opted to confront the whispering head on, appearing on the nation's most popular television show. "If I was going to make it to the top, I had to be straight with the public and say, 'dis is my position,'" he said. "I didn't set out to lead a campaign, but . . . I said to myself I'm not going to live a lie."[5]

Ahern's political timing, as always, was good. Though the Irish remained faithful churchgoers, the church was losing much of its moral authority. Within a few months of Ahern's public remarks, Bishop Eamonn Casey of Galway—who had introduced the pope to the Phoenix Park crowd in 1979—was revealed to have had a 19-year affair with an American woman and to have fathered a son by her. Casey also had used church funds to support the woman, Annie Murphy, and their son in America. As Ahern moved to address his personal situation, the contrast with Haughey's handling of his own extramarital activities years earlier illustrated the shifting public sentiments. For most of his career, Haughey had carried on an affair with Terry Keane, a journalist who frequently referred to her married lover in her well-read column, identifying him only as "Sweetie." Since Keane and Haughey could often be seen sharing a table in Dublin's finer restaurants, the Irish elite were never in any doubt as to "Sweetie's" identity, even if the average voter was. But Haughey never discussed his extramarital activities publicly. The Ireland of the 1970s and 1980s wouldn't have tolerated it. "We do denial better than anybody else. We see what's going on, but we turn a blind eye to it," said sociologist Tom Inglis.[6]

Ahern, who was granted a judicial separation from his wife in December 1993, was one of only two cabinet holdovers when Reynolds formed a new Fianna Fáil–led government alongside the smaller Progressive Democrats. There were two camps within the party now, Reynolds's so-called country and western faction and the Haughey loyalists. Ahern, almost alone, maintained good relations with both sides as well as with the free-market champion PDs. The new government's early weeks were consumed by pro-longed legal wrangling over a High Court decision to prevent a 14-year-old rape victim from traveling to Britain to obtain a legal abortion. But on June 2, attention in Ireland and across Europe swung to Denmark, where voters had rejected in a referendum a landmark European treaty.

THE PRESSURES ARE DREADFUL

Sealed in the Dutch city of Maastricht at the end of 1991, the treaty es-tablished the European Union and paved the way for the planned single Eu-ropean currency. To prepare the 11 participating economies to share a common coin, the treaty required them to meet specific targets for infla-tion, interest rates, government budget deficits, and exchange rates. In-vestors had taken the treaty as a sign that the various European states would quickly converge on the agreed targets. The Maastricht treaty's stunning defeat at the polls, which suggested they had been overly sanguine, thus roiled world markets.

At the time, the 11 currencies were linked in the Exchange Rate Mech-anism (ERM), a sort of single currency with training wheels. Each national currency—the Irish pound (or punt), the Spanish peseta, the French franc, and so forth—was permitted to trade within a specified range. If a currency rose or fell by too much, the country's central bank was obligated to inter-vene in foreign exchange markets. The difficulty was that, unlike a genuine national economy such as the United States or Brazil, Europe remained frag-mented, and conditions in Germany, France, and Belgium, for instance, were quite different from those in Italy or the United Kingdom. To global investors, the higher interest rates in the latter countries represented an all-but-guaranteed way to make money. They could invest in higher-yielding se-curities in those countries confident—or so they thought—that there would be no sharp changes in the currencies' values that would erode their profits.

After all, the ERM values had been fixed since 1987.[7] "While the ERM existed, it was a unilateral transfer from central banks to hedge funds. . . . It was a license to print money," says Marc Chandler, senior vice president for currency strategy at Brown Brothers Harriman in New York.[8]

The collapse of communism three years earlier had inaugurated a new era of globalization. Now, what had once been a fairly well-behaved, even sleepy corner of the financial markets was turning raucous and almost ungovernable. Daily turnover in foreign exchange markets of nearly $1 trillion had tripled in six years. A new type of American investor appeared, helming hedge funds that treated currencies as a separate asset class, utilizing sophisticated computer technology and complex investments called derivatives. The sheer volume of money surging across national frontiers threatened to overwhelm European finance ministers and central bank chiefs who were struggling to keep pace.[9] By August 1992, Federal Reserve board members were speaking behind closed doors of the likelihood of a "European currency crisis."[10]

At its heart, the gathering crisis reflected a failure of European governance. The exchange rates that valued Europe's currencies had been set years before and hadn't been changed since, despite epic events, including German unification. The Germans had spent lavishly to knit the former Communist East back into the national fold and now were battling the resultant rising prices with high interest rates. Outside Germany, however, most European economies had the opposite problem: idle factories and armies of jobless workers. To prevent investors fleeing to the stronger deutschmark, countries such as Italy and the United Kingdom had to maintain high interest rates even as their businesses and consumers demanded relief.

While Europe's leaders sought to maintain their customary summer vacation schedules, the strains within the ERM neared the breaking point. On August 28, the Italian lira fell below its permitted low for the first time. Ahern joined his fellow finance ministers in Bath, England, over the weekend of September 5–6 to discuss the gathering clouds. The summit broke up in barely concealed acrimony after Norman Lamont, Britain's chancellor of the exchequer, repeatedly pressed the president of the German central bank to lower rates to relieve pressure on the pound.[11] The meeting, Ahern later said, "was wasted in futile rhetoric and recrimination."[12] Two days later, the Finnish markka was forced off its peg, further ratcheting up the pressure. Now back in Ireland, Ahern and his team watched nervously as emboldened currency traders turned their guns on the United Kingdom, still Ireland's largest trading partner and the destination for nearly one-third of its exports. The Brits were in an especially vulnerable position vis-à-vis the deutschmark. In 1992, the United Kingdom was suffering through its deepest recession since the 1930s yet was running a deficit in its current account, a symptom of a nation consuming more than it produced and a sign of an overvalued currency.

Market pressures rose in the days leading to a September 20 French referendum on the Maastricht Treaty. On Wednesday, September 16, global investors, including George Soros, attacked the beleaguered pound. British authorities spent £6 billion (the equivalent of almost $12 billion at the time) and raised interest rates by five percentage points in a doomed bid to prevent the pound from falling beneath its permitted floor. By midafternoon, with the British economy screaming beneath interest rates of 15 percent, the government of Prime Minister John Major was forced into a humiliating climb-down. "Speculative market pressures against sterling," one official postmortem concluded, "rapidly became overwhelming."[13]

Sterling's fall left Ireland perilously exposed. At first, traders had targeted countries whose exchange rates were too high given their economic performance. But now, no one seemed safe; the market sentiment resembled a fever, a contagion spreading from currency to currency. In such an environment, tiny Ireland seemed a likely next target. "I remember coming in one morning to discover that overnight someone in Tokyo had made a IR

£50 million bet against our currency. These were frightening times," Ahern recalled.[14] The next day, the central bank intervened to support the punt, but investors still fled Irish government bonds. Tensions spiked as the weekend neared since traders knew that any planned devaluation would likely come when the markets were closed. So they could take a position on a Friday betting that a given currency would fall and wait for officials to make it a re-ality. On Friday, September 18, Ireland hiked its overnight loan rate to 300 percent. The astronomical rate was a deterrent, the market equivalent of a loaded shotgun. "It was a pretty awful time . . . when Britain fell out of the [ERM] arrangements. We were flabbergasted that they actually let it hap-pen. . . . They fell out of it and, of course immediately then the focus came on us. Were we going to fall? Were we going to devalue? What were we going to do?" said Michael Somers, head of the National Treasury Management Agency and a member of Ahern's informal "war cabinet."[15]

As Europe's currencies gyrated, the real economy howled. In Ireland, unlike the United States, most mortgages carried variable interest rates. So as the central bank jacked up the cost of borrowing to defend the Irish punt, homeowners' mortgage rates rose by up to four percentage points. Sterling's depreciation also acted as an effective price cut for British companies that competed with Irish manufacturers in the United Kingdom, Ireland, or third countries. Clothing makers, saw mills, furniture companies—even the taoiseach's former business, a pet food manufacturer in Longford—felt the squeeze.[16] To staunch the bleeding, the government in early October estab-lished a IR £50-million-pound (or about $95 million) fund to help Irish companies avoid layoffs, a political imperative now that unemployment, after briefly moderating, had climbed to nearly 16 percent.[17]

To currency traders, the extensive trade links between the United Kingdom and Ireland meant that the Irish punt simply could not avoid de-valuation in the wake of sterling's collapse. Before the Bath meeting, the punt had been worth 94.7 pence. One month later, it had risen to £1.10, an increase of 16 percent.[18] Irish companies, it was apparent, could not indefinitely survive with their prices nearly one-fifth higher than those of their British competitors. Hopes for an early end to the political uncertainty that was fueling market volatility evaporated on September 20, when French voters gave the Maastricht Treaty a tepid 50.1 percent "yes" vote dubbed the *petit oui.* In the ensuing days, the German Bundesbank teamed with its French counterpart in a coordinated campaign to bolster the franc. French Finance Minister Michel Sapin, recalling the bloodshed of the French Revolution, mused publicly that an earlier generation of financial speculators had faced the guillotine.

Irish officials who hoped for similar allied help were to be disappointed. Ahern ultimately enacted exchange controls to prevent speculative capital—what would be called in a later era "hot money"—from rushing out of the country. Ahern and the other four members of the Irish war cabinet—Michael Somers, Central Bank Governor Maurice Doyle, and top finance department civil servants Sean Cromien and Maurice O'Connell—saw no economic reason for the punt to be devalued. They believed that maintaining the currency's existing relationship to the deutschmark was essential to continued success in reducing inflation, government borrowing, and the public debt. The country's credibility as a charter member of the ERM and eventually the single currency was at stake.

Domestic politics acted to narrow Ahern's room for maneuver. As the financial crisis bubbled, Reynolds's government, riven by infighting, fell in early November on a no-confidence vote. Given the open enmity between Reynolds and Des O'Malley, the head of the Progressive Democrats, it had been obvious for weeks that the coalition was doomed. The three-week election campaign saw Fianna Fáil pledge to support a strong punt even as Ahern privately was moving closer to accepting the inevitable. "He called me at home one night in the middle of the election campaign and said, 'You know, the pressures are dreadful.' He said, 'I think we're going to have to devalue,'" recalled Somers. "I said, 'You're the boss'; I said, 'I wish you luck knocking on people's doors [during the campaign] and telling them you just devalued the pound.'"[19]

Even as Irish voters were leaving their polling stations, the Spanish peseta and the Portuguese escudo were devalued. Only exchange controls and sky-high interest rates were keeping the punt from the same fate. Ahern continued to resist devaluation pressures, believing both that Ireland's European partners would object and that succumbing would only whet traders' appetite for a second devaluation in the weeks ahead. Yet it seemed clear that the punt couldn't hold out indefinitely now that sterling was free of the ERM. Eventually, the Irish currency would have to be revalued, and every day of delay was simply raising the cost to Irish households and businesses. The prolonged defense was also severely eroding Ireland's foreign exchange reserves. From a peak of $6.9 billion in May, they had shrunk to $3.6 billion in November.[20]

Preparing to enter a new coalition with the Labour Party, Reynolds on December 12 won what he portrayed as an important victory in Brussels. The EU agreed to provide $13.6 billion over seven years in so-called structural and social cohesion funds for Ireland, one of four poorer European nations to get help. European money was important in upgrading Ireland's outdated infrastructure, paving new highways, laying rail track from Dublin to Belfast and modernizing airports in the capital, Cork, and Shannon. But its economic impact would often be exaggerated.

The arrival of 1993 meant Ireland was compelled by European Commission regulations governing the introduction of the single currency to abandon its exchange controls, thus permitting speculative capital to exit. At a January 6 press conference, Ahern reiterated his opposition to devaluation, but spooked nervous markets by adding: "We cannot stagger on like this indefinitely."[21] Britain's *Financial Times* interpreted the comment as a hint of softening resolve, sparking the biggest attack on the Irish pound since the worst days of the previous autumn. When Britain unexpectedly cut its benchmark lending rate by a full percentage point on January 26, Ahern could no longer maintain the defense. Publicly, the Finance Ministry held fast, arguing that for every 1 percent cut in the punt's value, the national debt would increase IR £100 million (or more than $150 million.) But the pain caused by the high interest rates defending the currency could no longer be endured. Small businesses were paying 19.5 percent for loans, and major banks were preparing to raise mortgage rates from 14 percent to 18 percent.[22] At a final meeting of the war cabinet, Maurice Doyle, the central bank governor, gave voice to the emerging consensus: "Look, there's a point at which courage turns into stupidity. And we fought the good fight. There's no point in us fighting a battle that's going to destroy us on another front."[23]

Over January's final weekend, Ahern put in motion a 10 percent devaluation. Interest rates quickly fell while reserves returned to health by April. The pressures on Irish exporters mercifully eased. In an especially startling shift, by May Irish short-term rates, which had ballooned to a multiple of the comparable German rate in the depths of the crisis, actually dipped below German levels.[24] Investors, if only briefly, somehow saw Ireland as a better credit risk than the famously reliable Germans. Ahern saw his handling of the currency crisis as a defining moment; "the devaluation crisis was the making of me," he would later write.[25] By permitting interest rates to drop to levels that encouraged growth, devaluation provided another critical ingredient for the emerging Irish economic recovery. "The big trick in the currency crisis for us was not giving in to the speculators early on, not devaluing like Spain and Portugal and other countries did in September '92 or December '92, but getting into January '93 when we were in the strong position where nobody expected us to do it," Ahern said. "And then getting a 10 percent devaluation, which was a competitive devaluation on our terms. And then interest rates came tumbling down dramatically and then we took off."[26]

He had resisted for months out of conviction that the fundamentals of Ireland's economy were sound and that the punt was the victim of market misperception and speculative frenzy. But a later IMF study disagreed: "Speculation in the Irish pound market from 1987 to 1993 was driven mainly by changes in Ireland's 'fundamentals'—namely, the evolution of its real effective exchange rate."[27] In other words, as economic conditions in Europe—including the value of other currencies—changed, the competitiveness of the Irish economy was affected in ways that investors were sure to notice. Further, if the eventual benefits of devaluation were as great as advertised, why had Ahern resisted for so long? Critics argued that the government could have acted earlier and saved Irish taxpayers and businesses enormous pain. Ahern saw prolonged resistance to the market as establishing Ireland's credibility in the councils of Europe. But Fine Gael leader John Bruton, who had publicly called for an early devaluation, accused the government of putting "pride before jobs" and said Ahern had made the economy a hostage to German economic policy. "Thousands of jobs were sacrificed, never to be returned; the indebtedness of many businesses and mortgage holders was needlessly increased by virtue of high interest rates in recent weeks; and the reserves of the Central Bank were run down in a vain and foolish attempt to defend what the Government itself by its actions demonstrated it believed to be indefensible," Bruton told the Dáil.[28]

Whatever it said about the wisdom or agility of Irish policymaking, the ERM crisis left in its wake important lessons about the emerging global financial landscape. An official postmortem by experts from the G10 industrial nations noted the rise of market forces that were too powerful to be quelled by individual nations and were themselves given to irrational twists and turns. "Investors seemed to be excessively confident in the prospects for a particular asset, and to pay insufficient attention to the development of fundamentals," the report concluded.[29] Modern capital markets, able to allocate capital swiftly from one side of the globe to another at a keystroke, enabled global growth. But the experts, including future U.S. Treasury Secretary Larry Summers, Bundesbank President Hans Tietmeyer, and future European Central Bank chief Jean-Claude Trichet of France, fretted that as markets grew in size and sophistication, the danger of more frequent financial crises would also grow. Shortfalls of liquidity in one market, they concluded, could "spill over into others with possible systemic consequences."[30] For Ireland, it was a warning that the foreign investors it counted upon to fuel its economic development could be both bane and benefactor. What global markets gave, they could also take away.

WARM SMILES AND FIRM HANDSHAKES

As Ireland began the slow climb out of its economic malaise, business conditions brightened, and Anglo Irish Bank's bottom line glowed. In Sean Fitzpatrick's first full year as CEO, the fast-growing institution had earned a modest after-tax profit of $935,000. Just three years later, in 1990, profits were more than seven times greater at $7 million. "We suddenly then became the bane of Irish banking. Why? Because Irish banking was like it is now, very conservative. It wasn't lending money and suddenly we were," Fitzpatrick said.[31]

Fitzpatrick drilled his small team on the need to handle the bank's money as if it truly were their own, repeating as a mantra: "Lend real money to real people." John Rowan, a chartered accountant who had joined Anglo after working at Ernst & Young, said a profound conservatism colored the bank's formative years. "We could never afford to lose money. We were too small and too fragile," he said. "So deals had to work. We were very risk averse."[32]

The bank grew by finding and servicing a new class of Irish businessmen outside the state-dominated industries that long had defined the Irish economy. "Seanie," as Fitzpatrick was known around Dublin, remained laser-focused on this niche strategy. Anglo didn't aspire to do everything: it had no sprawling network of retail branches to compete block by block with its larger rivals, and it didn't offer credit cards or provide routine check-clearing operations for its corporate customers. The bank might not have as much visibility into its customer's overall cash flow as a consequence. But instead, Anglo built a wildly profitable loan business through swift decision making and personal relationships. The bank owed its success as much to eye contact, warm smiles, and firm handshakes as to traditional green eyeshade skills. By 1993, its outstanding loans of about $1.6 billion were nearly three times the 1989 figure, though still just a sliver of the $24.6 billion on Bank of Ireland's balance sheet. Customers were happy to pay more, in fees and sometimes higher interest rates, in return for the Anglo treatment. Rather than wait for borrowers to approach them, Anglo officials would sometimes bring potential deals to local property developers and suggest the necessary financing. "It was obvious to anybody who had eyes in their head that this was a bank that was going places. . . . It was all right when they were nibbling at our lunch, but they're now nibbling at dinner as well," said a board member of a larger rival.

From the start, Fitzpatrick nurtured outsized ambitions for his small bank, setting a goal in 1989 of eventually reaping half the bank's profits from its then-miniscule operations in the United Kingdom.[33] After Anglo's embryonic London team was poached by Riggs Bank in 1988, Fitzpatrick approached John Rowan on the Friday before the bank's Christmas break and asked if he would take over the U.K. beachhead. "I said, yeah, I possibly would [but] I'd just been married and I'd have to speak to Annette, my wife. This was like 3 o'clock. He said, well, can you tell me by about 5 or 6?" Rowan made a quick call home and then accepted the job. Three days later, he was in London, working all day and sleeping on the floor of a colleague's apartment.

Fitzpatrick acquired the loan book of a small Canadian bank, formed a new company to provide short-term bridge loans to investors, and moved into asset-backed leasing. At home, he also saw an opportunity to expand

Anglo's range of services by moving into stockbroking. So he acquired and later merged two small Dublin brokerages—Porter & Irvine and the well-regarded Solomons. But he didn't fall in love with his own ideas. After consuming an inordinate amount of management attention, the stockbroking initiative faltered and was closed down in the fall of 1992.[34]

It wasn't hard to see why Fitzpatrick had chosen to build a bank on the strength of personal relationships. He was open and friendly, gifted with a blunt and often profane wit. Everyone who met him could see he was a man on the move. The charm was married, however, to a very visible chip on his shoulder. He had the schoolboy athlete's contempt for the smartest students in the class, disparaging those who'd earned good grades to an extent that seemed odd for someone whose only sibling was an accomplished academic. "I have a very healthy disrespect," he once said, "for really bright people."[35] In place of book learning, he valued the "hunger" that kept ambitious men and women working beyond the undemanding 9-to-5 hours of Anglo's more established rivals.

As it grew, and at a pace that startled the clubby world of Dublin banking, Anglo found itself the object of a rumor campaign. Fitzpatrick began hearing talk around town that Anglo was a pirate bank that was taking outsized risks and wouldn't last. The industry's leading powers were the blue-blooded elites of Allied Irish Bank and Bank of Ireland, which traced its lineage to a royal charter in 1783. Getting into a brawl with a farmer's son from Wicklow over who could make faster loan decisions was not their idea of high finance. "There was a rumor campaign from the banks to undermine us . . . rumors that we were going to go bust, that we didn't have deposits, things like that," Fitzpatrick said.[36]

Though that buccaneering image would dog the bank for years, Fitzpatrick insisted Anglo's approach was deeply conservative. It evaluated potential borrowers with "very cautious and prudent criteria," he said.[37] Anglo at the time was taking in more than enough from depositors to fund its loans to customers. It had no need to take on the additional risk of borrowing from other financial institutions in wholesale markets to support its growing loan book. Fitzpatrick kept a tight rein on hiring; over the 1990 to 1993 period, even as assets almost doubled, the number of employees increased by just 8 to 217. Thanks to prudent management, the bank managed to gain market share and avoid damage during the ERM crisis, despite wildly gyrating interest rates. "We've never had it so good," Gerry Murphy crowed two weeks before the devaluation.[38] Likewise, though the deep recession in the United Kingdom lasted longer than Anglo officials had expected, Fitzpatrick moved quickly to shelter the bank. From 1991 until late 1993, despite his hopes to diversify away from Anglo's still-heavy dependence upon Ireland, he froze new U.K. lending.

All of that sensible business-building, however, was little help in January 1992, when simmering doubts about Anglo flared into an episode that posed a mortal threat to Fitzpatrick's creation. A hazy *Sunday Telegraph* report on January 26 alleged that an unidentified U.K. company was involved in laundering money for the Irish Republican Army and that a small Irish bank was involved. The next day, as rumors of the firm's identity spread through the City of London, shares in the printing company Wace began to sink. John Clegg, then 33, the company's managing director, was a member of Anglo's board of directors, prompting clients to call Rowan and repeatedly press for assurances that the published reports were wrong. "It was very alarming. . . . It would have been a death knell for the business if it had been true," he said.[39] The episode was especially uncomfortable for Rowan. His London office was one floor below that of an Australian law firm that had seen two of its lawyers murdered in Holland not long before by IRA gunmen who mistook them for off-duty British soldiers.

Clegg resigned a few days later, while denying any link to the IRA. His family, which owned 15 percent of Anglo's shares, was not without controversy. Before Clegg had joined the board, officials of the Irish Central Bank

had raised questions about his father, who had a criminal record. "My attitude was: that's his father, it's got nothing to do with him," said Murphy.[40]
Anglo executives had wanted the family to pare its sizeable stake in the bank
even before the IRA episode, because such a large single holding acted as a
lid on the small bank's share price. But the reported IRA ties, at a time of
weekly bombings in Belfast and shortly after a terrorist bombing within
blocks of No. 10 Downing Street, elevated concerns to a different level. "I
was shocked. I didn't actually believe it. Because I couldn't see the logic of
it. But having said all of that, the fact that it was out there, you can't sort of
dismiss it," Murphy said. "So therefore I was of the view, ok, we've got to
get rid of him. We've got to get rid of his shareholding."[41]

The IRA chatter ultimately turned out to be nonsense, but Fitzpatrick's efforts to unravel the details of the family's holding were complicated by the Cleggs' odd and worrisome proclivity for using aliases and
describing cousins as siblings and vice versa.[42] Rowan recalls Fitzpatrick's
"frustration in trying to get to grips with exactly who owned the
shares. . . . It was a bit of a Russian-doll type situation. . . . Sean really
took this on as a personal crusade."[43] Fitzpatrick eventually flew to Dur-
ban, South Africa, where he met with the senior Clegg and finally convinced him to unload his holdings. That long-anticipated sale in July 1993
removed the fetters from Anglo's shares, which doubled in value over the
course of the year. Anglo boasted that, in place of family investors such as
the Cleggs, institutions now held 80 percent of its shares, a sign that the
upstart bank was seen as a solid corporate holding.[44] "It was a huge relief
to everyone in the bank when it was sorted out . . . that was a big, big
turning point in the bank's reputation because we always fought against
suspicion because you're small, etc., etc.," said Rowan. "Anything that fueled the flames of suspicion, as this certainly did, was hugely damaging. So
sorting it was equally hugely positive."[45] Having increased profits for eight
consecutive years, and having weathered a potentially fatal scandal, Anglo

might have deserved a respite. But the bank, and its aggressive CEO, were only getting started.

DOYLE CARRIES THE DAY

An economy stirring, with a new generation of businessmen and bankers, was one indication that Irish identity was in flux. The election in 1990 of Ireland's first woman president, Mary Robinson, who spoke in her inaugural of "a time of exciting transformation," was another. Art, too, was showing the world an Ireland that little resembled the bucolic idyll of *The Quiet Man,* the 1952 John Ford film that memorably portrayed for a global audience an apparently timeless image of Éire. For Roddy Doyle, these years witnessed success upon success. His first novel, *The Commitments,* had been published in the United States and then made into a feature film by the director Alan Parker. Released in 1991, it became a surprise hit—the Los Angeles premiere drew celebrities including Bruce Springsteen and Kevin Costner—and was followed by two more well-received novels that also became movies. His crossover Hollywood success sparked sniping that Doyle's dialogue-rich novels were really just thinly disguised screenplays—jibes the author resented. But no criticism rankled quite so much as the allegation that Doyle was exploiting his students and using Dublin's working class as a prop to entertain its social betters. "The novel critics were a lot tougher, a lot tougher. The work was just so popular and the books were hopping off the shelves," said Paul Mercier. "A lot of people felt, why is he getting such a big readership and I amn't? Let's start with that. Call it begrudgery."[46] Asked how he would answer charges that his coarse and foul-tongued portraits stereotyped the working class, Doyle said: "I don't. That's how I'd answer it. Full stop."[47]

The prolific Doyle continued to teach at Greendale, regarding his students as an audience that deserved to be engaged like any other; teaching, he would later write, "was a branch of show business."[48] Anton Carroll, the principal who hired him, said his classroom enthusiasm never flagged. "I don't think he ever diminished his commitment to teaching. Maybe he worked harder. . . . [There was] no celebrity stuff during school time," he said. "He was very, very loyal to his school, very loyal to his students."[49]

Doyle's fiction likewise stayed true to his vision of spotlighting Dublin's neglected suburbs and their working-class inhibitants. Doyle and novelists such as Dermot Bolger were showing readers an Ireland they hadn't seen before. Since the literary revival of the early 1900s, Irish fiction had obsessed over a rural tableau of farmers, tweed caps, and thatched roofs. Doyle's Ireland, in contrast, was a landscape of unremarkable postwar housing developments clinging to Dublin's northern rim. After *The Commitments,* band manager Jimmy Rabbitte's family reappeared in Doyle's second and third books. In 1990's *The Snapper,* Jimmy's sister Sharon becomes pregnant and decides to keep her baby, but will not identify the father. The following year, the Rabbittes' patriarch, Jimmy Sr., is laid off from his construction job in *The Van.* His friend Bimbo likewise loses his job, and the two idle breadwinners go into business for themselves, operating a mobile fish-and-chips stand from a dilapidated second-hand van.

The Van earned good reviews and was short-listed for the Booker Prize, one of English literature's most prestigious annual awards. Still, among literary critics for whom popularity almost disqualified a writer from consideration, there remained an ambivalence about Doyle. "Roddy Doyle's work is a powerful antidote to the myth that all Irishmen are entertaining raconteurs, their knowledge of joists and girders equaled only by their familiarity with Goethe and Joyce. It's hard to imagine even the most determined Hibernophile enjoying an evening down at the Hikers Nest [pub] with the heroes of *The Van,*" the *Times Literary Supplement* sniffed.[50] The same reviewer ultimately conceded that Doyle had brought a "ghastly authenticity" to his depictions of "the desolation of the unemployed."[51]

In February 1991, a few weeks after Doyle and his wife Belinda celebrated the birth of their first child, he began writing a new novel. *Paddy
Clarke Ha, Ha, Ha* would be a stylistic departure from his Barrytown tril-
ogy, written in the voice of a 10-year-old child growing up, as had Doyle,
in a Dublin suburb of the late 1960s. Like Doyle's earlier work, the book
reflects Ireland's immersion in American culture rather than the traditional
Irish trinity of land, religion, and nationalism. Bits of Americana such as
Napoleon Solo (*The Man from U.N.C.L.E.*), *Voyage to the Bottom of the
Sea*, The Three Stooges, Daniel Boone, and John Wayne litter the text
where earlier Irish novelists would have deployed the farm, the priest, and
the tricolor.

This was not Yeats's "Romantic Ireland." Doyle brought an unsentimental gaze to the poverty, repression, and casual violence of 1960s Ireland. Paddy's family doesn't have a telephone. His teacher, Mr. Hennessey,
routinely disciplines the children by hitting them. And beneath the uni-
form surface of an ostensibly Catholic morality lies an unruly social reality. Mr. O'Connell, a widowed neighbor up the street from Paddy's home,
loses his sons Liam and Aidan to an aunt after his middle-aged girlfriend
moves in. "Margaret was staying at the house and she shouldn't have been,"
Paddy notes.[52] This was an Ireland traditionalists liked to pretend didn't
exist.

The novel meanders until Paddy's world gradually collapses. His parents'
occasional verbal jousting becomes more frequent, cutting, and ultimately
physical: "He'd hit her. Across the face; smack. I tried to imagine it. It did-
n't make sense."[53] Domestic violence, like the themes that would animate
Doyle's later work, was an issue of universal rather than solely Irish concern.
But it also was something that lay hidden and unacknowledged in the Ireland of old. "In the Irish context, marital breakdown is often considered a
modern problem. And I wanted to force the reality that it's *always* been a
problem," Doyle said.[54]

Paddy Clarke was to be the last book for the teacher Roddy Doyle. At the end of the 1993 school year—"June 4, 1993, half twelve"—Doyle quit the classroom he had inhabited for 14 years. A full-time job, a thriving writing career, and two children meant the demands on his time were getting out of hand. Something had to give. "It got down to a choice between teaching and writing," he said. "It was becoming a bit boring. I was reading the same texts and I didn't want to do it anymore."[55]

Any doubts he entertained about ditching his day job surely must have evaporated on October 26, 1993, when several hundred of the literati filed into London's fifteenth-century Guildhall for the annual Booker Prize ceremony. Entering the chamber, they passed 50 picketing workers from a Booker subsidiary, Middlebrook Mushrooms in Yorkshire. (The Booker chairman was moved to assure the black-tie crowd, "we do not oppress people.")[56] The award, which often ignites furious second-guessing by advocates of the losing nominees, sparked controversy even before guests tucked into their plates of venison and mixed fruit. *The Economist* found the judges' decision to overlook Vikram Seth's *A Suitable Boy* so incomprehensible that "the prestige of the prize will be much diminished when the winner is announced."[57] Auberon Waugh, son of the novelist Evelyn Waugh, attacked the Booker in a televised broadcast as a grotesque that frequently applauded "obscure foreigners who write badly" rather than the lions of British literature.[58]

At table 16, Doyle endured two hours of speeches before Lord Gowrie, who headed the judging, rose to announce the winner. "In the end," his lordship intoned, "Roddy Doyle's extraordinary creation of a 10-year-old boy—funny, humane and sad—carried the day." Doyle gave brief acceptance remarks, thanking his father for the loan of his cufflinks and tweaking Waugh for his anti-foreigner comments. He was the first Irish writer to win the award—Taoiseach Albert Reynolds sent a message of congratulations—and he took home £20,000 (or roughly $30,000) in prize money. (Doyle donated half of the winnings to Greendale and half to a Kilbarrack women's self-help group.)[59]

By 1993, such an affirmation of Ireland's modern literary renaissance was overdue. A series of Irish writers—John Banville in 1989, John McGahern and Brian Moore in 1990, William Trevor in 1991, and Patrick McCabe in 1992—had been short-listed, but ultimately went home empty-handed. Their extraordinary achievements seemed proof of what Declan Kiberd labeled the "necessary link between social creativity and cultural self-confidence."[60] At the same time, in the conflicted critical reaction to his work, Doyle glimpsed a distinctively Irish phenomenon. "There's an enormous inferiority complex. . . . Success isn't mentioned until you succeed abroad," he said.[61]

The Booker may have demonstrated to an audience beyond Ireland that something was stirring in Irish culture. But it didn't silence the Doyle doubters. Novelist and critic John Banville, who would later win his own Booker, said he'd quit reading *Paddy Clarke* after 70 pages. Of its author, he said, "I've no interest in him. I think he is less a literary figure than a phenomenon of popular culture. And popular culture is easy and immediate. That's fine, but let's not confuse pop culture and art. And the way in which something like the Booker Prize has come to be regarded as an arbiter of good literature is nonsense. *Ulysses* would not have been short-listed for the Booker Prize, Beckett's *Molloy* would not have been short-listed, Proust would not have been short-listed. So we have to keep a sense of proportion as to what is really good in literature."[62]

Perhaps those establishment voices would never be stilled. But they had no more claim to speak for Ireland than did Doyle, who ended his post-Booker publicity tour of the United States by doing something the best Irish artists in the past had rarely done: he came home. Beckett had decamped for Paris; Joyce, too, along with Zurich and Trieste. Now, artists such as Brian Friel, author of the plays *Translations* and *Dancing at Lughnasa,* the director

Neil Jordan, and the poet Seamus Heaney, soon to be crowned with a Nobel, stayed in Ireland. Before, artists effectively had faced a choice: toil anonymously and unappreciated in Ireland or move abroad for success. No longer. In this newly self-confident era, it was possible to succeed, and to do so on a global scale, without leaving Ireland.

CHAPTER 4

A DIFFERENT
COUNTRY

B Y THE BEGINNING OF 1994, Jack Byrne was living proof of the gradual emergence of a new, more prosperous Ireland. Like tens of thousands of other Irish men and women, Byrne had chosen to try his luck outside the country after tasting unemployment. In 1986, the computer specialist departed Cork for Geneva, leaving behind his girlfriend of three years, Mary. But after six months, he returned for the young woman he would soon marry. "I missed her so much I came home and asked her to come with me, and thankfully she did," he said.[1] The footloose young couple spent the next five years enjoying Europe before returning to Ireland for good.

Almost the first thing they did upon arriving in Dublin was to buy a home, a comfortable four-bedroom residence in a middle-class suburb called Blackrock. The tree-lined neighborhood, full of detached, two-story brick dwellings, was home to the city's doctors, lawyers, and other professionals. Byrne had been earning a six-figure salary in Germany, where he had moved after Switzerland, and was a committed saver. So when he and Mary bought a $187,500 house, they put down a two-thirds deposit. Even so, with mortgage rates above 15 percent, the purchase left family finances a bit tight. By June 1993, the couple also had two small children, a two-year-old boy and a baby girl, and Jack was making significantly less money in his new job with an Irish high-tech startup.

In their almost subconscious urge to own a home, the Byrnes betrayed an instinctive Irish trait. Historically, a largely Protestant landlord class had owned the land, leaving the displaced Catholic population mere tenants. Only with the Land War of 1879–1882—which one historian judged a "virtual civil war"—had the peasant farmer gained the right to stay on the land he farmed and to pass it on to his heirs.[2] Vestiges of the chronic uncertainty bred into the Irish could still be seen in contemporary attitudes toward property. The rate of home ownership—almost 80 percent of the country's 1 million dwellings were owner-occupied—far exceeded the level in countries such as the United States or Germany.[3] "Culturally, everybody bought a house. So you do the cultural norm. . . . If you said, 'I'm renting a house,' your friends or your parents would say, 'What the hell are you doing that for? That's a complete waste of money,'" Byrne said.[4]

The year that the Byrnes purchased a home, 1993, Dublin's average house price of about $97,000 was actually a few thousand dollars less than it had been in 1990.[5] Buying the house was a financial stretch, however, and once the deal went through, the Byrnes lived frugally. They furnished the home one room at a time, starting with just the essentials: beds and a crib; kitchen table and chairs; and carpeting for the children's playroom. Jack and Mary sat on lawn furniture for six months, while the spare bedrooms stood empty. For the first few years, vacations and even nights out were unknown. Such sacrifice was nothing to be embarrassed about; the Byrnes' neighbors were doing the same. "People back then did not spend money they didn't have," he said.

If Ireland was no longer the moribund land of the mid-1980s, even savvy commentators by early 1994 saw little reason to anticipate a boom. "It may still take many decades for Ireland to narrow the gap with her richer EU neighbors," wrote the British journalist and author John Ardagh in a typical assessment.[6] The recovery from the crisis years had been slowed by the global recession of the early 1990s; gross national product expanded by just 2 percent in 1991 and 2.5 percent the following year. Worse, the tepid expansion drove little job creation. But by late 1994, the labor market finally brightened as the economy added twice as many new jobs that year as during the previous 12 months. It was a prelude to the greater improvement still to come.[7]

Byrne was working as director of engineering for the European arm of ISOCOR, a Santa Monica–based start-up that developed instant messaging software. He felt lucky to have landed work with the three-year-old company, which had established a software development and engineering facility in the Irish capital.[8] Technology companies, especially American technology companies, were emerging as central players in Ireland's economy. Over the past decade, employment at U.S.-owned companies had increased by 44 percent—four times as fast as overall employment growth in non-Irish firms—and now accounted for almost half the jobs at foreign-owned businesses in Ireland.[9] Lured by a 10 percent tax rate on corporate profits and the well-educated English-speaking workforce, companies such as Microsoft, Hewlett-Packard, Gateway, and Apple had flocked to the Emerald Isle. Soon, 40 percent of the computer software sold in Europe would come from Ireland.[10]

ISOCOR's revenues climbed quickly to $10 million and as the company prospered, Byrne was rewarded with promotions and salary increases. Ireland was doing better and so was he. "Our lifestyle was good," he said. "We had two cars, one vacation a year, and my wife could stay home and watch the kids."[11] Its first brush with prosperity also was turning Ireland into a different place from the land Jack had known as a youth back in Banagher. In the 1980s, even major cities had few restaurants, usually just a token Chinese or Italian eatery. His parents' limited social life had revolved around "going to the pub and smoking cigarettes." During his years abroad, Byrne had developed a taste for cappuccino and had all but abandoned beer in favor of wine drinking, a continental practice he shared with increasing numbers of his neighbors. "Our culture now is very, very European," he said.[12]

In March 1996, as a global technology boom lifted stock markets from New York to Dublin, ISOCOR went public. The move was a potential bonanza for employees, who received stock options as part of their compensation. At first, Byrne and his colleagues celebrated as their shares, after opening at $9, zoomed past $13. But investor interest cooled, and before employees were legally permitted to sell their shares, ISOCOR sank toward $1. As late as December 1997, the stock was mired below $3.[13] Byrne's hopes of a windfall had evaporated.

Any regret was short-lived. Frustrated with his job at ISOCOR, Byrne quit to accept an offer from Netscape, the American high-tech company that had come to symbolize the emerging dot-com mania. Just two years earlier, Netscape's initial stock offering had ignited an investor frenzy. It opened at $28 a share, touched $75 before its first trading day ended, and hit $171 four months later. The Mountain View, California–based company was a cash-flush Wall Street darling. When Byrne traveled from the Dublin office to company headquarters, he flew first class. "There was money everywhere," he said.[14]

A LOT OF WORK TO BE DONE

By late 1994, Ireland was earning its first investor plaudits. The economy was expanding at an annual rate of 6 percent, and an analyst at the investment bank Morgan Stanley likened Ireland to the fast-growing nations of East Asia, dubbing it the "Celtic Tiger." The improving economy, however, was all but overshadowed by the political drama that finally consumed the government of Prime Minister Albert Reynolds. The fatal blow-up came in a dispute between Reynolds and his coalition partners in the Labour Party over his plans to appoint Attorney General Harry Whelehan to the vacant presidency of the High Court. Whelehan remained politically radioactive for his handling of the 1992 "X" case, involving an unidentified 14-year-old girl he had tried to prevent from traveling to the United Kingdom for an abortion. At first, Whelehan's nomination seemed a routine, if potentially acrimonious, political dispute. Then, revelations of the attorney general's fumbling of the case of a notorious pedophile priest named Father Brendan Smyth hit the press. Smyth, 67, a Norbertine priest, had returned voluntarily to the North to face 17 counts of child sexual abuse and, in June 1994, was jailed for four years. Over a 29-year period, his victims had included both boys and girls; an Ulster TV report found that at least five later suffered broken marriages and two attempted suicide.

In October 1994, after months of horrifying disclosures about Smyth's decades of serial child abuse, the public learned that Whelehan's office had inexplicably bungled an earlier request to extradite him. Whelehan sat on the May 1993 request, he later said, because the offenses involved had allegedly been committed by Smyth 20 to 30 years in the past.[15] But voters were stunned by reports that the Irish attorney general's office had ignored nine warrants for the extradition to Northern Ireland of Smyth, then living in Ballyjamesduff, County Cavan. Whelehan ineffectually explained he had not been personally aware of the extradition request until it became public knowledge. The chairman of Reynolds's coalition partner, the Labour Party, however, rejected that explanation and accused the conservative Catholic cabinet officer of having acted to protect the reputation of the church.[16]

The episode took its toll on the already tattered reputation of the Catholic Church. Just one year earlier, Father Michael Cleary, one of the country's best-known priests and host of a popular radio call-in program, was revealed to have fathered a child by his longtime housekeeper. Catholics were perhaps growing accustomed to tales of such hypocritical, if human, behavior. In the Smyth case, however, outrage fastened upon the failure of the church hierarchy to act despite repeated warnings over a period of years. Rather than discipline or treat Smyth, his clerical superiors had shuttled him among different parishes in the United Kingdom, Ireland, and the United States—often without informing Smyth's new superiors of his criminal tendencies, thus allowing him to victimize more and more children. For the bishops, the priority clearly had been preventing reputational damage to the church rather than safeguarding their flock. Church officials, including the head of the Norbertine Order, were caught in obvious lies about their handling of the priest a Belfast tabloid called "Father Filth."[17]

As the political crisis intensified, Labour leader Dick Spring and his ministers walked out of the cabinet meeting that approved Whelehan's High Court appointment. With the breach between the coalition partners now open and irreparable, Reynolds on November 17 resigned as taoiseach. His was a dizzying fall. Less than three months earlier, he had been hailed for his role in achieving a historic IRA ceasefire; now, he was yesterday's man. His obvious successor, Finance Minister Ahern, quickly consolidated his support and emerged as Fianna Fáil's new leader. For a few weeks, it seemed that he and Spring would unite to keep the coalition government intact. But then on December 5, the *Irish Times* reported that Reynolds and his entire cabinet, including Ahern, had known of a second extradition case involving another cleric accused of pedophilia when Reynolds had defended Whelehan's nomination.[18] The report revived the air of political crisis and prompted Ahern to rush back to Dublin from a European finance ministers' meeting in Brussels.

Still expecting that he would soon be taoiseach, Ahern went to sleep late that evening at St. Lukes, his Drumcondra constituency office. But at 2 a.m., the ringing phone woke him. Spring was on the line, calling to say that he'd decided against remaining in government alongside Fianna Fáil. As Ahern fell back onto his pillow after the five-minute exchange, he knew his chance to be prime minister had vanished. Fianna Fáil would instead go into opposition and a new coalition government of Labour, Fine Gael, and the Democratic Left, dubbed "the Rainbow," would take over. "It wasn't just Bertie. The trust had broken down completely between ourselves and Fianna Fáil," said Spring.[19]

It wasn't immediately apparent, but the breach with Labour would have important consequences for the Irish economy. Fianna Fáil in the future would look for a coalition partner to the neo-liberal, market-oriented Progressive Democrats. That alliance would reorient Irish tax policy, and thus the economy, in a decidedly American direction. But all that lay in the future when on December 15, Fine Gael's John Bruton took over as taoiseach. He inherited an improving economy and a Northern Ireland peace process that finally appeared to be bearing fruit. Four months earlier, the Irish Republican Army had announced a historic cease-fire, intended to provide negotiating room for a settlement that would return governing authority to the British-ruled province's local leaders. In October, loyalist paramilitaries, who wanted the north to remain within the United Kingdom, had laid down their arms. People in both Catholic and Protestant communities reveled in the absence of killing, but Northern Ireland remained a long way from peace. Speaking in Irish, Sinn Féin President Gerry Adams had answered congratulations by saying, "Ta a lán obair le déanamh—There is a lot of work to be done."[20]

THE SMALL MATTER OF A DOOR

While the new government was scrambling to assemble its team, Linda O'Shea Farren and her husband, Brian, were settling into their new home in Dublin. The couple had returned the previous year from their jobs at high-powered New York law firms. Like Jack Byrne, Linda and Brian Farren reflected one of the most historically resonant changes affecting Ireland. "We were one of the first to come back," said Brian. "And we timed it perfectly. . . . Property prices weren't completely out of control."[21] For generations, Ireland had been unable to support its population. Parents raised their children knowing there was a good chance they would not see them mature and raise their own families. Before leaving home, nineteenth-century emigrants were feted at bittersweet "American wakes" by relatives and friends who realized they would likely never see them again. Large-scale emigration began with the famine of the 1840s and continued as a defining feature of Irish life with far-reaching consequences for Ireland, the United States, and other countries. Of the millions of people born in Ireland between 1821 and 1991, one of every two moved away.[22] And once they left, unlike Italians, Swedes, or Germans, they usually didn't return. For every 100 Irish emigrants to the United States, only six ever came back. The English were twice as likely to see home again; Germans returned almost four times as often, while Italian returnees outnumbered the Irish nearly 10 to 1.[23]

Then, beginning in 1996, the Irish started to come home. That year saw the customary human traffic reverse: 39,200 people entered Ireland while 31,200 left. The 8,000-person net gain wasn't a massive flow, not yet. But it was the start of the largest sustained inward migration since the late seventeenth century and it signaled a fundamental change in the nature of Irish life.[24] After generations of going out into the world to find their place, the Irish now could stay home. Ireland had posted four consecutive years of robust growth, and the economy was more than one-third larger than in 1993. In 1997, unemployment fell to 10.3 percent; in 1993, it had been nearly 16 percent.[25] The country was beginning to offer the opportunities and even the lifestyle that previously had been available only in more advanced nations. Once having reversed, the flow would eventually grow to a torrent. In 1997, the net inward migration exceeded 19,000.

In the mid-nineteenth century, emigration had opened an escape route for people who might otherwise have slowly starved to death. In the twentieth century, it served as a critical safety valve during years of stagnation, bleeding off the discontented who might have threatened domestic stability. Jobless university graduates in the 1980s, like Farren and O'Shea, routinely grabbed their diplomas in one hand and an Aer Lingus ticket in the other. The astonishing turnabout in Ireland's human traffic was of more than sentimental import. Irish returnees in the 1990s brought with them management and technological skills that were crucial in elevating the economy's performance. For those who made it back in the late twentieth century, there were also obvious human benefits. They were happy to be home, happy to be close to loved ones. At the same time, they noticed that Ireland had changed in their absence. "At the height of the Celtic Tiger, it was very close to a 'Type A' New York lifestyle," said Brian Farren. "People were working very hard, like in New York, running around consuming like wildcats."[26]

With their well-compensated jobs and U.S. green cards, the Farrens were far from typical immigrants. Most of the Irish who went abroad in the 1980s were more likely to have tended bar or worked on a construction site than to have toiled in the rarified world of white-shoe law firms. With nothing to draw them home, thousands overstayed their tourist visas and lived in the shadows of American life. The Farrens, however, had prospered in New York, earning enough to afford homes in both Ireland and the south of France. With much of their savings in dollars or British pounds, the January devaluation had given them an immediate 10 percent windfall. Once back home, Brian, who had earned a comfortable six-figure salary in New York, was enduring a year of required "pupilage" or apprenticeship in a barrister's office that would net him a grand total of IR £86, or roughly $123. So Linda, who had parlayed her corporate law experience into an investment banking position, was supporting the family while also several months pregnant with their second child, Devin.

Amid the year-end frenzy of deal closing, she got a call from a man who had interviewed her for a job the year before. He was now advising the incoming government and wanted to sound her out about a position as program manager. Each Irish government came to office having pledged to enact a "program for government" or what, in U.S. terms, would be called a platform. When Fianna Fáil and Labour formed their coalition under Reynolds, Labour pushed for appointment of individual "program managers" in each department to make sure that the coalition actually delivered what it had promised. Fianna Fáil chose its program managers from the Irish civil service; Labour ministers handpicked theirs from the ranks of politically loyal experts. When the Rainbow coalition took office in December 1994, Bruton followed the Labour model.

Farren, a political junkie, was immediately intrigued. "I didn't care what the salary was. . . . I'd have paid him for the job. I was made to do that job," she said. Meanwhile, Nora Owen, a veteran Fine Gael politician slated to become the new minister of justice, was keen to hire a female program manager. Within days, she arrived at the Farrens' fashionable Raglan Road home, which was in the midst of a major renovation. Scaffolding filled the front hallway and canvas was draped across the furniture. As the two women talked, Brian served tea.

A grandniece of the Irish revolutionary Michael Collins, Owen was a living link to the country's nationalist past. She had been impressed by what she'd heard about Linda, but she wanted to make certain the young attorney was right for the job. The program manager played a critical role in any ministerial office, serving as a minister's gate-keeper and political alter ego. Getting what the minister wanted when she wanted it would require a willingness to knock civil service heads together when necessary. It wasn't a job for the timid or insecure. "You needed people who had a bit of gumption that they might have to get a little cross with people. There's no doubt that a particular aspect of her personality [is that] she would be quite persistent. A man would say pushy, but I'd say persistent," said Owen. "Linda was definitely a confident young woman with her law background and was clearly interested and involved in Fine Gael. So I knew I was getting somebody who was not a spy in the camp. And that's an important element, too."[27]

Farren got the job and, after a break to have her baby, started working in the minister's office on St. Stephen's Green. But almost from the start, she felt excluded from Owen's inner circle. The problem was largely a physical one: the principal entrance to the minister's office suite led to a central chamber staffed with half a dozen civil servants and the minister's private secretary. From there, a door opened into Owen's personal office. As a newcomer, Farren was quarantined in an adjacent office, with no door into the office crossroads where everything happened. She was literally walled off from the action.

But not for long. Farren had already gotten to know the minister of public works during periodic meetings to discuss planned prison construction. So at their next meeting, "I mentioned the small matter of a door," she said. Over a weekend, a crew from public works obligingly descended upon the Justice Ministry and carved a passage between Farren's office and the inner sanctum, giving her the access she needed. "I was kind of quite admiring of her," Owen said. "[Though] I got the sense that maybe the staff in my private office wasn't quite so amused."

For more than two decades, amid the constant threat of an IRA attack, the Justice Ministry had been a security-conscious fortress. There wasn't even a nameplate on the building's exterior, though it was difficult to believe any self-respecting IRA gunman would have been unable to find it. By the time John Bruton took office, however, the ceasefire was four months old and nerves that had been guitar-string taut since 1969 were beginning to relax. Owen even chose to forego the offer of a full-time police guard outside her home.

Bruton had met with British Prime Minister John Major within a week of becoming taoiseach, and the two leaders had agreed in February 1995 on a roadmap known as the "framework document." It set out a vision of a future Northern Ireland, still within the United Kingdom, but with a greater role for Dublin in representing the province's largely Catholic nationalist community. The peace process was perhaps the single area in which Bruton most differed from his predecessor. Along with Fianna Fáil's traditional tilt toward the nationalist/republican point of view, Reynolds had brought to the talks a businessman's instinctive zest for a deal. Fine Gael historically was cooler toward the nationalist cause, reflecting the conflict that had divided Irish politics since the 1921–1922 civil war. To traditional supporters of a united Ireland, Bruton seemed excessively interested in accommodating the North's pro-British unionist community and overly dismissive of what he called "the mythology of Irish republicanism."[28] By that, he meant a view—common in both the nationalist community and among Irish Americans—that the Unionists were a wholly artificial creation of the British state and thus could be controlled by London politicians. On May 31, 1995, the taoiseach welcomed Britain's Prince Charles to Dublin, the first official royal visit to the Republic of Ireland since its founding. Bruton was criticized for an overly effusive toast to the queen at the state dinner that evening, held at Dublin Castle, formerly the seat of British rule in Ireland. But the visit of Prince Charles, whose favorite uncle, Lord Louis Mountbatten, had been assassinated by the IRA, underscored the gradual progress the island was making in putting its past to rest.

To Dick Spring, Bruton's foreign minister, the peace process was important for its own sake as well as for the intangible gains it would bring the Republic. "I'd always felt that the north was a big stain on this island," Spring said. "What did people know about Ireland? Even my [wife] Kristi's relations in Virginia: 'How close to Belfast are you? Will she be safe in Kerry?' And it's worlds apart." Spring had been born in 1950 and so was on the cusp of adulthood when the north erupted in 1969. On his last day of law school, May 17, 1974, loyalist paramilitaries detonated three bombs in the center of Dublin. Sitting in a lecture hall, Spring and his classmates heard the blasts and felt the windows rattle. In the Dublin attacks, and in a bombing the same day in Monaghan, 33 people were killed, including a pregnant woman. The Parnell Street bomb, which exploded less than half a mile from Spring's law school, wiped out an entire family, the O'Briens. Husband John, 24, a worker in a popsicle factory; his wife Anna, 22; and their children, 17-month-old Jacqueline and her five-month-old sister Anne-Marie, were among the victims of a tragic conflict that seemed likely to persist indefinitely.[29] "My roommate, who was a medical student . . . was coming back to college and the bombs went off. And as a medical student, he felt he should go and help," Spring said. "He went over and picked up a body and the head fell off."[30]

By 1995, people north and south had grown accustomed to politically inspired killing. But they still found the wanton loss of innocent life abhorrent. The IRA had implemented its ceasefire with an expectation that the British government would admit the republicans' political wing, Sinn Féin, to talks on the province's future. But Major reacted tepidly to the historic cessation of violence, complaining that the IRA had not described it as "permanent." The British prime minister had little room to maneuver politically. He was wary of alienating hard-line Unionist politicians, whose support he needed in Parliament in order to maintain his razor-thin majority and remain in power. British officials spent much of 1995 demanding that the IRA begin surrendering its weapons before Sinn Féin could join the negotiating process.[31] Linda Farren, though engaged with numerous other policy issues, accompanied Owen on her frequent trips to the North for meetings with British officials and the mainstream unionist and nationalist parties. "Progress was so slow, that it was almost like having the same meeting constantly," she said.[32]

The foot dragging and political skirmishing continued into early 1996. On the evening of February 9, just before 6 p.m., an IRA spokesperson telephoned RTE studios in Dublin and read a statement announcing "with great reluctance" that the ceasefire was over. The caller accused the British government and Unionist politicians of "bad faith" for what he called "the failure thus far of the Irish peace process."[33] Little more than an hour later, at 7:01 p.m., a brilliant flash of light followed by an enormous debris cloud raked Canary Wharf in London's east docklands. After 17 months and 9 days, a half-ton truck bomb signaled the resumption of the IRA's military campaign. Two men working in a newsstand across the street from the blast—Inan Bashir and John Jefferies—were killed in the attack; 39 people were injured. Peace in the North seemed as distant as ever.

"We had no intelligence about that. We knew the IRA was not dead and buried but we didn't have intelligence about Canary Wharf and it came as an awful shock," Owen said. The justice minister telephoned Bruton, who called a meeting within the hour at government buildings. Dazed officials struggled with the question of whether the peace process could continue, before deciding that the IRA and its political allies in Sinn Féin could not be permitted to dictate the pace. Farren was at a reception with coworkers at the Grey Door, a tony Dublin restaurant, when she got news of the bombing. In an awkward bit of timing, she was scheduled that evening to attend a small dinner party at the home of the British defense attaché at Glencairn House. She briefly agonized over the appropriate course. "It was decided one should just continue business as usual," she said.[34]

SHILLELAGHS AND LEPRECHAUNS

On April 30, 1994, a crowd including President Mary Robinson and Prime Minister Albert Reynolds packed Dublin's Point Theatre for the annual Eurovision song contest. This somewhat schmaltzy, pan-European sing-off had emerged as a popular favorite in recent years, showcasing acts from 25 countries. When Paul Harrington and Charlie McGettigan outpointed their rivals with a song called "Rock n' Roll Kids," they became the third consecutive made-in-Ireland winner.

But their fame, such as it was, was short-lived. The act that stole the show that night was not even entered in the competition; it merely filled the seven-minute intermission between the singing and the judge's scoring so that the live audience would not be unduly bored. But when the troupe of dancers and musicians finished performing what would become known as "Riverdance," the crowd leapt to its feet in a standing ovation as raucous as it was spontaneous. "The cultural shockwave" created by the performance reverberated all the way to London's West End, Broadway, and eventually the world.[35]

The object of this adoration was an innovative fusion of traditional Irish dance and choral songs with up-tempo music. Before Riverdance, Irish dance was a stodgy pastime for freckled Catholic girls decked out in white socks and lace-fringed wool costumes. This was different. With its rows of lithe young women scissoring their legs, short black skirts flying, arms held straight at their sides, Riverdance was a blend of a genuine Irish art form and the sex appeal of a Las Vegas chorus line. From its modest origins, the act blossomed into a full theatrical performance, opening in Dublin in February 1995. By June, after a sold-out five-week run at home, Riverdance had moved to London. It reached Radio City Music Hall in New York in time for St. Patrick's Day 1996. The following year, the show's composer, Bill Whelan, won a Grammy for Best Musical Show Album.

The Irish traditionally had been stereotyped as feckless, violent, often inebriated, and rough to the point of primitive. Now, suddenly, the Irish had another identity: they were cool. In Ireland, there was enormous pride in the accomplishment and professionalism of the exuberant performance. "It was special since it indicated we could do something as well as anybody.

For a time, Ireland didn't think like that."[36] To a global audience that had largely been oblivious to Irish entertainers, Riverdance signified the need to give Ireland a new look. The country was stirring, visibly throwing off the shackles of traditional forms that had lost their relevance. Independent Ireland had long been "notable for a stultifying lack of social, cultural and economic ambition."[37] From the founding of the state, a homogenous people, overwhelmingly rural, Catholic, and conservative had failed to create an environment conducive to experimentation. What was done today was what had been done yesterday and would be done tomorrow. Certainly, it was difficult to imagine this high-stepping, percussive blend of custom and innovation emerging a decade earlier when the entire society had been stalled. "There was a moment in time in the '90s. Things were moving forward," said Moya Doherty, the show's producer. " . . . There were the seeds, I think, of a whole lot of different things happening, none of them directly connected, but in some way fused together by just happy circumstance."[38]

The economic turnaround had not "caused" the cultural flowering. Ireland was populated by writers and artists even during the bleakest years. But surely it was no coincidence that suddenly in the mid-1990s Irish figures seemed to be atop so many global rankings: U2, Jim Sheridan, and Seamus Heaney, among others. What enabled Ireland to punch above its weight in cultural terms was a robust new confidence. For generations, the Irish had been saddled with a pervasive sense of inferiority, the most visible and enduring residue of colonialism. They spoke freely of it themselves, and the second-rate economy only seemed confirmation. So when the economy turned around, at some level, it simply had to feed into, and be expressed through, popular culture. "The great renaissances of national culture in the past have flowered right across the globe against a background of economic confidence—ancient Greece and Rome, Shakespeare's London, the United States in the age of Whitman and Emily Dickinson and the United States again now," wrote Declan Kiberd in 2005.[39] By that metric, Ireland's achievements were all the more remarkable. Greece, Rome, England, and the United States were the dominant powers of their day, armed with enormous advantages in the race to win global notice of their cultural attainments. Tiny Ireland had only its art.

Three days after Riverdance wowed the crowds at the Point, Ireland confronted the darker side of cultural awakening. Fresh from his Booker Prize win, Roddy Doyle showed no signs of resting on his laurels. While writing *Paddy Clarke,* he had simultaneously been working on a screenplay for a television series about yet another north Dublin working-class family. Entitled simply *Family,* the four-part broadcast, airing on Ireland's RTE and the United Kingdom's BBC, was Doyle's most overtly political drama to date. The series trained an unflinching eye on the breakup of a fictional family told in sequence from the perspectives of the father, son, daughter, and mother. *Family* shocked viewers with its stark portrayal of domestic violence; the father, Charlo, is a casually brutal alcoholic who beats his wife, Paula, in front of their children. In the first episode, angered by a mediocre fish-and-chips dinner, Charlo is shown dragging Paula by her hair across the kitchen floor. Near-ubiquitous profanity and occasional nudity—including a hint of incest—disoriented viewers expecting Doyle's customary affectionate, good-humored portrait of the working-class.

From the outset, *Family* drew large audiences; more than 1.1 million viewers tuned in to the first episode in a nation of 3.6 million people. The ferocity of the initial public response staggered Doyle, in part because many people faulted the victim of violence more than the perpetrator. A writer once revered for his faithful re-creations of working-class Dublin life was now being assailed for sullying the same community's image. Among those complaining were residents of the sprawling public housing development where the series had been filmed. Ballymun, a north Dublin cluster of seven 15-story high-rises, each named for a leader of the 1916 Easter Rising, was unmistakable—at least to local audiences who recognized it as the only high-rise neighborhood in Dublin. Though some of the inhabitants felt slighted, the series was a pointed reminder that the Celtic Tiger tide was failing to lift all boats.

Doyle had been denigrated as more entertainer than artist. But *Family* exceeded the limits of mere amusement. The series represented a frontal assault on the venerable Irish tradition of pretense, of willful blindness to troublesome realities. Doyle was making his case by tackling an institution at the core of traditional Irish identity. "I deliberately called it *Family* because it is a holy word here in Ireland," he told one interviewer.[40] Indeed, it was codified in the founding document of the state. Article 41 of the 1937 Irish constitution explicitly recognizes the family "as the natural primary and fundamental unit group of Society, and as a moral institution possessing inalienable and imprescriptible rights, antecedent and superior to all positive law." Conservative Catholic groups such as the Family and Media Association attacked Doyle for undermining the family and violating "Catholic Christian principles."[41] One priest wrote Doyle in what can only be described as un-clerical language. "The sheer hatred in it was quite staggering. As I do with all letters like that, I threw it in the bin. It finished up, 'We don't want you here, Mr. Doyle. In your own words, fuck off!'" Doyle said.[42]

But others understood that Doyle was holding a mirror to a society that, like many others, was marred by domestic violence. Even as traditionalists howled, the bruised and battered emerged from the shadows. Calls to a domestic violence helpline operated by the charitable organization Women's Aid soared in the days after *Family* appeared. "To want to deny its existence here in Ireland typifies the blinkered attitude that still prevails in this country of ours. . . . As an image of Ireland, I'd swap [*Family*] for shillelaghs and leprechauns any day," one Killiney woman wrote the *Irish Times*.[43]

The public reaction revealed a society at once eager and reluctant to take an honest look at how far it had fallen short. Seven decades after independence, and despite the burgeoning prosperity, too many Irish families were like the one Doyle depicted: wracked by violence, swimming in alcohol, mired in dysfunction. For some, the country's recent economic achievements created space for consideration of society's unaddressed ills. "Our brilliant Irish minds are making a success of our economy and our creative talent is blooming. We are creating an identity as a people. We are off our knees," one woman wrote.[44]

From the nineteenth century onward, Catholicism had been intertwined with nationalism and Irish identity. Practicing the faith was the single most unambiguous way that individuals could differentiate themselves from the British. Since the days of British rule and the first decades of independence, however, the church had seen its hold on society slip. Journalist Sam Smyth had once written that the church held Ireland in "a drowning man's grip."[45] But thanks to the Celtic Tiger, Ireland in the 1990s was becoming a much more secular society in the image of the United States and continental Europe. One of the era's biggest television hits was an absurdist sitcom called *Father Ted,* featuring three misfit priests sharing a home on a remote island off the Irish coast. Father Dougal is a childlike naïf who has trouble correctly making the sign of the cross. Father Jack is a foul-mouthed alcoholic who awakes from his daily stupor to bellow "drink!" or "girls!" And Father Ted is a vain, not terribly religious man, with a habit of narrow escapes, such as leading to safety a group of priests who had "accidentally" wandered into the lingerie section of the local department store. Remarkably, though there were a few mumbled gripes from the clergy, in a country where 9 of every 10 people were Catholic, no one seemed to mind a program that routinely ridiculed both priests and the fundamental beliefs of the faith. "That whole loaves and fishes thing, it's completely mad! You're not supposed to believe it, are you?" the oblivious Father Dougal asks Ted at one point.

It is impossible to imagine such a program airing in the Ireland of the 1980s. It wasn't just economic progress that changed the country. The church, which once dictated public policy on everything from health care to the censorship of published material, lost its stranglehold on society as its own hypocrisies were exposed. In 1994, when Father Brendan Smyth was arrested for pedophilia, it turned out his immediate church supervisor and several bishops had been aware of his abuse of children for decades and had shuttled him from parish to parish rather than alert the authorities. Revelations of behavior that was so fundamentally at odds with the teachings of the faith eroded the authority of the institutional church. Even as Mass attendance remained well above international norms, and people retained a deep emotional attachment to a Catholic identity, the church's shadow over Irish society dissipated.

In 1995, the clergy and other supporters of traditional Ireland mounted one more campaign against the Rainbow government's proposal to amend the constitution to permit divorce. The bishops and their allies had defeated decisively a similar initiative under the Fitzgerald government in 1986. Now, as then, the "yes" campaign began with high hopes and even higher poll numbers. It seemed a certainty that nearly an additional decade of material progress and secularization would carry the reform effort to victory. But for those who had lived through the earlier loss, nothing was taken for granted.

Raised a Catholic, Doyle had been an avowed atheist since his youth. His writings treated religion with a mixture of disinterest and ridicule. One character in the play *War,* about a pub quiz night, receives a bottle of holy water from Lourdes as a wedding gift and uses it in mixed drinks "when they ran out of tonic the Christmas before last."[46] Doyle had never been publicly active in politics, never tried to use his fame as a political weapon. But he and his wife, Belinda, were not raising their children in the church and resented the implicit compulsion in the church's insistence that its religious teachings be codified in the state constitution. "It basically was the Catholic Church against everyone else," Doyle said. "It was this insistence that if you're Irish, you're white and you're Catholic as well and if you're not both of those things then you're not fully Irish. Ultimately, that is what it was about."[47]

He was worried about the implications of another "No" campaign triumph, seeing a fresh rejection of divorce as merely the start of a possible rollback of Ireland's progress. Doyle had grown up in a near-theocratic society where the church controlled the schools, ran the hospitals, and censored the books—and he had no interest in going back there. If in the closing years of the twentieth century, divorce was again confirmed as legally impossible for the Irish, if society again chose pretense over reality, then Doyle vowed to take his family to live abroad.[48]

"Hello Divorce, Goodbye Daddy." In the days leading to the November 26 balloting, that was the warning that appeared on billboards all over Ireland. In case that message was too subtle, opponents of the proposed constitutional amendment helpfully castigated its supporters as "wife-swapping sodomites."[49] For all the acrimony, voters were hardly being asked to endorse quickie Vegas-style divorces. The proposed amendment would only allow marriages to be dissolved if the husband and wife had been living apart for four of the previous five years. In the week before the voting, a passionate Doyle appeared at a "Youth For Divorce" press conference in Dublin. "I am also voting Yes because I am frightened and angry," he said. "My country is an open, warm tolerant place, a place that respects the differences between people. I believe that there are people involved in the No campaign who want to take my country away from me."[50]

In the campaign's waning days, Pope John Paul gave a pointed endorsement of marriage in remarks to a group of Irish pilgrims at the Vatican, and Mother Teresa publicly urged a "no" vote. An Irish bishop warned that if the measure passed, Catholics who remarried could be denied communion. (No one could recall the church issuing similar threats against IRA bombers or pedophile priests.)[51] When the votes were counted, and then recounted, the Irish had chosen to allow those with ruined marriages a second chance. But the verdict was closer than many had expected even hours before the polls closed. The "Yes" campaign won, but by the narrowest of margins: 818,842 (50.3 percent) to 809,728 (49.7 percent). Just 9,114 votes separated the two sides in an election in which more than 1.62 million votes had been cast. If the historic nature of the change was striking, so too was how close Ireland had come to embracing the status quo.

CHAPTER 5

FAMINE TO FEAST

WITH THE GAIT AND POSTURE of an enormous teddy bear, big Ben Dunne was difficult to miss—especially when he was high on cocaine, hog-tied to a pole, and being carried through a hotel lobby by a pair of policemen. Several days earlier, Dunne had flown to Orlando, Florida, with several pals for a convivial mid-February week of golf and booze. In his $1,200-per-night suite at the Grand Cypress Hotel in Orlando, the wealthy Irishman, heir to a supermarket fortune, spent much of the time snorting lines of white powder, guzzling the contents of the hotel minibar, and unburdening himself to local working girls. The frenetic partying eventually degenerated into a paranoid mania. Dunne retreated to his balcony, and somebody called the cops. To get the plus-sized Irishman through the lobby and into a waiting ambulance, police had to cuff him hand and foot.[1]

It didn't take long for that 1992 incident to become front-page news back home. Apart from the personal humiliation, the resulting scandal provoked a lengthy fight for control of family-owned Dunne Stores, which Dunne ultimately lost. But before he did, his secrets, including details of lavish payments to top politicians such as Fine Gael's Michael Lowry, then the minister of transport, energy, and communications, spilled into public view. In February 1997, three months after Lowry had been forced to resign, and following published reports that the beneficiaries of Dunne's largesse also had included the then-taoiseach Charles Haughey, the Dáil established a tribunal of inquiry. High Court Justice Brian McCracken was charged with investigating links between Dunne Stores and the nation's leaders. Press leaks made it clear that Dunne would confirm for the tribunal that he had given Haughey a total of IR £1.3 million (or roughly $2 million) over several years, including IR £210,000 that he had hand delivered.[2]

For Haughey's protégé Bertie Ahern, the tribunal posed an inescapable challenge. A general election loomed in June 1997, and defeating the incumbent Rainbow Coalition government already seemed a tall order. Bruton's government had defied the skeptics, holding together and presiding over an impressive economic boom. Three weeks before the balloting, *The Economist,* which in the 1980s had lampooned Ireland as a nation of idle spendthrifts, celebrated its achievements and underscored just how daunting was the task facing Ahern. Ireland, the British publication raved, had "enjoyed an astonishing economic success" and was "getting richer all the time."[3]

To have any chance of victory, Ahern needed to somehow separate himself from Haughey. Though he enjoyed a good working relationship with both the Haughey and anti-Haughey factions in the party, Ahern unmistakably owed his rise to the legendary figure. Haughey had elevated him from obscurity, given him his first political role of any consequence, and nurtured his career from then on. "He was great to work with. . . . He was a pleasant guy, but tough most of the time, didn't deal with fools easy . . . was certainly demanding," Ahern said.[4] It wasn't personal style that bound the two men. Haughey fairly oozed an appetite for the good life while Ahern was a Manchester United football fan with a taste for Bass ale and anoraks. But Haughey had made no secret of his admiration for the younger man's political wiles. After Ahern hammered out a difficult agreement with the Progressive Democrats, the party's coalition partners in the 1989–1992 government, Haughey interrupted a briefing Ahern was giving for political journalists to proclaim of him: "He's the man. He's the best, the most skillful, the most devious and the most cunning of them all!"[5]

The praise, such as it was, dogged Ahern thereafter. But he retained a deep respect for his political patron, even after the McCracken tribunal's official verdict in August 1997. The 112-page report lambasted Haughey's testimony as "strange," "untrue," "quite unbelievable," and "incomprehensible"—all but branding the country's former taoiseach a liar. McCracken concluded that Haughey's lavish lifestyle had been funded by gifts from prominent individuals, including Dunne, with much of the proceeds hidden from the tax authorities in offshore bank accounts in the Cayman Islands. Dunne hadn't received or solicited special favors, McCracken said, but added, "If such gifts were to be permissible, the potential for bribery and corruption would be enormous."[6]

Well before the report's publication, Haughey's dealings were both an open secret in Dublin and a potentially mortal threat to Ahern. The younger man may have been loyal, but he was also ambitious. As the Fianna Fáil party convention, known as an *ard fheis* (ar-desh), got underway on April 18, Ahern was under pressure to disavow his mentor. Reluctantly, he did so. "No one is welcome in this party if they betray public trust. I say this and mean this with every fiber of my being," he told delegates.[7] An Ahern government, he said, would have no tolerance for the seedy blurring of public and private realms that had characterized the Haughey era.

Ahern had decided to fight the election in harness with the smaller Progressive Democrats. The PDs had burst onto the political scene in 1985, founded by Des O'Malley, a veteran Fianna Fáil politician who had clashed with Haughey one too many times. Derided as "Thatcherite" by union leaders and others on the left, the PDs had a clear identity focused around neo-liberal economic policies. Their ideological anchor made them an un-usual presence on the Irish political scene, where the two major parties had emerged from divisions over the national question in the 1920s and re-mained impossible to locate along a traditional left-right spectrum seven decades later.

On June 6, voters went to the polls and handed Fianna Fáil what once would have seemed an improbable victory. The Labour Party vote had im-ploded in the final weeks, leaving Ahern in position to form a new govern-ment. His would-be partners, the PDs, however, also had performed poorly. The PDs were discouraged after taking just four seats, but the parliamentary math still put them in government and thus tilted Irish economic policy to the right. On June 26, Ahern, 45, was sworn in as Ireland's youngest-ever taoiseach. "We believe tighter economic management is needed to safeguard the gains of recent years and maximize further growth so it will pay divi-dends for all," he told the Dáil in his maiden address. "We need to correct course so the dynamism of the Irish economy does not go off the rails."[8]

The first order of business was an ambitious program of tax-cutting, re-flecting the influence of the PDs. In American parlance, the tiny party's phi-losophy was based on supply-side economics, the counterintuitive theory that cutting tax rates will lead to higher, not lower, tax revenues. In the 1980s, Ireland's top income tax rate had been 65 percent. It had been re-duced to a still high 50 percent in the '90s, but both Fianna Fáil and the PDs promised further cuts. "There was no future, as I saw it, in Ireland contin-uing to be a high tax economy. . . . The personal taxes were an appalling disincentive to effort and contributed to high unemployment and lack of en-terprise," said O'Malley.[9]

The new government cut taxes across the board. The standard and top rates of personal tax fell, from 26 percent and 48 percent to 24 percent and 46 percent, respectively, as did corporate taxes, cut from 40 percent to 32 percent. Finance Minister Charles McCreevy made his biggest splash, however, by halving the capital gains tax from 40 percent to 20 percent. Mc-Creevy slashed the gains levy over the objections of his department's senior professionals, who feared a plunge in revenue. Instead, the government's take soared: from IR £84 million in 1996 to IR £609.2 million by 2000.[10]

On the other side of the world, a financial crisis was brewing that would make Ireland a rare bright spot on the global scene. In July, Thailand was forced to devalue its currency, the start of turmoil that spread across Asia, battering Malaysia, South Korea, and Indonesia, before reaching Brazil and Russia the following year. Before it ended, the episode shook governments on three continents, upended the conventional wisdom about how developing countries should pursue affluence, and gave global central bankers mistaken confidence that they could manage their way through even the worst difficulties.

Ireland's robust performance, meanwhile, was beginning to revive old fears of inflation. As the country entered its fifth consecutive year of strong growth, there were signs that annual price increases would near 3 percent. The currencies of Ireland's trading partners, including the U.S. dollar, had strengthened amid the Asian tumult, meaning imported goods that played a large role in the economy cost more. A tight labor market threatened to push wages up, and in the first quarter of 1998, new home prices were up 25 percent from one year earlier.[11] But Irish officials weren't overly concerned; the rising housing prices, they said, could be explained by strong economic growth, favorable demographics—including the annual arrival of thousands of immigrants—and low interest rates. The government tried to remove some of the froth from the market by eliminating a tax break that encouraged excessive investment. But the impact of the change was barely perceptible.[12]

Overall, Ireland was enjoying the best sustained economic climate in its history, but officials realized that no country could keep growing at this pace indefinitely. "It is essential to avoid making the presumption that the current boom should or could continue unabated. If growth is not kept to a sustainable level, the inevitable outcome would be the emergence of adverse economic conditions," including a "very serious deterioration" of international competitiveness, the finance department mandarins warned.[13] The Central Bank added its voice to the cautionary chorus, arguing that the economy's "exceptional" performance should be regarded as "something of a catch-up phenomenon."[14] After lagging behind the rest of Europe for so long, it was natural that once it got its act together, Ireland would grow rapidly for a time. The economy had expanded by more than 8 percent in 1998; in the future, growth should moderate to around 4 percent to 5 percent.

In its first year, the Fianna Fáil government concentrated on growing employment while preparing for what it hoped would be an eventual "soft landing" for the hard-charging economy. A soft landing is the palm-fringed oasis of economics, often glimpsed but rarely experienced. In this case, the chief impediment to the desired soft landing was the white-hot housing market. In April 1999, the Central Bank sent a letter to all Irish credit institutions reminding them of the dangers to the wider economy of "a lending policy that is excessively flexible."[15] Complicating the policy challenge for Ahern's government, the Central Bank was about to lose one of the principal tools for managing an economy: control over its money supply. Ireland was proud to be among the first 11 countries that would participate in the planned single European currency, the euro, when it debuted in financial markets on January 1, 1999.

Euro membership was a reaffirmation of Ireland's attachment to the European project and a validation of its sound economic management. But joining the euro meant surrendering to the planned European Central Bank (ECB) control over both the country's interest rates and the value of its currency. In the future, if Ireland's economy either languished or revved too high, Irish officials would be unable to respond by lowering or raising interest rates. If Irish products became profoundly uncompetitive, Central

Bank officials on Dame Street would be helpless to adjust the exchange rate. Those fundamental decisions now would be made in Frankfurt by officials attuned to the broader continental economy, not to the fortunes of 4 million people tucked away on Europe's periphery. In the short term, the process of joining the euro would involve a massive jolt of adrenaline for the already supercharged Irish economy. To bring the Irish economy in line with Germany, Europe's dominant economy, interest rates needed to drop sharply.

With the economy already running hot, Irish Central Bank officials were wary of dropping rates too quickly and inviting a surge of activity that could push prices higher. For the first nine months of 1998, the Central Bank maintained its benchmark lending rate at 6.19 percent, roughly twice the rate it needed to reach before the euro launched. Then, in quick succession, it cut the rate by 125 basis points in October and again in November, before lowering the rate to 3 percent in December.[16] The cuts were like adding gasoline-soaked logs to a raging fire. The economy leapt ahead, growing at a nearly 10 percent annual rate in 2000 and reaching an annualized average since 1994 of an astounding 8 percent.[17] Increasingly, Ireland was both the envy of Europe and a role model for small economies from Colombia to the Baltics.

"The economy was ticking over o.k., but we still weren't getting the jobs growth we needed," Ahern said.[18] Indeed, after a full decade of social partnership agreements and several years of robust growth, unemployment in 1997 remained above 10 percent. Then, after years in which Ireland seemed incapable of generating an adequate number of jobs for its people, help wanted ads suddenly blossomed. The economy might be overheating, but at least it was finally producing jobs. By the end of 2000, the number of those working was 40 percent higher than it had been just six years earlier. The microscopic 3.75 percent unemployment rate was a mere fraction of the double-digit rates of the early 1990s.[19] "The big thing for me was to see low unemployment. If you look at the period around '97, I was still unhappy with 10 percent unemployment and still some emigration. Really at that time I was saying: 'we need more investment. We have to get more investment. Have to be productive, have to keep the cost base right,'" Ahern said. "If we do that, we can really get unemployment down."

There was a fine line between an economy hitting on all cylinders, however, and one that was in danger of flying to pieces. Warnings from the green eyeshade corps at the Central Bank were growing more numerous. The economy was running above capacity. Unemployment was now "significantly below" the level associated with stable prices. Sure enough, inflation in 2000 had hit a disturbing 5.5 percent, more than double the eurozone average. Property prices also were getting out of hand. Where once the economy had grown thanks to exporting, it was now deriving three quarters of its forward momentum from domestic demand. That was a sign that the nature of the Irish boom was changing, shifting more toward consumption than production, and that the government needed to either raise taxes or cut spending to cool the economic engine.

HOW MUCH HAD CHANGED

The unfamiliar sense of economic achievement was having a profound effect on the Irish psyche, spawning a new willingness to confront one of the most painful episodes in the nation's history: the Great Famine of 1845–1847. The result of a fungus that caused the potato crop—the staple food for millions of peasants—to blacken into putrescence, the famine killed 1 million people and sent an additional 1.5 million into involuntary exile. In so doing, it remade both nineteenth-century Ireland and the countries of the new Irish diaspora, chiefly the United States.

There was no argument about the awfulness of the disaster that struck Ireland in the middle of the nineteenth century. Multiple near-total failures of the potato crop led to starvation for an impoverished population whose hold on the land lasted only so long as they could make their rent payments. At its peak in July 1847, more than one of every three people in the country subsisted on daily soup rations. Some non-Catholic aid groups gave food to the starving only if they first converted to the Protestant faith. In the poorest regions in the southwest, the famine swept away one quarter or one third of the population.[20] The deaths came so fast in parts of County Kerry that coffins equipped with hinged bottoms were utilized in multiple funerals. From a population of more than 8 million in 1841, Ireland over the next two decades shrank to just 5.7 million inhabitants. Across the Irish Sea, the famine was instrumental in cementing in the Anglo-Saxon mind an image of "an innate Irish inferiority."[21] As the Irish died, their colonial masters were confirmed in their belief that the race was inherently lazy as well as violent and thus responsible for its own plight. In the fall of 1846, *The Economist* told its readers that Irish suffering was "brought on by their own wickedness and folly."[22] This was an image that would follow the Irish across the seas to their new homes. Among the involuntary exiles, including those who took refuge in the United States, Britain's miserly relief efforts fed enduring emotions, from nationalist anger to suspicion of genocidal intent.

The famine's imprint could be seen to the present day. In Skibbereen, a town in Cork where victims died in droves, their bodies left to rot in the streets, local people were still known as "donkey eaters" because of what their ancestors had done to survive. For generations, the descendants of those who had survived and remained in Ireland were too ashamed to speak of the calamity. There had been almost nothing done to mark the famine's centennial; in the 1940s children who asked about the famine were "spanked or put out of the room," said Minister of State Avril Doyle.[23]

But the Irish of the late 1990s were a far more self-assured tribe than those who had come before them. For the 150th anniversary, the Irish government embarked upon an official multiyear program of commemoration.

Artists constructed a replica of one of the ships that carried those lucky enough to leave while volunteers reclaimed famine graveyards. Historians published more than 50 books on the subject. A new museum opened in Strokestown, County Roscommon, and drew 60,000 visitors in a year. The exhibits were housed in the stable yards of an eighteenth-century mansion that was once the home of Major Denis Mahon, a landlord who paid for a thousand of his impoverished tenant farmers to emigrate before social tensions boiled over and he was assassinated. The official commemoration ended on July 20, 1997, when President Mary Robinson unveiled a bronze sculpture of a famine ship with its rigging composed of ethereal, life-size skeletons.[24]

"The country had become rich enough to face how poor it had been," said Terence Brown, a prominent social historian. "If you're still struggling to get out of the lifeboat, you don't commemorate the sinking."[25] Academics had studied the famine for decades, but this period marked the first sustained public consideration of the cataclysm. The societal reflection would go on so long that some would detect a kind of "famine fatigue," but the effort provided a vital cultural context for the country's modern economic achievements.[26] Prosperity was welcome, of course, for its own sake. But affluence meant more when measured against the heartbreak and deprivation Ireland had once endured.

The famine attracted the attention of Roddy Doyle, who began a quixotic attempt to develop a movie on the great national trauma. A big-screen rendering of the deaths by starvation of poor, often illiterate peasants didn't exactly scream "box office success," as his producer, Andrew Eaton, acknowledged. "There is a danger (and obviously we don't want to dodge the horror of it all) that the film would be unremittingly grim," he wrote Doyle.[27] But after acquiring the film rights to the classic 1937 novel *Famine* by the Irish writer Liam O'Flaherty, Doyle began work on a screenplay. The 448-page novel is set near Galway during the famine's first two years and tells the story of a poor couple, Brian and Mary Kilmartin, struggling to survive in a ramshackle village called Black Valley. Doyle had long admired O'Flaherty's work, but he found it difficult to adapt. By the fall of 1996, he finished a first draft. "I think you have paired [*sic*] down the book brilliantly, but my main feeling was that it is, at present, too much Liam O'Flaherty and not enough Roddy Doyle," Eaton told him.[28]

Doyle eventually hammered the story into shape. But a bigger difficulty loomed: financing. Potential backers were interested only if he agreed to make significant changes in the plot. "I've had a series of bad meetings with people who want a love story about a couple beating the British Empire single-handedly while going a little bit hungry at the time," Doyle complained. " . . . It involves throwing away Liam O'Flaherty's work and writing something that you don't want to write."[29]

Doyle had already made one important change in the original story. The villain of the novel is Captain Jocelyn Chadwick, the dissolute and doomed English land agent, the landlord's representative, who sneers cruelly at Ireland's tenant farmers as "howling savages."[30] In Doyle's version, however, the land agent is Irish, not English, a change with echoes of a central debate over the Irish national narrative. "It's so easy to blame the English. Of course, some of the things they did at the time were appalling, quite outrageous. . . . But an awful lot of what happened, like the enforced evictions, were organized by Irish people," Doyle said.[31]

That sentiment placed Doyle firmly in the camp of historical revisionists, who took issue with the traditional Irish narrative of a poor and pure people victimized by British oppression. To the revisionists, the classic nationalist account was simplistic, obsessed with the past and overly forgiving of the Irish nation's own errors. Revisionists attributed much of what ailed modern Ireland to its stagnant blend of Catholicism and nationalism. In the case of the famine, nationalists traditionally blamed the disaster on the British: "The Almighty, indeed, sent the potato blight, but the English created the Famine."[32] British officials, motivated by laissez-faire ideology and disdain for a people they viewed as inferior, failed to respond in anything like the dimensions required, nationalists believed. Revisionists, however, saw the famine as the impersonal, if predictable, result of overpopulation in rural districts coupled with a dangerous dependence upon a single crop. The dispute between the competing interpretations of Irish history was of more than academic interest; it was particularly relevant in contemporary debates over the troubled North. Traditional nationalists, concentrated in the ranks of Ahern's Fianna Fáil, saw the conflict in the North as rooted in the evil of British "occupation" while revisionists viewed the pro-British unionists there as a community with its own legitimate identity. (The taoiseach's father, Con, was a staunch republican who had fought in the civil war on the anti-treaty side.) In a nutshell, revisionists boiled the myth and romance out of Ireland's rich national brew, leaving behind a dry residue of social forces and what they saw as objective reality.

The historical dispute ultimately spilled into the realm of popular entertainment. In late 1996, director Neil Jordan released a film version of the life of Michael Collins, the IRA intelligence chief who negotiated the treaty that ended the war with the British and was then killed by the anti-treaty forces in the civil war that followed. The movie sparked sometimes vicious attacks by revisionist figures such as the writer Eoghan Harris, the author of a competing screenplay, who described the film as a veiled effort to boost the armed republican cause in Northern Ireland. The sometimes outsized reaction was a reminder that Irish history remained something to be contested and fought over in contemporary politics. Doyle, too, took aim at nationalist myths with his sixth novel, *A Star Called Henry.* Told in the first person, it is the story of Henry Smart Jr., the tough, good-looking son of a one-legged bouncer at a Dublin whorehouse. His father dies, his mother is overwhelmed, and Henry and his little brother Victor strike out for a life as

thieving "street Arabs." Theirs is a harsh existence with little room for nationalist pieties:

> "–Do you love Ireland, lads? . . .
>
> They got no answer.
>
> We didn't understand the question. Ireland was something in songs
> that drunken old men wept about as they held onto the railings at three
> in the morning and we homed in to rob them; that was all."[33]

Henry grows up to become a sort of Zelig of Irish history, living on the
filthy streets of Dublin's notorious slums before joining the 1916 Easter Rising. As the bullets fly along O'Connell Street, he fights in the General Post
Office alongside the heroes of Ireland's bid for independence: Connolly,
Pearse, Collins, and Clarke. But this is no sentimental paean to self-
determination. Henry's tone is cynical and sardonic, utterly bereft of the
standard Rising hagiography. At a critical moment in the battle, he can be
found in the GPO basement having sex with his former schoolteacher, Miss
O'Shea. Of de Valera, hero of the republic, Henry says, "He was wearing red
socks and he smelled of shite."[34] Henry fights for Ireland's independence in
the GPO, in the guerilla conflict against the British that follows the doomed
revolt, and in the subsequent civil war. But he's clear-eyed about the class-
riven nature of the independent Ireland that will result—not a united Gaelic
homeland, but a land divided between ruler and ruled, just as it ever was.

One historian saw Doyle's historical fiction as "a crude debunking of
the 1916 Rising."[35] Yet its commercial success was just one indication that
traditional nationalist attitudes were proving themselves surprisingly muta-
ble. This ongoing evolution of the increasingly prosperous Republic also
was influencing the long quest for peace in Northern Ireland. Unionists,
who wanted the province to remain part of the United Kingdom, historically
were motivated in part by their fear of what life in the Republic was like. The

British-ruled corner of the island was industrial, urban, secular, and, most important, modern—unlike the theocratic, backward, rural state to its south. The North was factories and shipyards; the south thatched cottages and dim pubs. Among leading Unionist politicians, this stereotypical view would linger long after it lost the slightest resemblance to reality. "Contrast the United Kingdom state—a vibrant, multi-ethnic, multi-national liberal democracy, the fourth-largest economy in the world, the most reliable ally of the United States in the fight against international terrorism—with the pathetic, sectarian, mono-ethnic, mono-cultural state to our south," said David Trimble, leader of Northern Ireland's largest Unionist party.[36]

In the 1980s, Garrett Fitzgerald, Fine Gael's leader and twice taoiseach, had argued that the Republic needed to change both for its own sake and to make Unionists comfortable with the idea of sharing power with Catholics. The partition of the island in the 1920s had created two sectarian states on the island, the Protestant British enclave in the north, which openly discriminated against its Catholics, and the southern republic, which, if it practiced no such explicit favoritism, nonetheless was governed in strict accordance with Catholic principles. Promising a "constitutional crusade," Fitzgerald took the first abortive steps toward eliminating the Republic's claim to govern the entire island, codified in Articles 2 and 3 of the constitution, "in the interest of peace in Ireland and the removal of obstacles to Irish unity."[37]

Fitzgerald's crusade was cut short by his government's premature end. But even absent official action, societal changes in the Republic—now increasingly secular and cosmopolitan—became an important backdrop to diplomatic efforts. By the late 1990s, it was increasingly difficult for unionists to cite economic backwardness as proof of Irish inferiority or justification for their fears of a united Ireland. To the contrary, the economy in the southern half of the island was notably more dynamic than the rust-belt English dependency in the north. Thanks to the supercharged Celtic Tiger, the Irish economy was growing more than twice as fast as its northern counterpart. The average Irishman in 1999, by one measure, was actually better off financially than his counterpart in England—an astonishing turnaround in the historic relationship. As recently as 1984, the typical Irish income had been barely 70 percent of the British figure.[38]

Ahern moved within weeks of taking office to accelerate the peace process. In July 1997, the IRA restored its ceasefire, and two months later, the republican movement's political wing, Sinn Féin, entered multiparty talks in Belfast. From Christmas on, Ahern felt that genuine negotiations on a comprehensive deal were finally taking place. The Belfast talks, chaired by the former U.S. Senate Majority Leader George Mitchell, hurtled toward an April deadline. In the final days, amid the high-stakes negotiating, Ahern's mother died. But after marathon, all-night sessions, the parties reached an eleventh-hour bargain hailed as the "Good Friday Accord." The historic agreement provided for the establishment of a power-sharing government, cross-border agencies and a new council of the British Isles. It was, said an exhausted Ahern, "a day we should treasure." For the first time in three decades, an end to a bitter conflict that had killed 3,500 people and injured more than 37,000 others seemed at hand.

Less than two months later, the Irish people underscored just how much had changed. In simultaneous referenda on May 22, 1998, more than 71 percent of northerners and 94.4 percent of those in the south approved the deal. Both votes were of monumental importance, but the balloting in the Republic, by formally abandoning the constitutional claim to rule the entire island, seemed especially profound. Where once the Republic of Ireland had asserted that every individual on the island shared an "Irish" identity, it now accepted that its inhabitants could be "Irish," "British," neither, or both. No longer was a united Ireland assumed to be the natural state of affairs, interrupted only by an illegitimate British presence. Now, the rewritten constitution would acknowledge that a united Ireland could come about only with the explicit consent of the northern electorate—something all sides agreed would not happen anytime soon. What Irish voters had erased in the polling booth was "a constitutional claim to the six northern counties, a claim which they had been taught since childhood was a force of nature and a recognition that God had made our island a singular space, destined for unification."[39]

Though it had been decades since the Troubles physically spilled across the border, the fact that Belfast was seen globally as Europe's answer to Beirut habitually sullied the Republic's image. "Around the world, what was known of Ireland was not the Celtic Tiger miracle or the booming Irish economy; it was 'the Troubles.' So straight away I had to convince you when I came in to talk to you, that no, there isn't a war in Ireland," Ahern said.[40] The Good Friday Agreement's impact on the economy was "enormous," the taoiseach said, especially insofar as it encouraged continued strong inward investment from American multinationals. By 2000, U.S. companies such as Intel and Citigroup employed almost 75,000 Irish workers, roughly twice their payroll from a decade earlier.[41]

A MINNOW BESTS THE SHARKS

American cash had provided the main financial propellant for the 1990s Irish boom. The major manufacturing firms at the center of the Irish miracle usually relied upon internal funds from their corporate headquarters back in the United States or the United Kingdom rather than on bank financing. "The whole Irish growth story hadn't much to do with the banks," said Patrick Honohan, an economics professor at Dublin's Trinity College. Now, however, Irish banks gradually began assuming a more prominent role. Irish individuals and businesses were increasing their borrowings at a dramatic rate. In 1994, total private-sector credit amounted to barely more than 40 percent of gross domestic product. By the end of the decade, it had soared beyond 114 percent and showed no sign of reaching a plateau. "Such a rapid build up in credit would be a cause for concern for the stability of the whole system if borrowers were to find themselves unable to service these higher levels of debt," the Central Bank cautioned in 2000.[42] Even with Irish incomes growing more rapidly than they ever had, households were falling deeper into debt. Only four other European countries—Portugal, the Netherlands, Luxembourg, and Germany—had higher borrowing ratios. For now, however, the danger remained hypothetical.

Few financial institutions were surfing the boom as adeptly as Sean Fitzpatrick's tiny bank. Anglo Irish still specialized in the underserved midsection of the business market. A typical customer might be a solicitor in Athlone who needed financing to buy an office or a developer in Dublin who wanted to put up a string of retail shops. Anglo loved these loans, since repayment would be backed by an income stream tied to the property. There was nothing speculative about them. With every passing year, the bank reported record profits. From $29 million in 1996, after-tax earnings clocked steadily higher until they reached $100.6 million in 2000. "The real drive came about '96, '97, '98," Fitzpatrick said.[43]

By now, the bank was attracting attention beyond Irish shores; top institutions such as Fidelity Investments and Morgan Stanley were among Anglo shareholders. Still, with only $10 billion in assets in 2000, Fitzpatrick's operation was dwarfed by the traditional stalwarts of Dublin's banking scene, a "minnow" said the *Irish Times* to "the sharks" of Allied Irish or Bank of Ireland. (The latter boasted $63 billion in assets and was itself dwarfed by the giants of global banking; Citigroup, for example, was closing in on $1 trillion.) There was talk on the street that Anglo might be acquired as the European banking sector consolidated in preparation for the single currency. But it was Fitzpatrick who was on the prowl, adding Ansbacher Bankers Ltd., the loan book from Smurfit Paribas, and Royal Trust Bank of Austria, a private banking unit in Vienna serving wealthy

Americans. In 1999, he dispatched a young banker named David Drumm to open a representative office in Boston. "We'll be cherry-picking the best real estate investment deals," Drumm told an interviewer.[44] But in 2000, Fitzpatrick stumbled over a proposed merger with First Active, a small mortgage bank with a network of more than 50 retail branches in Ireland. Linking up with the smaller operation would broaden Anglo's product offerings and give it access to another deposit pool, but the markets reacted warily. First Active was a much higher cost operation than Anglo, in part because of its retail network—precisely the sort of expensive infrastructure Fitzpatrick had previously shunned. In May, Fitzpatrick appeared to have nailed down a deal that would make him CEO of the merged entity reporting to First Active Chairman John Callaghan. But the Anglo board balked, demanding both of the top jobs. First Active refused and the marriage collapsed. "Sean was very much keen on that. . . . He spent a lot of time giving out hell about the fact that it didn't happen," said Gerry Murphy, Anglo's chairman until 1999. "He thought he had it all on board."[45]

For years, Ireland's conservative bankers had expanded lending in line with the growth of their deposits, but no faster. As the Celtic Tiger roared on, however, demand for new loans was outrunning deposit growth. "We used to lend our customer deposits. . . . It was always our ambition to say our total lending was covered by our customer deposits," said Murphy.[46] The advantage of that strategy was its safety and predictability. It was hard for a bank to fail lending out the money it took in from savers. At the same time, it was also hard to make astonishing profits. The alternative to lending only customer deposits was to raise additional sums by selling short-term securities to investors or by borrowing in global markets. Anglo at first tiptoed down the riskier path, but by 2000, the bank raised almost $900 million selling such securities, up from just $119 million the year before. In a review of Ireland's financial sector, the International Monetary Fund noted the industry-wide change: "Banks are generally liquid; however, there has been a tendency towards a decline of funding from deposits and an increased reliance on wholesale [interbank] funding."[47] Still, Anglo ended the decade with $7 in deposits for every $1 it raised from global markets. There seemed little reason to worry—especially since Anglo, despite its go-go reputation—put such a premium on collateral. Fitzpatrick repeatedly emphasized that loan officers should make decisions on lending as if they were handling their own money. "In times of strong economic growth and a competitive environment the banking industry is in danger of taking on board risk assets of a poorer quality," he warned in one annual report. "We have implemented strong controls to ensure that this will not happen."[48]

Certainly, the supply of money available to banks such as Anglo appeared almost inexhaustible. Well into the 1990s, Irish banks had operated amid implicit limits on their lending growth. After all, there were only so many Irish pounds (or "punts") circulating, and the Central Bank kept a close watch on what banks did with them. Borrowing on the interbank market was possible, but there were transaction costs in converting deutschmarks or sterling into Irish currency as well as the risk that sudden exchange rate movements would erode profits. But with the 1999 introduction of the euro, all that changed. "Once you joined the euro, there was an infinite amount [of funding]. That made a total difference on the interbank market because now you had access to a huge pool. . . . In the old days, the pond was quite small because it was Irish punts," said Murphy.[49]

With the introduction of the euro, the Central Bank had lost control of interest rates and the money supply. But it remained responsible for regulating Ireland's financial sector. The need for adult supervision was manifest: Ireland's banks for two decades had staggered from scandal to scandal. In 1985, a subsidiary of Allied Irish Bank (AIB) called Insurance Corporation of Ireland (ICI) collapsed and left the Irish taxpayer with a hefty bailout bill. All of the major banks were involved in a subsequent scheme that allowed Irish citizens to avoid withholding tax on their bank deposits simply by declaring themselves nonresidents. (Bertie Ahern himself spoke of a "culture of tax evasion" in the country.) The Ansbacher bank ultimately acquired by Anglo had in the 1980s and early 1990s operated as a circuitous conduit for Irish citizens to shift money offshore and yet retain access to it in Dublin. Among those partaking: Charles Haughey, whose financial advisor routed the payments from Ben Dunne via an Ansbacher account.[50]

The global banking industry since the late 1980s had operated under a framework called Basel I, which specified how much capital banks must hold in reserve to guard against losses. But by the late 1990s, as bankers developed new and more complex financial instruments, it was becoming more difficult for regulators to assess the risks any institution faced. Traditionally, regulators had monitored banks' health by poring over individual loans, ensuring that each was backed with appropriate collateral, and scrutinizing a bank's entire portfolio to satisfy themselves that it was not excessively concentrated in one type of business. The problem now was that banks could reduce—some would say mask—their risks by using derivative securities or complex hedging strategies. Besides, markets were moving so quickly that an institution's risk profile could change in days or even hours. In response, regulators in the developed economies began focusing on a bank's internal systems, corporate governance, and formal risk-control processes rather than on the specifics of individual loans. The idea was to create the proper incentives for a bank to operate safely and ensure it had the internal ability to do so. The key, however, would be not to take such a "big-picture" approach that any sense of a bank's actual operations was lost.[51]

In April 2000, the Financial Stability Forum, representing central banks from the major world economies, examined 37 offshore financial centers and judged Ireland among the best-regulated, those "generally perceived as having legal infrastructures and supervisory practices, and/or a level of resources devoted to supervision and co-operation relative to the size of their financial activities . . . that are largely of a good quality and better than in other [offshore centers]." There was one cautionary note: the forum ranked Dublin among four locations that warranted "continuing efforts to improve the quality of supervision."[52] At Anglo, and its larger competitors, meanwhile, there was little fear of the regulator's bite. "All that the Central Bank could do was write and sort of say, 'you're expanding too fast.' But in effect, they had no control, real control compared to what they had [before the euro]," said Murphy. " . . . Everybody would ignore it."

As the bank grew, Fitzpatrick's profile rose accordingly. He joined the head of the Irish Stock Exchange in judging *Business & Finance* magazine's Entrepreneur of the Year Award and began speaking at corporate events alongside government ministers. In an April 1998 speech, following disclosure of banking scandals linked to offshore tax-avoidance accounts, Fitzpatrick called on the industry to "enthusiastically embrace the concept of transparency."[53] By 2000, he had risen to head the Irish Banking Federation, the industry's main trade association, where he promulgated a sober industry code of ethics. Introducing it in the wake of revelations of the banks' role in facilitating widespread tax evasion, he said, "The industry must do everything in its power to ensure that we do not warrant in the future the degree of criticism that has been meted out to us in recent times."[54]

The speeches were standard captain-of-industry pablum. What really distinguished Fitzpatrick was his role as an Irish Catholic in building a home-grown financial powerhouse. Until "Seanie" came along, Catholics were not the ones deciding who got money; they were the ones asking for it. Ireland's traditional banking powers had emerged from the waning days of the Protestant Ascendancy, the period beginning in the late seventeenth century that established an overwhelming Protestant dominance of Irish life. The Bank of Ireland, the nation's leading modern financial institution, began operating in 1783, at a time when Catholics still awaited the full repeal of the noxious Penal Laws, which had proscribed their faith and forbidden them to bear arms, buy land, teach, or fill most professional occupations. Enforcement of the anti-Catholic statutes varied over the years, but was most strict in depriving Catholics of "economic and political power and social position."[55] Catholics were left free to engage in trade, since Protestant gentlemen disdained such grubby endeavors. But the genteel professions, notably including finance, were off-limits. Almost two centuries later, "Most Irish banks and insurance companies had no Roman Catholics at senior or board level," Mary Kenny wrote in *Goodbye to Catholic Ireland*.[56]

To Fitzpatrick, the rise of Anglo Irish was more than merely a commercial success. The bank's outsider struggle to subdue its Protestant rivals was the financial equivalent of Glasgow's Celtic football club taking on archrival Ranger—a clash he'd traveled across the Irish Sea more than once to witness firsthand. From vindicating his father, who had been labeled a deadbeat by a Protestant lender, to establishing a physical presence on English soil with Anglo's London operation, he had redeemed and advanced the native Irish. "He would see himself as the absolute quintessential Irishman, a Gael. . . . It's a kind of revenge," says social historian Terence Brown.[57] During the Celtic Tiger era, Fitzpatrick was not alone in finding deeper meaning in what others might regard as prosaic transactions. When Derek Quinlan, a former tax inspector turned property mogul, bought London's Savoy Hotel Group in 2004, one of his Irish employees ordered the tricolor flown from the roof of London's landmark Connaught Hotel. Quinlan gently wept when he was told.[58]

By the year 2000, after almost a decade of energetic growth, Irish pride was swelling toward hubris. Jobs were so plentiful, developers were luring English workers to Dublin construction sites in a reversal of a generations-old pattern even as visiting delegations from China and Colombia, Singapore and Slovenia trooped to Dublin to learn the secrets of the Irish miracle. Deputy Prime Minister Mary Harney boasted publicly that the Irish didn't have to choose between the American and European ways of life. Rather than follow "Boston or Berlin," they could have the best of both, the robust economic growth of the United States with the generous social safety net of Europe. "Ireland is now the fastest-growing country in the developing world," Harney crowed in a July 2000 speech to the American Bar Association. "And did we have to pay some very high price for pursuing this policy option? Did we have to dismantle the welfare state? Did we have to abandon the concept of social inclusion? The answer is: No, we didn't.

At least, not yet.

CHAPTER 6

HAVING IT ALL

*I*T WAS EARLY AFTERNOON ON A CRYSTALLINE autumn Tuesday when state broadcaster RTE first aired the terrible images from New York. And just like that, the good times threatened to come to an abrupt end. The terrorist attacks of September 11, 2001, plunged global markets into crisis and seemed certain to trigger a recession in the United States that would profoundly chill the Irish economy. The taoiseach, who was meeting with U.S. diplomats to discuss the next steps in the Northern Ireland peace process when an aide interrupted with news of the attack, swiftly declared a national day of mourning. On Friday, Ireland—alone in Europe—shuttered its government offices, businesses, and schools in tribute; at one point, an estimated six thousand people queued to sign a book of condolence at the U.S. Embassy.

When the Dáil assembled in special session the following week, "atrocities in the United States of America" was the first order of business. Bertie Ahern spoke of a "clear and shockingly defined moment in history." Fine Gael's Michael Noonan said the attacks underscored the need for Sinn Féin and the IRA to "get off the fence" in the North and begin putting their weapons beyond use. Ruari Quinn of the Labour Party was eloquent on the ties between Ireland and the United States: "For generations America has been the haven for those fleeing economic want and political oppression here. Is there a family in this country, let alone in this House, who does not have a relative in the United States?"[1]

Left unsaid were the likely consequences for the Irish of what had just happened. In the wake of the dot-com bust, the U.S. and global economies had already been deteriorating for a year even before the planes hurtled into the Twin Towers. Now, the shock of the attack and the disruption to finely tuned global supply chains threatened to compound the economic palsy. Sears executives privately told the Federal Reserve their September 11 sales were down 50 percent from the same day in 2000. In Lower Manhattan, both the idled New York and NASDAQ exchanges could not resume trading until Consolidated Edison restored power supplies destroyed in the attack. Crews ultimately resorted to the equivalent of an enormous extension cord, laying thick cables along Wall Street's curbs. At the New York Federal Reserve Bank, the nerve center for the nation's financial institutions, harried officials could make but not receive telephone calls two days after September 11. In the markets, the dollar tumbled, and the Dow Jones Industrial Average, which had closed at 9,605 on September 10, quickly surrendered 1,400 points in the first days after trading resumed. Amid the danger of renewed attacks and the prospect of prolonged global war involving the world's largest economy, worried central bankers struggled to divine the future. "This event came at a most inopportune time if one really wants to look at it purely from an economic forecaster's point of view," Alan Greenspan, the chairman of the Federal Reserve Board, told Fed governors on a hastily arranged conference call.[2]

Ireland had grown at a nearly double-digit annual pace in 2000, its seventh consecutive year of jaw-dropping economic performance. The unemployment rate in early 2001 dipped to 3.7 percent, an astonishing achievement, but the Irish boom was living on borrowed time. The bursting of the Internet bubble, rising oil prices, and a synchronized slowdown in the United States, Japan, and Germany all combined to halve global growth, producing "the sharpest slowdown in global economic activity in two decades."[3] As an extremely open economy dependent upon global trade, Ireland was especially hard hit. Central Bank Governor Maurice O'Connell said in November that the turbocharged "Celtic Tiger phase is now over."[4] By the end of 2001, growth had "effectively ceased."[5]

However inevitable, any prolonged slowdown would be bad news for Bertie Ahern with an election fast approaching. But the Irish prime minister was about to get some help from friends in America. To prevent the post-attack upheaval from capsizing the U.S. and global economies, Greenspan slashed interest rates to 1 percent and kept them there. That put pressure on the European Central Bank (ECB) to follow suit, which it did, lowering rates from 4.75 percent in 2001 to barely 2 percent two years later. Low interest rates meant massive financial stimulus for Ireland, at times making borrowed money effectively free. Because inflation in Ireland was higher—often much higher—than the eurozone average, interest rates set in Frankfurt were too low for Irish conditions. On average, the ECB's benchmark lending rate was six percentage points lower than an Ireland-only rate would have been, according to a standard formula called the "Taylor rule." At times, the discrepancy was even greater. In early 2003, when the ECB rate was 2.75 percent, the Irish economy warranted a rate in excess of 10 percent.[6]

For political reasons, the government poured fuel on the economic fire with its own free-spending ways. Both the number of workers on the public payroll, and their pay, began to soar. Ahern added nearly fifty thousand workers to the government ranks by 2002, a jump of 22 percent in just four years.[7] By the late 1990s, public-sector pay was spiraling out of control. Nurses, for example, won pay hikes between 1996 and 1999 of 26 percent to 47 percent. In 2000, the government introduced a process called "bench-marking," which was intended to align compensation for government work-ers with prevailing rates for similar jobs in the private sector. In theory, the new pay system would be coupled with improvements in public-sector effi-ciency. In practice, the head of the major teachers' union gleefully compared the results to "going to an ATM." In mid-2002, the first report of the new pay-review board recommended salary increases of up to 25 percent.[8]

On December 5, 2001, Finance Minister Charles McCreevy, known to friend and foe alike as "Champagne Charlie," went to the Dáil to introduce the government's 2002 budget. Ahern deferred to his finance minister, a neo-liberal who had flirted with the Progressive Democrats in the 1980s before remaining with Fianna Fáil, in crafting the government's financial plans.[9] McCreevy was still smarting from opposition gibes that he had grossly un-derestimated spending the previous year. The new budget, he insisted, was aimed at "carefully managing" the public's money and did not require a sin-gle euro of borrowing. "Careful economic and budgetary management pro-vides the soundest basis for our future," McCreevy told the Dáil. Earlier that year, the finance minister had launched a new national pension fund that would receive 1 percent of economic output each year to cover the future costs of a rapidly aging population. Despite the nod to prudence, what fol-lowed was a veritable laundry list of giveaways: more generous old age pen-sion checks, fatter child benefit payments, a 20 percent increase in provisions for free electricity for qualifying households, and even a sharp cut in the bet-ting tax. Along with those goodies, McCreevy offered personal tax cuts worth $568 million as well as reductions in corporate levies valued at $311 million. In the event, government spending in 2002 would increase 6.3 percent after taking inflation into account, on top of an even more lavish 12.1 percent real increase the previous year. If this were prudence, it was hard to conceive of profligacy. At a time when prices were rising in Ireland at a pace more than twice the eurozone average, the government was stepping on the economic accelerator. IMF experts tried repeatedly to dissuade the Irish from their free-spending ways but were ignored.[10]

The tax cuts were also notable for reshaping the tax base in a manner that would ultimately have profound implications for the government's finances. Fianna Fáil was consciously removing individuals from the tax rolls, leaving the government increasingly reliant upon revenue sources other than personal income tax, such as the transaction charge associated with the buying and selling of homes. Since coming to office in 1997, Ahern's government boasted that it had removed more than 380,000 people from the tax rolls. The tax tinkering didn't stop there. Several property-related tax incentives were scheduled to expire in 2002, but the government opted to extend them for two years. That left in place provisions allowing investors to deduct from their tax bill costs associated with everything from urban renewal projects to construction of multistory parking garages. McCreevy also reversed course on the deductibility of mortgage interest for residential rental properties, which he had stripped from the tax code only two years before, after what Ahern described as "an outcry."[11] Now, amid signs that new construction was failing to keep up with roaring demand, Fianna Fáil suddenly wanted investors back in the game.

Yet the criticism from the opposition benches was not that the government was doing too much, but too little. Fine Gael complained of lengthy waiting lists for medical treatment and public housing, a national road system that remained a "shambles" almost a decade into the boom, and a school system starved for funds. "Ireland is the sixth worst funder of primary education in the OECD," said Fine Gael's Jim Mitchell. "Congratulations, we are ahead of Mexico and the Czech Republic."[12] Ahern & Co. could afford to take a relaxed view of the opposition brickbats; as voters headed to the polls in June 2002, the economy was showing signs of renewed life. One statistic above all others shaped Ahern's reelection campaign: the number of those working had soared by 20 percent, or more than 300,000 since Fianna

Fáil came to power in 1997. The taoiseach could rightly boast that Ireland had finally solved a problem—an inability to provide gainful employment for its people—that had plagued the country since its founding. Sure enough, when the counting was done, Fianna Fáil had romped home with a massive vote, though short of an outright parliamentary majority. Once again, Ahern would require the PDs' support to form a government.

The economy grew by only 2.9 percent in 2002, its weakest performance in a decade, and what growth took place was predominantly in the construction and housing sectors. In 2002, John Hurley, the governor of the Central Bank, wrote the heads of all the major lending institutions to underscore "the need to maintain high lending standards" and began sending his inspectors to check the bank's loan books.[13] The Central Bank, among others, had been concerned about overly liberal credit growth and signs of froth in the housing market for some time. Signs of excess abounded: in tiny Castletownshend, in West Cork, for example, developers were pushing ahead with plans for 100 new homes in a village consisting of just 98 dwellings. "This development is wrong for here," one resident told the *Irish Times*. "The village is going to double in size at one fell swoop."[14]

Still, there were legitimate complaints about the inadequacy of housing supply. Much of Ireland's housing stock before the boom was old and dilapidated, clearly unfit for the cash-flush masses of the Celtic Tiger. The planning process, especially in Dublin, was notorious for corruption and spawned a seemingly endless series of national scandals. Developers often held back vast tracts of land in an effort to promote the scarcity that fed higher prices. "House prices were growing by too much and the demand was too strong; that's why they were growing by too much. Our supply side wasn't strong enough. The general view was that we needed about 45, 50 thousand houses a year, you know, all the time and we weren't producing that," said Ahern. "So our first pressure was to try and get more houses built to try and dampen down the prices."[15]

Easy money from the banks coupled with stimulative government policies encouraged limitless building. In 2002, for the first time in any 12-month period, Irish builders threw up more than 50,000 homes. In 2003, more than 62,000 were built, a record quickly surpassed the following year, when more than 72,000 arose. It was as if the engine of construction, once started, could not be stilled. Despite the supply increase, prices kept rising, too. They were up 14 percent in 2003 alone and had roughly tripled since 1996.[16] The pace was insane, clearly speculative, and unsustainable. And yet the building frenzy roared on. Buying and selling homes became a national obsession. Wags dubbed the ad-rich *Irish Times'* weekly real estate section "property porn." When local boosters buried a stainless steel time capsule beneath the new Spire landmark on O'Connell Street, the newspaper's full-color property supplement was one of the ten items left for future generations to ponder.[17]

Home ownership soared toward 80 percent of the population, well above the roughly 65 percent reached at the height of the boom then unfolding in the United States. Irish land hunger derived from a rural ethic that continued to shape the culture, even as villages emptied and people thronged the cities. "Land is all that matters, Tadhg boy, own your own land," advised Bull McCabe, the iconic character in John B. Keane's play *The Field*.[18] To historian Diarmaid Ferriter, contemporary Ireland's hunger for property had roots in the Irish peasantry's history of dispossession. To this day, Irish tenants enjoy fewer protections against arbitrary evictions than do renters in the United States or continental Europe. "Down through the years, there would be a sense that money spent on rent is wasted money. This goes right up to the present day," he says. "There's an important cultural angle to this. A detestation for landlords is drilled into us from a very young age."[19]

Warnings that Ireland was about to repeat the mistake of other countries that had overindulged in property began to sound. Goodbody Stockbrokers in March 2003 said the country only needed 38,000 new homes annually and was heading into "bubble territory." The IMF followed suit later that year, noting that Irish house prices had risen by more than 130 percent since 1993, and criticizing the government's on-again, off-again use of tax incentives for making prices more volatile.[20] William Slattery, former deputy head of banking supervision at the Central Bank, published an article in *Business & Finance,* a widely read Dublin business magazine, warning that unsustainable credit growth was creating a danger of a crash of 30 to 50 percent in property prices. "A substantial decline in property prices is inevitable," he wrote.[21]

But the cautionary notes were lost in a blizzard of otherwise positive reviews. The IMF, in the same report that obliquely raised housing concerns, praised Ireland's "enviable achievements" and "sound policies."[22] And there were always those who saw the housing glass as more than half full. "There is no evidence to suggest that Dublin house prices will see a fall," wrote Michael Grehan, managing director of Sherry Fitzgerald Residential, a prominent realtor. " . . . There is nothing to suggest that we are facing some sort of economic Armageddon that would see large scale job losses or the sort of collapse in personal income that would drive people to desperate measures."[23]

WE AREN'T GOING ANYWHERE

It took money to build that many houses, and lots of it. Fortunately, Ireland's banks were happy to oblige—especially Anglo Irish, which continued to raise enormous sums in global markets. Its sales of short-term commercial debt—essentially borrowings from global investors—grew to more than $8 billion in 2004 versus less than $1 billion in 2000.[24] That gave Anglo's lending division the wherewithal to satisfy growing demand from Ireland's increasingly busy development industry. Anglo's borrowers read like a "Who's Who" of the property business: Liam Carroll, the taciturn skinflint billionaire known for dotting urban Ireland with ranks of cheap shoebox apartments; Bernard McNamara, the construction mogul who built up the family business he had inherited from his father; former stonemason Sean Mulryan, known for his love of football and interests in eastern Europe; the financier Derek Quinlan; and Joe O'Reilly, the developer behind the Dundrum Shopping Centre.[25] Many of these men, like Sean Fitzpatrick, were self-made successes from the countryside, "new money" rising in defiance of established wealth. Anglo took a remarkably proactive approach to its developer clients, sometimes approaching them with both potential land deals and the financing needed to pull them off, according to a senior banking industry executive.

Fitzpatrick was presiding over the rise of a rare home-grown financial success. There were a few genuine Irish corporate stars in this period, such as Michael O'Leary's discount airline Ryanair, which eventually grew to be Europe's largest. But in global business circles, Ireland was known more as a locale for, and beneficiary of, foreign direct investment. When businessmen thought of Ireland, it was often Intel, rather than any genuinely Irish company, that came to mind. But Anglo was Seanie and Seanie was Anglo. Where one stopped and the other began was impossible to tell. The farmer's son was identified with his bank every bit as much as Bill Gates was with Microsoft or Jack Welch with General Electric. And he loved the limelight. In 2002, Fitzpatrick was "delighted" to be named Irish Businessman of the Year by *Business & Finance* magazine. At the black-tie dinner presentation at Dublin's Four Seasons hotel, he was seated at the head table alongside Mary Harney, the deputy prime minister.[26] "It would have very much been seen as Sean's bank. . . . People were just absolutely cheering Anglo all the way along," a former colleague said.

Anglo's success was now reaching the point where the bank could no longer be ignored. The traditional powers of Irish banking had once condescended to Fitzpatrick's scrappy little operation, deriding it as a fly-by-night outfit that probably wouldn't last. With $42 billion in assets in 2004, Anglo remained about one-third the size of Bank of Ireland or Allied Irish Bank. But it was growing much faster than either. Between 2000 and 2004, Anglo's assets more than tripled; the $29 billion it added to the balance sheet over those five years exceeded AIB's new loans during the same period. Fitzpatrick was gaining ground on the establishment banking powers, and he was doing it while increasing his profits more than five times as fast as either AIB or Bank of Ireland.[27] "Anglo was always out there making the running, making the running on pay, making the running on bonuses, making the running on loans and so on," said Phil Flynn, the then-chairman of Bank of Scotland's Ireland operations. " . . . They were very, very heavy into property and of course we were all chasing after them."[28]

Anglo wasn't the only competitor worrying Bank of Ireland and Allied Irish. New players in the residential mortgage market, notably Halifax/Bank of Scotland and Ulster Bank, were attracting loads of new business with their cut-rate loans. The big boys, under pressure from restless shareholders and stock analysts, felt obliged to fight back. "Anglo was so successful, though it was in a very narrow sphere of an incredible property boom. . . . When you're losing market share, when your profitability rate is below Anglo's—which is much smaller than you [and] which is rapidly growing up to your size, you have to say to [yourselves] what are we going to do about this?" said one of the directors of an Anglo rival. "We must now enter the market, which is basically the development market that Anglo were in, because otherwise they'll kill us."[29]

In 2004, Michael Buckley, the chief executive of Allied Irish, established a "win back" team to recapture lending business that had been lost to Anglo.[30] Bank of Ireland lured Richard Boucher from Bank of Scotland to head up its corporate banking unit, "specifically to do Anglo-type lending," said one former Anglo executive. Indeed, Irish banks as a whole plunged into the property game in a big way. In 2001, real estate loans accounted for about 38 percent of domestic banks' total lending. Three years later, they exceeded 54 percent and continued to rise.[31] To get enough cash to really play in the development world, the banks needed to tap global markets. Bank of Ireland, which in the 1990s had funded its loan book from customer deposits, now waded into the swift currents of global financial channels, raising almost $25 billion in 2004 by selling its own debt securities and an equivalent amount in loans from other banks. That total haul funded a bit more than one-half of the bank's new loans that year, leaving it even more dependent upon the goodwill of deep-pocketed global investors than the buccaneers at Anglo.[32] In a world awash with cash—what Fed Chairman Ben Bernanke would later label a "global savings glut"—it was easy for the banks to tap this pool of liquidity. And they would need to tap it and keep tapping it, since much of their borrowing was short-term. More than $2.8 billion of Anglo's debt, for example, needed to be paid off in three months or less; an additional $2.1 billion was due within a year.[33] So long as fresh money was available, the banks' business model worked like a charm. The IMF noted that of all European banks, Irish banks were the most dependent upon wholesale funding markets—and the most profitable, with a return on equity more than twice the eurozone average.[34] Inside Anglo, the former executive said, there was a "sense of invulnerability."

Whatever private fears may have been aired in bank boardrooms, they were easily dispelled. At one major bank, a board member says he expressed concern about the pell-mell expansion of the balance sheet, but was assured by auditors that there was nothing to worry about. The banks certainly had little to fear from their government minders. In the final quarter of 2003, the Central Bank ran a stress test of the Irish banks to see if they could withstand a sharp fall in housing prices along with unexpected difficulties obtaining their customary funding. The results, it said, were "positive." Regulators also launched an inspection of mortgage loan files at the major lending institutions and were cheered when they uncovered "no questions of financial soundness" at any of the banks.[35] The exams may not have been sufficiently rigorous, or they may have focused too much attention on the amount of capital that banks held in reserve and not enough on making sure the banks weren't running excessive risks by concentrating loans in a single industry, according to economist Karl Whelan of University College Dublin.[36] Within the banks, there was a sense of sanguine superiority toward the civil servants tasked with monitoring them that bordered on arrogance. "There was extraordinarily incompetent regulation. There were a number of regulators, who were simple products of the civil service. And I have terrific regard for the public servants. But there are jobs they can do well and jobs they cannot do well," said one bank director. "They wouldn't have a notion what they were dealing with. They'd just come in and look at the books, have a nice lunch and chat about interest rate policy."[37]

As Ireland's financial industry boomed, and the banks heedlessly took on more risk, the nation's regulatory system was undergoing far-reaching change. From May 1, 2003, the Central Bank was reorganized into a hybrid structure called the Central Bank and Financial Services Authority of Ireland. Within the CBFSAI, the bank would continue to monitor the overall health of the nation's financial system, but it surrendered its traditional responsibility for policing Ireland's banks. A new organizational sibling—the Financial Regulator—assumed that role, promulgating a "principles-based approach" that aimed to police finance through a select number of general guidelines, the banks' self-interest and firm enforcement. Critics castigated the model as "self-regulation" or "light touch" in contrast to ostensibly stricter rules-based systems such as that of the United States. The distinction between the two approaches often was less dramatic than the rhetoric would imply; in practice, under either type of system, much depended upon the aggressiveness of the regulators. Under Alan Greenspan, the Federal Reserve opposed efforts to regulate investment contracts known as "derivatives," for example, opting instead to rely upon "the overall effectiveness of private market discipline."[38] Irish regulators, for their part, sought to balance twin (and potentially contradictory) objectives, which were set out in new legislation. They wanted to both safeguard the financial system and promote the country as a location for the global investment industry. Dublin's International Financial Services Center, which had opened in 1987, defied the skeptics and grew to employ more than twenty thousand people. At the same time, companies operating there—multinationals such as Citigroup, Merrill Lynch, and State Street—did not want to end up with Dublin as a seedy tax haven, a sort of Cayman Islands sans sunshine and beaches. Liam O'Reilly, chief executive of the Financial Regulator, explained the competing impulses in a 2004 speech. "A regulatory environment which is too light or non-existent leads to reputation questions, which can be a competitive disadvantage. On the other hand, an overly intrusive environment can be costly and off-putting. We strongly believe that this circle is best squared by maintaining a principles-based approach, placing responsibility on boards and top management who are expected to be competent, conscious of risks and are responsible for inculcating a culture of probity throughout their organizations. What I am saying is that industry must strive for excellence in corporate governance," he told an industry group.[39]

Yet corporate governance was precisely the issue in December 2004, when Fitzpatrick ended his extraordinary run at the helm of Anglo. The charming glad-hander, who announced in July he would retire as CEO at the year's end, had humbled the naysayers, turning in 19 consecutive years of rising profits, from barely $1 million in 1986 to $627 million in his final year. "We weren't any brighter than our peers or our counterparts. We were hungrier," he told one interviewer. "We have arrived and we aren't going anywhere."[40]

Indeed, Fitzpatrick himself was only leaving the corner office to move upstairs and become chairman of the board. Corporate governance experts, worried about a potential lack of accountability at the helm of the fast-growing bank, tut-tutted. A company's chairman is supposed to represent shareholders by riding herd on the chief executive, the hired help tasked with running the business day to day. Would a former CEO, who had had a hand in selecting his replacement, provide the sort of independent perspective required in that role? Or would he be more concerned with making sure that his policies and his successor were seen as successful? With Anglo operating as a veritable profits machine, no one seemed terribly concerned with what were—for now anyway—only hypothetical dangers.

THE POSSIBILITIES ARE FANTASTIC

Sustained prosperity was making itself felt in ways that were transforming what it meant to be "Irish." Construction jobs were so plentiful that Ireland, in a reversal of historic experience that would have seemed impossible a decade earlier, began importing workers. Government officials fanned out across Europe on labor recruitment road shows that their ancestors would have found as unfathomable as space travel. Tens of thousands of eager laborers from eastern Europe saw in Ireland the same opportunity for advancement that the Irish had seen in the United States a century earlier. So many Poles came to Dublin that during Poland's presidential election, Polish-language campaign posters sprouted on street corners like mushrooms after a spring rain. And foreign workers were not appearing only on building sites. At Mater Hospital, where Bertie Ahern had once worked as an accounts clerk, 80 percent of the nurses had been born overseas, many in the Philippines and India.[41] Celtic brogues were being replaced at any service job—including the local pub—by Slavic accents. Chinese students, frustrated by tougher U.S. visa requirements in the wake of 9/11, began matriculating at Trinity College and University College Dublin. Likewise, those fleeing conflict or persecution at home increasingly headed for Ireland, where they could anticipate that the country's own experience of emigration and its newfound affluence would assure them of a warmer welcome than anywhere else in the European Union. In 1992, about three dozen asylum-seekers had presented themselves to Irish immigration officers at Shannon Airport. By 2000, the annual total reached 10,938.[42]

They say the past is a foreign country, but for Roddy Doyle, it was the present that felt unfamiliar. "I went to bed in one country and woke up in a different one," he wrote. "I'd written a novel, *The Van,* in 1990 about an unemployed plasterer. Five or six years later, there was no such thing as an unemployed plasterer. A few years on, all the plasterers seemed to be from Eastern Europe. In 1994 and 1995, I wrote *The Woman Who Walked into Doors.* It was narrated by a woman called Paula Spencer, who earned her money cleaning offices. She went to work with other working class women like herself. Ten years later, I wrote *Paula Spencer.* Paula was still cleaning offices, but now she went to work alone and the other cleaners were men from Romania and Nigeria."[43]

Doyle was intrigued by the changing face of Ireland. So in April 2000, when a pair of Nigerian journalists launched *Metro Éireann,* a monthly paper dedicated to chronicling the rise of multicultural Ireland, he offered his services. "We were so happy," said Chinedu Onyejelem, one of the founding editors. From then on, Doyle fed them an 800-word short-story chapter each month. They were quick hits, not as well thought out as his novels. But they were good reads, and they brought Doyle's customary acute observations and humor to the experience of the new Irish. Doyle, one observer wrote, "is the only major contemporary Irish writer tackling the subject of the social and cultural impact of the Celtic Tiger on Ireland in a committed manner."[44]

The first story, appearing in May 2000, was "Guess Who's Coming for the Dinner," a takeoff on the 1967 Sidney Poitier film; it centered on an Irish father's reaction to his daughter's bringing home a Nigerian man. Larry Linnane, the good-hearted father, struggles with his instinctual racism, but gradually comes to like and even admire "Ben." By the end, Larry is disappointed when he learns that the Nigerian and his daughter are no more than friends—and he is proud of himself for the sentiment[45]: "He was happy enough. He wasn't a racist. There was a black man sitting across from him and he wanted to be his father-in-law. He wasn't sure why, but that didn't matter. Larry was happy with himself." A version of the story later appeared in *The New Yorker,* but only after Doyle ignored an editor's advice to change the title to "Chocolate."[46]

"Deportees," the second story, provided the long-awaited sequel to *The Commitments,* reprising the character of band manager Jimmy Rabbitte, who is now married and the father of three children. He places a "help wanted" ad seeking musicians for a band designed to represent multicultural Dublin: "Brothers and Sisters, Welcome To Ireland. Do you want the Celtic Tiger to dance to your music? If yes, The World's Hardest-Working Band Is Looking For You. White Irish . . . Need Not Apply."[47] That is an ad that would have read like gibberish not so long ago, when Ireland's few black faces inevitably belonged to visitors. Onyejelem, who went to Dublin in the late 1990s for training in the airline industry before becoming a freelance journalist, remembers standing at one end of O'Connell Street, scanning the length of the boulevard and seeing only one other black person. "It was not common to see black people around," he said. By the turn of the millennium, however, growing numbers of Nigerians had fled ethnic tensions, corruption, and political unrest at home for the comparative ease and safety of life in boom-time Ireland. The Irish had strong historical ties to Nigeria, where Irish missionaries ran schools and served the poor. During the 1967–1970 Biafran war, aid efforts led by an Irish priest had been critical in preventing starvation in the secessionist Biafran province. So the first waves of Nigerian refugees were greeted warmly. "At the beginning, it was welcoming because people could easily stop you on the street to chat with you, to talk about the Biafran war. People could talk to you about religion, people could talk to you about what kind of tea you drank back in Nigeria. People were very curious," said Onyejelem.[48] But as the number of Nigerians mounted, and as they remained idle during the sometimes lengthy asylum application process as the law required, irritation grew. Only a sliver of those applying were allowed to stay permanently, but black faces became far more common on Dublin streets.

One area where tensions flared was Bertie Ahern's north side bastion of Drumcondra. In some electoral wards there, the new Irish outnumbered the natives, according to Ahern. "The Irish are like anybody else, if they're in here and they're working and doing their bit, they like them. If they think they're in here dossing on the dole, they don't like them and the Nigerians, I suppose, are not top of the list because a lot of them are illegal. They haven't come in here the proper way," Ahern said.[49]

Historically, Ireland was a place people fled, not a refuge or a destination. Now, as people flocked to Dublin seeking work or sanctuary, the country confronted unfamiliar questions of race and identity that had long bedeviled other advanced societies. Who was Irish? Who could become Irish? Under what conditions would the country allow people to enter and for how long? These were precisely the questions that animated Doyle's third story for *Metro Éireann*, "57% Irish." Ray Brady, a young graduate student, is hired by the "Minister of Arts and Ethnicity" to devise a test to measure "Irishness." The minister, whose office is bedecked with Irish totems including a manuscript page from *Ulysses* and a U2 gold album, wants to distinguish between aspiring immigrants who should be allowed to stay in the country and those who need be expelled. Ray develops a polygraph-like device to measure Irishness by gauging an individual's physiological reactions to video clips of the Irish national soccer team, the fictional porn star "Shamrock Chambers," and Pope John Paul II. Those who take the test receive a grade called the "Fáilte Score"—a play on the traditional Irish greeting "Céad Mile Fáilte" or "a hundred thousand welcomes." In the end, Ray deliberately skews the test to allow 800,000 Africans and eastern Europeans to win Irish citizenship.

Happy endings were harder to come by in real life. Ireland welcomed the newcomers as needed workers for the hot-running economy, granting them temporary permits that allowed them to stay in the country for a year. The unspoken assumption was that once the economy cooled, those no longer needed would simply return home. Bruce Morrison, a former U.S. congressman, warned Irish officials they risked repeating the errors of countries such as Germany, which had consigned its largely Turkish guest worker population to a multigenerational shadow existence. The German approach, which defined citizenship on ethnic or racial grounds, bred resentment between the hosts and their often exploited or marginalized labor force. Morrison's was a respected voice in Ireland, stemming from his role in authoring legislation in the 1980s that created 48,000 U.S. green cards for Irish immigrants to the United States. He urged Irish officials instead to follow the American approach of offering immigrants a legal path to full citizenship. "Look to Boston, not Berlin," Morrison told his Irish contacts. "The Germans have made a hash of it."[50]

Since the 1950s, under Irish law anyone born in the country became a citizen. Their parents, in turn, could seek citizenship through their child. (The constitutional changes approved as part of the Good Friday Agreement in 1998 extended the same rights to people born in Northern Ireland.) Public ire flared over reports of "citizenship tourism" involving pregnant women from Nigeria or non-EU countries in eastern Europe circumventing EU immigration channels by traveling to Ireland to give birth. The Irish self-image was of a sympathetic people, happy to extend a welcome to those who had left their homes much as the Irish of 1980 or 1880 had left theirs. Occasionally, however, the color-blind mask slipped, and the antagonism toward the small but growing black population became visible. In March 2004, a paper in Galway became notorious after publishing this advertise-

ment: "4 Bedroom House, no coloured, Fully furnished." The manager of
the property agency rather incredibly blamed a "misprint."[51] Likewise, black
immigrants who were eligible to seek work were at a "severe disadvantage"
in the labor market and were nine times as likely as Irish nationals to be unemployed.[52] Doyle's "White Irish Need Not Apply" was, after all, fiction.

In June 2004, Ahern's government proposed a constitutional change to
drop the automatic birthright to citizenship. In the June 11 balloting, voters approved by 79 percent to 21 percent a requirement that only those children whose parents had lived in the country for three of the four years prior
to their birth would automatically become citizens. Supporters saw the revision as a common-sense move to bring Irish law into conformance with the
rest of the EU; opponents decried the move as racist.[53] Perhaps it wasn't sur-
prising that discomfort with the pace and extent of the change that had
swept Ireland over the previous decade sharpened in response to the most
visible indications of that change: the physical presence of the new Irish, especially those whose skin color marked them as the "other." Even after the
referendum, however, Ireland remained a reasonably welcoming place, especially compared with other European countries. Whatever political tensions there were had not yet given rise to any explicitly nativist or
anti-immigrant party like those that could be found in virtually every other
European nation. Doyle, for one, was enthusiastic about prospects for an
Irish melting pot. "We are opening ourselves to different cultures," he said.
"The possibilities are fantastic."[54]

MONEY, MONEY, MONEY

On the same day that voters endorsed rewriting the constitutional definition
of citizenship, they also dealt a resounding blow to Ahern and Fianna Fáil.
In elections for local offices and European parliamentary seats, the governing party suffered its worst loss since 1927. The debacle had been brewing

since Ahern's reelection two years earlier, which occurred only after Fianna Fáil repeatedly promised there would be no end to its spending spree. Yet, in a post-election turnabout that carried uncomfortable echoes of the party's 1987 fingers-crossed approach to campaign promises, McCreevy almost immediately began tightening the public belt. By November, when details of the cuts became public, "Screwed By Liars" was the unforgiving headline in the *Daily Star*.[55]

The ensuing controversy soured voters on the government they had just reelected; much of the anger was aimed at the almost deliberately confrontational McCreevy. By 2004, Ahern had concluded that voters saw his government as excessively pro-business. Too much attention had been lavished on developers and other well-heeled types gathered in the Galway Races tent, too little spent on the have-nots. "It was becoming clear that sections of the population were doing extraordinarily well. Sections of the population were doing well, but by comparison they were being left behind. I wanted to pump far more resources into people I represent, people who were not poor but certainly come within the category of the less well off," Ahern said. " . . . I was trying to get guys off just everyone wanting to be making money, money, money and trying to get more into the left behind."[56] So at the party's annual fall retreat, held in Inchydoney, County Cork, Ahern staged a deliberate left-turn media event. He invited Father Sean Healy of the Conference of Religious of Ireland, a frequent critic of widening inequality, and Harvard University political scientist Robert Putnam, author of *Bowling Alone,* to lecture the party on what Ahern called "the social capital 'ting." But the political chameleon then strained public credulity by proclaiming himself one of the last "socialists" in Ireland.

The changes occurring in Ireland sometimes seemed so all-encompassing and, more important, so rapid that it was difficult for people to get a handle on them. But even as the country raced toward the future at a breakneck pace, the past would not quite release its grip. As he sought to recast

Fianna Fáil's image, Ahern increasingly was being drawn into the quickening whirlpool of corruption investigations. In September 2002, Justice Fergus Flood released the second interim report of his investigation into the planning process, savaging Fianna Fáil's Ray Burke. Ahern had named the party stalwart foreign minister in his first government, despite widespread rumors for 20 years that he had accepted bribes in return for rezoning development land in the Dublin area to benefit prominent developers. Burke had always denied the charges, but he resigned in October 1997 after press reports detailed the allegations. Ahern publicly mourned his departure in a statement of "profound regret," which assailed "the persistent hounding of an honorable man to resign his important position on the basis of innuendo and unproven allegations."[57]

Now, the Flood report—the product of three years of work, 313 days of hearings, 170 witnesses, and a transcript that ran past 35,000 pages—shredded the pretense that Burke was anything other than deeply corrupt. In 1973, while a member of Dublin County Council, Burke had received a new house and land in return for acting on behalf of Oakpark Developments Ltd. (Burke later sold the property for more than $4 million.)[58] Offshore bank accounts opened for Burke on the Isle of Man and island of Jersey served as conduits for at least £160,000 sterling (or more than $222,000) in corrupt payments from Oakpark directors. And while serving as a cabinet minister in 1989, Burke had received IR £80,000 ($114,000) from a pair of developers who wanted a North Dublin parcel of land rezoned.[59] Flood's verdict was uncompromising.

When the report went on sale for €1, the line of people waiting outside the government printing office on Molesworth Street stretched around the corner; more than 100,000 people downloaded it in the first weeks of publication. As farms were paved over for soulless housing developments, people were increasingly irate over the lack of official foresight. Row upon row of new homes were being slapped together with little thought of the schools,

stores, or transport residents needed. Now they knew why. "No political report published in my political lifetime has caused such public anger and re-
vulsion," said Fine Gael's Simon Coveney. The report, he added, was "a
damning description of bribery and corruption at the top of Irish politics
and business under the Fianna Fáil banner."[60] Ahern came under fire for
having placed Burke in the cabinet. In the well of the house, the taoiseach
felt compelled to defend his own honor, saying: "I have never received a
bribe in my life."[61]

There was one witness, however, who disputed that defiant assertion
and publicly claimed that Ahern had solicited a political "donation" after
smoothing the approval process for a land sale. Developer Thomas Gilmartin
first met Ahern in 1988 to discuss a proposed development in a rundown
corner of his constituency before abandoning that idea in favor of developing the largest shopping center in Europe outside the city. The proposed
mall, an enormous undertaking in the depressed Ireland of the time, was to
be on a site called Quarryvale, where a proposed Dublin beltway would cross
an existing east–west artery. At the time, Gilmartin complained to numerous politicians and business people that he was getting nowhere with the
project because he refused to bribe local officials. When the sale was finally
approved in June 1989, he said he called Ahern to thank him for his help.
During the conversation, Ahern reportedly asked him for a donation to Fianna Fáil. The developer said he responded that he already had given IR
£50,000 ($67,500 at the time) to another Fianna Fáil minister, and Ahern
let the matter drop.

The tribunal, now helmed by Justice Alan Mahon, who had replaced the
aged Flood, continued to churn forward until, on April 7, 2004, Ahern was
called to testify. It was the first time a sitting taoiseach had found himself in
the witness chair, though Ahern had appeared before an earlier tribunal
while in opposition. Ahern agreed that he had met Gilmartin in his Drumcondra office, then located above Fagan's pub, and spoken with him on the

phone a couple of times. But he denied asking Gilmartin for money. "I would not ever ring up asking somebody to give a donation, whether I had done something for them or not, or even friends. I just wouldn't do it," Ahern testified. "It's not my practice."[62] Ahern also disputed the developer's account of an alleged February 1 or 2, 1989, meeting in Leinster House with Haughey and other ministers. The gathering emerged as a key point of contention in Ahern's and Gilmartin's accounts of their dealings. Put simply, both could not be telling the truth.

Fianna Fáil's Mary O'Rourke, then serving as minister of education, testified that she recalled the meeting that Gilmartin described and remembered Ahern as among the attendees. Under questioning, Ahern grudgingly conceded that it was possible he might have briefly encountered Gilmartin in the halls of the ministerial offices and engaged in "chitchat." But he insisted that no formal session had taken place. "I have no recollection of ever a group of ministers meeting anybody, not least Mr. Gilmartin, in the parliamentary party room," he testified.[63]

After more than five grueling and often repetitive hours, the Irish leader arose at 7:17 p.m. and walked out of the chamber almost entirely unscathed. He had been forced to amend his original account, but only marginally. The events at issue were all so very long ago and besides, the economy was still pumping right along, which was all most people cared about. Ahern could be forgiven for feeling that he had outmaneuvered his enemies. But the taoiseach's problems were only just beginning. And they would soon get much, much worse.

CHAPTER 7

PEOPLE LOST THE RUN OF THEMSELVES

B Y 9:30 A.M. THAT THURSDAY, there were already five thousand people milling about at one end of the main road that wound through the ancient village of Dundrum. Standing in the cool morning air, they listened intently as the priest intoned his blessing and then, to the strains of the U2 anthem "Beautiful Day," surged forward—and started shopping. The date was March 3, 2005, and a new mall called Dundrum Town Centre, looking like something that had been airlifted in from Southern California, was opening its doors for the first time. Hewn from Sardinian granite and sheathed in terracotta tiles from Germany, the gleaming venue boasted 160 stores, including staples of the American consumer experience such as Starbucks and McDonalds as well as the high-end British chain House of Fraser. There also was a "state of the art car parking facility" for people too lazy to walk a block to the Luas light rail line, a Thai restaurant, Mao-themed café, and a 15-screen cinema.

Dundrum Town Centre was visible proof that midway through the new millennium's first decade, the prosperous Irish themselves had begun to

change. And as they did, healthy economic growth was morphing into speculative excess. In the decade to 2001, the Celtic Tiger had been about real
prosperity, based on making competitive products and selling them to customers outside Ireland. The expansion that resumed in 2002, in contrast,
was showing itself to be almost entirely a function of easy money. Private-
sector credit had risen steadily for years and now equaled 161 percent of
gross national product, roughly twice the early 1990s figure. Elsewhere in
Europe, only people in the Netherlands were deeper in debt; even the undisciplined Greeks (79 percent) were more restrained.[1] The economy was still
growing at a healthy pace, but Central Bank officials feared runaway borrowing threatened financial stability.[2]

Erica Cash, 26, was one of the "yummy drummies" who came to Dundrum for the shopping, but stayed for the lifestyle. "It was just super. It's so
big; it's brilliant," enthused the young mom. "You can just stay there the
whole day." Inside the airy modernist structure, an almost entirely female
midmorning crowd could meet at Butler's Chocolate Café ("Purveyors of
Happiness") to sip cappuccinos and chat about their children or their ca-
reers. It was a long way from the old Ireland of dank pubs smelling of stale
beer and cigarettes.

Fresh from quitting her software licensing position at Microsoft, Cash
had taken a job that would have been unimaginable in an earlier Ireland: selling residential and vacation properties in Bulgaria. "To be honest, I almost
didn't know where Bulgaria was," she said with a laugh. It hardly mattered.
People were so eager to invest that Cash was more of an order taker than a
saleswoman. She was making incredible money, around €150,000 a year
($187,000), and spending just as freely. She'd bought her first house at age
20, her second in 2005 for €685,000 (the equivalent of $850,000 at the
time). The bank didn't seem at all concerned about how much debt she was
taking on. Any time she felt the urge for a new car, a vacation, or another
Gucci bag, she simply tapped the equity in her ever-appreciating home. The

weeks were a blur of nights out with her fiancé, Glenn, enjoying the teeming restaurants and pubs of her native Dalkey. "I never saved for anything," she said. "Most of my friends never saved for anything."[3]

They were too busy spending. At the Brown Thomas department store on Dublin's Grafton Street, five hundred women placed their names on a waiting list for Hermes shopping bags that started at $5,000.[4] Michelin-starred eateries such as Restaurant Patrick Guilbaud—home of the $50 appetizer—were suddenly packed in a city where fine dining had once meant boiled potatoes and brown bread. Cash-flush Dubliners flocked to the airport to board flights to New York for weekend shopping trips in a disorienting echo of the sea journey their ancestors had taken more than a century earlier. Irish lenders were shoveling money at borrowers, courtesy of a global surplus of cash. Between 2002 and 2007, Irish banks almost tripled their lending, to €363.7 billion ($498 billion.) Four-fifths of the borrowing by individuals was for the swollen mortgages needed to cover the ever-increasing price of a new house. Though credit card debt was just a sliver of the overall figure, the balance Irish cardholders were carrying on their cards increased by 98 percent in just five years.[5]

Ready access to money marked a sea change for many Irish households. Credit had once been limited, rationed really, and reserved for only a select few. As a young graduate, Sean Fitzpatrick had been unable to secure a mortgage from the building society to which he had belonged for years. Likewise, Rory Doyle, the novelist's father, had once left Provincial Bank "humiliated [and] shaken" after the branch manager scoffed at his request for a $200 loan.[6] If working-class people wanted credit, they went to the pawnbrokers clustered in the city center, not to the banks.

Irish attitudes toward wealth historically were conflicted. Common people called those who sought it too obviously, rather than accept their God-given station in life, the "lace curtain Irish." Those who obtained wealth found themselves frequently viewed not with admiration, but with the corrosive mixture of suspicion and envy that the Irish called "be-grudgery." Said Dubliner Brendan Walsh: "You just don't want to be seen high up in case someone would pull you right down."[7] After all, poverty was virtually a totem of traditional Irish identity. Wealth was something the British Protestants possessed and the Catholic Irish lacked. The influ-ence of the Catholic Church, which encouraged in its followers a "preoc-cupation with the next world" at the expense of this one, also dampened entrepreneurial initiative.[8] "Being ambitious was seen as being greedy. . . . In the 1950s, in Ireland to be seen as greedy was called a 'gombeen man.' It was a subject of denigration to engage in anything that was ostentatious, to be self-indulgent," said sociologist Tom Inglis. "It wasn't that it was just a sin; it's that people would have frowned on it."[9]

But now, the Irish were much richer than they had ever been. Between 1984 and 1999, per capita gross domestic product doubled and then jumped an additional 38 percent over the following decade. By 2007, the inflation-adjusted average income of €43,731 was roughly triple the 1984 figure.[10] Amid the Celtic Tiger boom, a rural tradition of delayed gratification, born of necessity, was replaced by a culture of consuming. In nominal terms, the $105 billion the Irish spent in 2006 on personal goods and services was more than twice the amount they'd spent in 1998.[11] Consumption was mov-ing from fad to frenzy.

The entire look of the country got an upscale facelift. Cozy pubs, such as the venerable Davy Byrne's, scrapped their traditional wooden signage and smoked windows in favor of purple neon and enormous plate glass. O'Connell Street, formerly a drab boulevard running arrow-straight over the river Liffey into the city center, got a makeover with a gleaming hotel, a movie theater, and a phallic steel obelisk that earned the unfortunate moniker "the stiffy by the Liffey."

Much of the change was welcome, even long overdue. But the very pace of life was revving into overdrive. Where the Irish were once famed for their friendliness, they now spent too much time trapped in soul-crushing commutes to linger in conversation with a stranger. Even the traditional "full Irish" breakfast was reborn for those in a hurry as an appalling takeout concoction called the "JBR" or jumbo breakfast roll: a full-sized buttered baguette jammed with a fried egg, sausage, bacon, beans, pudding, tomatoes, cheese, and mushrooms. "People lost the run of themselves. They just got carried away," says sociologist Mary Corcoran.[12]

Others noticed that Ireland was changing. In 2007, the German ambassador to Ireland, Christian Pauls, poked fun at Irish conspicuous consumption in a speech to a business group. He marveled at the lavish salaries afforded junior government officials and teased the free-spending Irish with a joke about his recent visit to the National Concert Hall. An announcer, he said, had come on the loudspeaker to summon the driver of a 1993 model car that was blocking a fire exit. "Of course no one moved," said Pauls. "All the Irish are driving 2006 and 2007 cars. For all I know the car is still there." The ambassador's remarks, which an aide later insisted were offered in jest, drew laughs from the German businessmen in attendance—and a formal diplomatic protest from his thin-skinned hosts.[13]

Such sensitivity, bordering on defensiveness, started at the top. The Celtic Tiger was Bertie Ahern's economy, and he did not take kindly to criticism of it. The muted drumbeat of Central Bank warnings took on a more alarmist tone, but Ahern would later brush them aside as "their usual reports."[14] In June 2006, the bank publicly struck a succession of worrying notes: productivity was weak, the labor market was as dependent upon construction as any addict was its pusher, and overall competitiveness showed "significant deterioration."[15] Officialdom seemed surprisingly sanguine, but the data were unmistakable: after thriving because it was a cost-effective location for multinational companies, Ireland had grown fat and self-satisfied. In 1999, two small nations on Europe's periphery, Ireland and Finland, had earned almost identical scores on an ECB competitiveness assessment. Ireland's 97.5, in fact, was a shade better than Finland's 97.9. But eight years later, Finland had held its ground while Ireland, after an orgy of consumption and neglect of manufacturing, had slumped to 120. It was the worst performance of any EU member.[16] Ireland was rapidly pricing itself out of its key markets.

"Growth has become heavily reliant on building investment and competitiveness has eroded. The share of the construction sector in GDP is high and likely to fall over the next few years," the IMF said in 2006. "Rapid growth could lead to overheating and wage pressures, which would further undermine competitiveness. Ireland is also vulnerable to external shocks."[17] By the customarily mushy standards of such documents, that language represented a flashing red light. Ireland was speeding in the wrong direction.

The various official diagnoses served as fodder for Irish media commentators and academic economists, who were increasingly insistent that something fundamental was going wrong. George Lee, RTE's economics editor, and David McWilliams, a former Central Bank economist turned author, took the lead in debunking the myth that Ireland could boom indefinitely. Morgan Kelly, an economics professor at University College Dublin, issued Cassandra-like warnings about an impending 50 percent plunge in housing prices. Ahern's response was derisory. "Quite frankly, if you had taken the advice a year ago, you would have lost a lot of money. Everybody said we're going to see a huge downturn in 2005 linking into 2006—they were entirely wrong," he said in April 2006. "Really we should have an examination into why so many people got it so wrong. My view is there's not a great problem."[18] After an April 2007 RTE program forecast a housing crash, the taoiseach rounded on those suggesting the economy was heading over a cliff.

"Sitting on the sidelines, cribbing and moaning is a lost opportunity. I don't know how people who engage in that don't commit suicide," he said in a speech to the Irish Congress of Trade Unions.[19]

The red-hot housing market was at the core of the increasingly sharp debate over the economy's prospects. As the politicians bickered, people across Ireland confronted the consequences of years of government action and inaction. In bucolic County Leitrim, the government's use of tax incentives to encourage rural development was fueling housing supply well beyond any corresponding demand. Revered in song as "lovely Leitrim where the Shannon waters flow," the pancreas-shaped swathe of land lies in the northwest near the border with Northern Ireland. The county, which boasted a population in 1841 of nearly 160,000, had suffered some of the most extensive losses of the post-Famine era. By 1996, barely 25,000 people remained, spread across an area a little more than half the size of Rhode Island. The remote area was devoid of cities and prospects for growth. To combat the air of decline, the government in 1998 introduced a pilot rural renewal scheme that offered developers generous tax breaks for building or refurbishing homes and industrial facilities.[20]

The program was one flake in a blizzard of tax incentives that spurred construction projects of all types beginning in the late 1990s. The tax code was used to encourage urban and rural developments, seaside resorts, multistory parking garages, hotels, holiday cottages, sports injury clinics, park-and-ride facilities, childcare centers, nursing homes—only sand castles seemed to have been overlooked by Fianna Fáil. The ruling party enjoyed close links to the country's property sector; by one estimate, at least 40 percent of its campaign funds between 1997 and 2007 came from developers.[21] Many of the builders hailed from the countryside and shared a rural ethos with Fianna Fáil, which traditionally was stronger in farm communities than the more middle-class Fine Gael. Now the developers flocked to previously ignored areas such as Leitrim, replacing farms with new housing developments, big-box retailers, and office parks. Some building anticipated the effects of another Ahern initiative, which would decentralize government by moving selected departments from Dublin to rural areas. Leitrim officials, for example, expected the Central Fisheries Board to materialize one day.

In the county seat of Carrick-on-Shannon, Martin Dolan, the county's taciturn director of planning, struggled to cope with the torrent of paperwork unleashed by the new tax policies. In a typical year in the 1990s, Dolan might have received four hundred planning applications, almost all for individual houses. After the rural tax scheme was introduced, the total surged to a 2004 peak of 2,100, many for multiple dwellings. "Planning applications started to come in right, left and center. . . . Tax incentives were there for developers to come in and invest their money; the lending institutions were giving money without much difficulty. It became sort of fashionable: if you weren't in the building industry or building houses, there was something wrong with you," he said. "We began to get concerned there was a danger of too many houses being around."[22] One sign of the building fever: local professionals, such as dentists, doctors, and lawyers, began dabbling in property. Anyone who could lay their hands on a parcel large enough to hold a few homes was getting into the tax-friendly development game. In a half-hearted bid to tame the frenzy, the county in 2006 belatedly toughened planning requirements. But the change merely required developers to produce evidence of demand for any planned homes from local auctioneers. That was a decidedly modest imposition, since the auctioneers—who earn commissions from property sales—had a vested interest in seeing development go forward.

The helter-skelter building was putting the county's deserved reputation for unspoiled beauty at risk. Traditional Leitrim villages, like those elsewhere in rural Ireland, consisted of small clusters of stone homes along a two-lane paved road, with a few shops and a pub or two. Now, those same villages, places with names like Newtowngore or Keshcarrigan, were increasingly bookended by incongruous suburban housing developments with cookie-cutter designs and cul de sacs that appeared to have been lifted from a 1970s Spielberg film. "I fear for our villages, lovely, beautiful, picturesque villages dotted along the Shannon. They are the ones that will suffer greatly because of what happened. And what happened is inexcusable. Central government has a lot to answer for. While everybody was crying out for development, it went too far," said Enda Stenson, an Independent local councilor.[23]

The village of Newtowngore, about five miles from the border with Northern Ireland, was among the places that absorbed the brunt of the reckless building. In the fifth century, St. Patrick established a monastery where the village now stands. Later, it was a farming and commercial center for area residents. But it has never been more than a small settlement; in recent years, the population has hovered around 40, according to John McCartin, a local Fine Gael councilor. Until the early years of this decade, Newtowngore consisted of just 15 houses, a few shops, and a small restaurant. The local church sits on a hill outside of town. "There was absolutely no such thing as a speculative property trade in this area. If you wanted a house you bought a site, you got planning permission, you approached a builder and you built your house," said McCartin. That all changed with the rural renewal scheme. "We began to see the helicopters dropping out of the sky," he said, referring to the mode of transport favored by tiger-era developers.[24]

Construction workers, most from eastern Europe, poured into the village, giving a temporary boost to local shops and restaurants. But by 2007, the quaint village had been engorged with two new housing developments. Of the 24 semidetached homes in the first neighborhood, just off the main road to Carrick-on-Shannon, only three drew buyers. Another two would be rented out on short-term leases. Long after the developer had fled, the paving remained unfinished and the streetlights were dark. Around the corner, a second new development of 11 pastel-hued homes was entirely vacant. Some were unfinished, with pipes protruding from openings in the walls and deteriorating building materials piled nearby. A mile down the road, a trio of half-built homes—one sans roof—had been empty since

2004. In a village of 40 people, developers had thrown up 38 new homes, which it seemed almost no one cared to buy.

There wasn't much mystery as to how this had happened. Ireland was one of the few countries where mortgage interest payments were tax deductible, but there was no property tax.[25] Plus, the tax relief granted by the various property-related programs was incredibly generous. Depending upon the specific property, a taxpayer could deduct 50 percent or 100 percent of the cost of construction or refurbishment, with the benefits spooling out in annual increments over ten years. McCartin was an outspoken critic of the tax breaks, which he described as a political favor from the ruling Fianna Fáil party to its development industry allies. But he was also a businessman who knew a good deal when he saw one. So he spent almost $500,000 renovating a pub in Ballinamore, about five miles from Newtowngore. Under the rural renewal program, he could deduct that entire amount against his income from the pub, effectively allowing him to rent it out tax free for the next ten years. Likewise, by spending around $275,000 to renovate and expand his family home, his wife, who works as a schoolteacher, will end up getting, over the course of a decade, tens of thousands of euros back in tax refunds from the government. "It's absolutely crazy," McCartin says.[26]

Ahern would later defend the incentives as "the popular thing," backed by all the parties. Indeed, Dáil members of all political persuasions habitually lined up to plead for special consideration for their local constituencies. Forty-three towns and cities were selected for the urban renewal designation, for example, a program that was credited with rejuvenating rundown city centers across the country. "The cities in Ireland had got notoriously dilapidated: Cork, Limerick, Waterford, Dublin and the other big towns. There were old mills in the cities, old manufacturing plants; they were terrible," Ahern said. "We used the tax incentives to get the money into these spots. . . . All our cities have been modernized in the last 10 or 15 years because of that. It wouldn't have happened otherwise."[27]

Whatever initial justification had existed for the property-related tax breaks, as the housing boom raged, they seemed less and less necessary. The steroidal construction sector was swelling out of all proportion; by mid-decade, it accounted for nearly one-fifth of the nation's entire economic output.[28] The combination of easy money from the banks and government encouragement in the form of tax relief was spurring construction without regard to whether there were people prepared to live in the buildings constructed. In 2006, the national census estimated that 29 percent of the houses in lovely Leitrim were vacant, the highest percentage in the nation and almost twice the national average of 15 percent.[29] The tax break had succeeded in creating new buildings. Unfortunately, it hadn't been able to create new customers to buy them.

By the middle of the decade, Ahern's government realized belatedly that the tax breaks were doing as much harm as good. Shortly after replacing McCreevy as finance minister, Brian Cowen commissioned a study with an eye toward phasing out those tax breaks that were no longer needed. In early 2006, the Department of Finance released a pair of consultants' reports recommending major changes in the programs. Goodbody Economic Consultants, which examined the tax incentives focused on particular areas of the country, concluded they had cost the government more than $2.5 billion in lost revenue. But even as the government prepared to withdraw the measures, it was goosing housing demand by reducing the stamp duty on purchases by first-time buyers.

The taoiseach said the tax breaks "kept the money in Ireland," rather than allowing it to leak outside the country to non-Irish investments—an odd thing for the leader of a country heavily dependent upon the free flow of cross-border capital to say. But even in cases where the incentives did lead to useful investment, as in the case of the urban renewal program, they caused collateral damage. They mostly benefited a small circle of higher-income taxpayers and were responsible for "significant inflation of property prices," Goodbody found.[30] The rural renewal giveaway, in particular, promoted a good deal of development that would have occurred anyway while doing little to reverse the rural population decline—the stated justification for granting the tax relief in the first place. "There is evidence that much of the housing output has been taken up by existing residents, further increasing the dead weight associated with the Scheme. As a result, the Scheme has not represented value for money. This has been exacerbated by the tendency, on the part of a significant minority of participants to build relatively large houses. It is now evident that the very substantial increase in housing output has now resulted in excess supply and that house prices are softening and rents have declined," the report concluded.[31] Goodbody recommended eventually scrapping the rural renewal tax break, which it said flatly "is not a model that should be employed elsewhere in the country."[32]

In Ahern's telling, the incentives had resulted in only isolated abuses. Despite nearly one in six houses in the country sitting vacant, "there weren't many places" that shared Leitrim's overbuilding. "The reason we did away with the tax incentives in the end is because we were finished with that part of the work. It wasn't really to do with overheating of the market. The incentives had done their job," he said. In any case, the taoiseach was convinced that the housing market would come back to earth in an orderly way. The market, which somehow had failed to produce enough houses without the crutch of tax incentives, would sort itself out. But the tax incentives had been in place for eight years by this point, and housing was in the waning moments of a long boom. By 2006, with house prices having quadrupled in a decade, the damage, quite simply, had already been done.

A BRILLIANT PARTY

Almost a decade after leaving government with the Rainbow Coalition's demise, Linda Farren found herself unexpectedly caught up in the forces buffeting Ireland's booming credit industry. The episode set her on a twisting path that ultimately would provide a ringside seat at the eventual remaking of the nation's financial industry. The occasion was the April 2007 annual meeting of the Educational Building Society (EBS), one of the handful of remaining mutual savings organizations in Ireland. Organized to serve members, rather than the profit-seeking demands of shareholders, building societies had long been a staple of the Irish financial scene. In the pre-Celtic Tiger days of scarce credit, Irish parents would open building society accounts for their children as a first step toward establishing the savings history needed to secure a mortgage. Linda's father had opened one for her when she reached her thirteenth birthday and she had likewise opened EBS accounts for her three children. "There is a longstanding Irish tradition of opening children's accounts in the building society so that you can prepare yourself for your first mortgage. . . . It was always foreseen that you would want to buy a house," said Brian Farren.

When she read the official proxy statement for the society's 2007 annual meeting, however, it was with the eyes of a corporate lawyer rather than those of a mother. Farren was struck by the board's highly unusual recommendation against the re-election of one of its directors, Ethna Tinney. In Ireland, as in the United States, corporate boards typically are cozy institutions. Directors are almost invariably endorsed for re-election and when they do quit, a hand-picked replacement is generally standing by. But Tinney had become the bête noire of the EBS leadership, criticizing an abortive merger with another bank, management's overly generous compensation, and its dismissive treatment of members. "I just couldn't fathom this," said Farren. " . . . [From] a corporate lawyer perspective, I don't think I've ever seen proxy papers like this." Tinney was the only board member up for re-election to a rotating three-year term. So by urging members to reject her, the board would be able to appoint a replacement to hold the seat until the next annual meeting.

The EBS machinations came at a time of turmoil for the mutual institutions as the Celtic Tiger's "show me the money" ethic clashed with the societies' communal principles. Some building societies, including First Active
and Irish Permanent, had already opted for a process called "demutualization," which allowed members to cash out their stake in the societies through
a public stock offering. Individual Irish Permanent members, for example,
had walked away with a $7,200 windfall when their society demutualized in
1994.[33] EBS had resisted the demutualization trend thus far, but with the
only other building society, Irish Nationwide, pursuing such a course, pressure to reconsider was inevitable. Already, EBS management had succumbed
to the lure of easy riches by pushing into commercial property investments,
which were far afield from the institution's original purpose.

Farren was one of more than 400,000 EBS members entitled to vote in
director elections and question management at the annual meeting held at
the Burlington Hotel. Wearing an eye-catching red outfit that earned her the
sobriquet "The Lady in Red," she challenged CEO Ted McGovern from
the floor on his plan to sack Tinney: "Tell us who you're going to put in if
she fails to be re-elected?" Farren never got a clear answer. In the end, Tinney was defeated for re-election, and the dysfunctional EBS executive team
staggered onward. It would not be their last controversy. Before the meeting room emptied, several dozen members approached Farren and urged
her to run for a board seat in 2008.

For now, however, Farren's EBS foray was just a sideline. In 2000, she
had opened her own legal practice, doing pro bono work on issues affecting
the disabled and serving smaller Irish businesses that wanted more personal
treatment than they could get from Dublin's large law firms. After leaving
government in 1997, Linda had joined the Irish Wheelchair Association as
director of legal and corporate affairs. Personal experience had left her with
a profound interest in those less fortunate. A sister had needed special education, and two of her children had suffered serious illnesses. Daughter Lara

was born with a heart condition, which required extended hospitalization and eventual open-heart surgery, and her youngest son, Devon, was treated with antibiotics for two and a half years while battling chronic pneumonia.

With two professional incomes—husband Brian was now well along in his barrister career—the Farrens were more than comfortable. A prized 1969 Bentley sat in the driveway outside their handsome Ballsbridge home. That the Celtic Tiger had spawned unprecedented Irish wealth on a wider scale was demonstrated on a rainy Saturday evening in November 2007, when the Farrens' home was the setting for an unusual fundraiser for Senator Hillary Clinton's presidential campaign. Irish America had enjoyed strong links to Bill Clinton since his 1992 bid for the Democratic nomination. When the Hillary Clinton campaign went looking for someone to host a Dublin event, the Farrens were a natural choice. During their time in New York in the 1980s, they had become close to other Irish American lawyers, some of whom stayed behind and got involved in politics. "I think just somehow or other they were going through, who's gone back, who has a big house and who would actually say in nine days time, yeah, [let's] have a big party," said Linda Farren.

In the old Ireland, money had flowed from America to the penniless relations at home. Now, the affluent Irish could return the favor. The evening, headlined by former President Clinton, marked the first time a U.S. presidential candidate had held a fundraiser in Ireland. The Farrens were nonplussed by the event's demands. Multiple security teams repeatedly sweeping the house. Excited local media attention. And a last-minute decision to expand the venue with a backyard tent, which required Brian to climb a ladder and amputate a protruding tree limb. On the night itself, less than two months before the Iowa caucuses, a veritable who's-who of the development industry, including developers Bernard McNamara and Noel Smyth, Irish Nationwide CEO Michael Fingleton, and Tom Parlon, a former member of Parliament now heading the Construction Industry Federation, were among those who paid more than $2,200 apiece to drink champagne and munch hors d'oeuvres. Also in attendance were well-known New York hotelier John Fitzpatrick, software entrepreneur Bill McCabe, and philanthropist Niall Mellon, whose efforts to build housing for the poor in South Africa were backed by volunteers including a banker named Sean Fitzpatrick. (Under U.S. election law, only American citizens or green-card holders could purchase tickets. Irish citizens could legally attend only by convincing an American friend to pony up on their behalf.)

Clinton, who had earlier played 18 holes at the legendary Portmarnock Golf Club and met with Ahern, was driven onto Raglan Road shortly before 6:45 p.m., past a pair of quixotic rain-soaked protestors shouting "investigate 9/11." Once inside, he worked the crowd, charming everyone from Linda's mother, who was volunteering as coat check, to the "bundlers" who'd rounded up the deep-pocketed guests. Outside, under the rain-splashed tent, Clinton gave a rousing speech touting his wife's candidacy. "He's incredibly charming. He connected with absolutely everybody," said Brian Farren. "Everyone here was quite certain that he or she had met Bill Clinton personally." After raising almost $250,000 for his wife's doomed presidential bid, the former president then left for a chat with Bono and a late dinner with the Nobel Prize–winning poet Seamus Heaney and his wife. "The atmosphere was electric—just a brilliant party," said Linda Farren.

SNEAKING REGARD

Irish politics was going through its own tumult. For Ahern, who faced a general election in 2007, allegations of irregularities involving his personal finances proved a mounting distraction. The latest controversy erupted with a front-page story in the September 21, 2006, *Irish Times* headlined "Tribunal Examines Payments To Taoiseach." During its investigation of Thomas Gilmartin's allegations that Ahern had accepted bribes from a developer, the Mahon tribunal uncovered sizeable unexplained deposits in the taoiseach's accounts. He explained them as the IR £39,000 ($47,000) proceeds of friends' efforts in 1993 and 1994 to help him navigate his marital breakup and a separate £7,800 sterling ($11,950) gift from a group in Manchester, England, to whom he had made brief remarks after a private dinner.

Ahern was irked by public disclosure of the probe. "What I got personally in my life is, to be frank with you, is none of your business," he told reporters.[34] According to Ahern, as his six-year marital separation became legally permanent in 1993, his friends grew concerned about his battered finances. His attorney then approached a select group of "close friends, people who were close to me for most of my life," in Ahern's words, and quickly raised IR £22,500 ($26,800). The cash was handed to Ahern, then serving as finance minister, around Christmas 1993. The following year, he received an additional IR £16,500 ($20,000), also in cash.

Ahern had at least three problems. First, this wasn't the first time allegations of financial shenanigans had been lodged. Gilmartin's bribe claim, though so far unsubstantiated, had been circulating for years, and just the previous month word had come that a separate investigative body, the Moriarty Tribunal, would criticize Ahern for routinely signing blank checks for Haughey's use in the late 1980s and early 1990s.[35] Second, among the good friends participating in what became known as the financial "dig out" were prominent businessmen with numerous interests before the government, including David McKenna, owner of a Dublin recruiting firm. Third, there was no paper trail to support his version of events, no written agreement covering what Ahern described as loans or a "debt of honor." People were openly skeptical of Ahern's explanation of what was at the time a substantial sum of money. The greatest incredulity was reserved for Ahern's description of his personal finances during the late 1980s and early 1990s, a period when he had been in his late 30s and early 40s. For several years after his 1987 separation, Ahern said he had no bank account in his own name.

He explained that he routinely cashed his government paychecks, depositing the bulk of the proceeds in a joint account controlled by his wife, and then stashed the leftover cash in an office safe. Public reaction ran from outright disbelief to a sense that the taoiseach's slippery personal finances were uncomfortably reminiscent of his mentor Charles Haughey's standards. "How could a fella have—particularly a minister of finance, a minister of labor—have no accounts all the way from 1987 to '93? Well, it wasn't that I had no accounts. I had me accounts; they were all in me wife's name and I didn't use them because I was separated," Ahern said in an interview. " . . . What I did was I saved most of it in my safe in the Department of Finance, which was protected by the Army."[36]

Before the week was out, a visibly uncomfortable taoiseach sat down with RTE's Brian Dobson for a high-stakes televised interview. Blasting "the false allegations, half truths [and] lies," Ahern said he had done nothing wrong: "There was no corruption in this." He conceded that in the dozen years that had elapsed since the most recent loan, he had paid not a penny of interest. His good friends, he said, had "refused to take it." But it was not the detailed refutation or the accusations of political skullduggery by his opponents that left the lasting impression. It was Ahern's emotion-laden peroration, ending in a choked near-whisper: "The Irish public [has] always been kind to me about being separated. They've always been understanding and, em, if I've caused offense to anyone—I think I have to a few people—em, I'm sorry."[37] After almost three weeks of constant pounding on his ethics, when results of the first public opinion poll were published, Ahern's standing had gone up—not down. Almost two-thirds of those polled thought he had been wrong to accept money while in office. But the percentage of those satisfied with his job performance rose, as did support for Fianna Fáil.[38]

It wasn't that the Irish were indifferent to morality. What historian Kevin Whelan called the public's "sneaking regard" for Ahern reflected both the fundamental organization of Irish politics, especially as perfected over the generations by Fianna Fáil, and deep currents in the country's history. Living at the whim of a colonial power had bred in the Irish a disrespect for what was seen as the oppressor's law as well as a keen faculty for skirting formal rules. In Irish eyes, someone who got away with something, even if it was wrong, was admiringly termed a "cute hoor." Ahern himself had spoken in 1999 of Ireland having "a culture of tax evasion," a fairly sympathetic rationalization for a series of jaw-dropping scandals involving offshore bank accounts.[39] "Irish cynicism about the forces of law and order has an ancient pedigree. . . . Irishmen's reputation for deceit and guile [was] the logical outcome of a life of political oppression," wrote Declan Kiberd.[40]

Power in Ireland is centralized to an extent that means national politicians are expected to deliver local benefits in a way that is unknown in the United States or other European states. An American voter who wants a parcel of land rezoned turns to a city councilman. In Ireland, he would look to his member of parliament or perhaps even a cabinet minister. About 80 percent of Irish voters will have personally met a candidate before voting for him or her for national office. For years, the country had been run as a cross between the intimacy of the New Hampshire primary and the ethics of Tammany Hall. "There is an expectation by the public that politicians will do things for them. So if they need to jump the waiting list in the hospital or if they need access to housing and there's a waiting list or [they need] a medical card. Then they see that as perfectly normal to go to their politician and ask them to do something for them. And they don't see that as corruption or improper influence," said Elaine Byrne, the author of a forthcoming history of corruption in Ireland. That helps explain why some Irish politicians caught in the most flagrant ethical or legal violations still retain strong local support.[41] Michael Lowry, the minister for transport, energy, and communications, for example, was forced to resign from the Rainbow Coalition cabinet in November 1996 after the disclosure that Ben Dunne had paid nearly $500,000 for an addition to Lowry's home. His company later was forced to pay more than $1.5 million in overdue tax bills while he was compelled to pay $250,000 to settle his personal tax affairs. In the wake of the blistering McCracken Tribunal report, his disgrace was so complete that he was drummed out of Fine Gael. Lowry refused to slink off stage, however, and ran for re-election as an independent. How did voters respond to evidence that their representative was a liar and tax cheat? They returned him to office in three consecutive elections as the greatest vote-getter in the constituency. He sits in parliament to this day.

WE'LL GET THROUGH THIS

In February 2007, housing prices wobbled and then turned down for the first time in a decade. Even as unsold homes piled up in suburban Dublin developments such as "The Grange," radio ads touted property in Dubai, of all places. Ahern led Fianna Fáil into the general election in May, seemingly gravely weakened by the whiff of scandal. Three weeks before the balloting, an opposition leader said of the taoiseach: "Politically, he's a dead man walking."[42]

Ironically, the financial tremors worked to Ahern's political advantage. For voters tempted to ditch Fianna Fáil, they provided a reason to hesitate before placing the government into the uncertain hands of Fine Gael. Ahern also got a break when the Mahon Tribunal, which was moving closer to a direct confrontation, suspended its hearings until after the election. The lingering ethical cloud ultimately did little damage to the "Teflon Taoiseach," who led Fianna Fáil to a third consecutive victory in May 2007. For the moment, Ahern could breathe a sigh of relief.

The calm didn't last. Ten weeks later, France's largest bank suddenly closed three hedge funds, preventing investors from withdrawing their money. The $2.2 billion funds were invested heavily in U.S. subprime mortgage–backed securities, which were suffering huge losses as homeowners began defaulting on their loans. Global financial pressures that had simmered for months were moving to full boil. Ahern was reading the *Financial Times* with mounting worry and, after returning from his summer holiday at the end of August, met regularly with Central Bank Governor John Hurley. The situation looked a "bit iffy up until Christmas," Ahern later recalled. But by early 2008, markets calmed and his advisers had a clear message: "It's okay. We'll get through this."[43]

WE BECAME TOO EXPENSIVE

For the moment, Jack Byrne was unfazed by the gathering storm. Since returning to Ireland from Europe more than a decade earlier, he had surfed serial and overlapping economic waves. He had been right in the middle of the Internet bubble at Netscape while, all around him, he could see Ireland's consumption boom unfolding. Unlike so many of his countrymen, however, Byrne was careful with his own money. "I came from a very conservative financial upbringing. . . . I just cannot get my head around anybody wasting money," he said. It was a good thing, too, because, despite the Internet frenzy, Netscape was having trouble replicating its early success. Over time, Byrne could feel the company's declining fortunes. Where once he had stayed in upscale hotels on trips to the company's Mountain View, California, headquarters, he later found himself lodged in a local Super 8 Motel.

Conditions improved temporarily in November 1998, when industry giant America Online announced plans to acquire Netscape for $4.2 billion. AOL was a digital pioneer: billionaire founder Steve Case was lauded as a visionary, and the company's ubiquitous user greeting, "You've Got Mail!," had even featured in a Tom Hanks film. In the peak years of the Internet craze, as AOL's stock price soared and everything seemed possible, Byrne and his coworkers enjoyed the fruits of the boom. The multinational's offices in the Citywest office park, a digital business campus southwest of Dublin, were a major step up from ISOCOR. "There was everything you could want from a working point-of-view. You just asked for it and you got it," he said. When he traveled to AOL's headquarters in Virginia, Byrne flew business class. As the Internet established itself as an essential part of commerce, recreation, education, and daily life, an air of reward and entitlement characterized the industry. One morale-building retreat for a small executive group took place at the plush K Club, a five-star hotel and golf resort complex nestled along the river Liffey 40 minutes west of Dublin. The resort's centerpiece is a grand estate house, which dates to 1832 and was modeled on a Parisian chateau. Byrne's room was draped in imported silk and outfitted with an elegant four-poster bed. The AOL group dined in a private room that boasted a personal sommelier and views of the 550-acre parkland outside. "We ate and we drank to the point of complete stupidity. . . . We ordered the most expensive wines we could drink," Byrne said. Cigars and a $1,700 bottle of Louis XIV brandy capped the meal. As the executives headed back to Dublin, they left in their wake an $11,000 tab. "All I got out of it was a pounding headache the next day," Byrne said with a laugh.[44]

By the first years of the new millennium, it wasn't just techies who were living well. The good life was also on display on the streets of Dublin and even in Byrne's own Blackrock neighborhood. As home prices steadily rose, many people tapped the equity in their homes to finance home improvements, a new car, or a vacation. Some of Byrne's friends spent several hundred thousand dollars that way, which they later regretted. "A lot of our neighbors revamped their houses. . . . There was a huge temptation for us to do that, but I could never get my head around re-mortgaging my house for €200,000 for a cosmetic thing," he said.

It was fortunate that Byrne resisted the siren's call because the once highflying AOL, which merged with TimeWarner in 2000, eventually lost its way. Once the Internet bubble burst in 2001–2002, the much-vaunted

AOL–TimeWarner merger fizzled. By 2002, the new company was reporting a $99 billion loss, then the largest financial loss in U.S. history. The fol-
lowing year "AOL" was dropped from the company's name and Case, the
visionary, was gone. By mid-decade, Byrne was harboring doubts about his
future. He felt overqualified for the work he was doing and as periodic lay-
offs swept AOL's Dublin operation, Byrne felt himself a potential target.
After the company's 2005 opening of an office in Bangalore, India, his team's
projects were gradually transferred out of Ireland. "I wasn't surprised," he
said. "I think we became too expensive."[45]

Still, when an AOL vice president arrived in Dublin before Christmas
2007 and said he had "great plans" for him in the New Year, Byrne relaxed.
He happily went off on his Christmas vacation, only to learn the day after
his return that he was being let go. It was January 4, 2008. He was nearly
50 and for the first time since the bleak 1980s, he was jobless. "It's petrify-
ing. . . . You think: 'Is this what it boils down to after all these years?' And
then you wake up the next morning and say, 'Now what? Where am I going
to get a job and how am I going to get a job?'" Byrne said.

Possibly the most difficult aspect of his sudden layoff was breaking the
news to his children. "When I did tell them, it was like I told them their
mother had died. You have to reassure them everything will be fine, but they
don't believe that," he said. Though rocked by the news, Byrne made a point
of rising each day at his customary early hour. He would go for a walk or
help get his kids, Steven, 17, and Heather, 15, ready for school. There would
be no wallowing. But it was difficult to keep his spirits up amid the daily,
fruitless calls to recruitment agencies. Two decades after leaving Ireland with
the country in the depths of recessionary gloom, Jack Byrne was again at
the bleeding edge of a major turn in the labor market. After dipping to a
rock-bottom 4 percent in the fourth quarter of 2006, the unemployment
rate had begun creeping higher. The number of those without full-time jobs
rose from 87,600 to almost 110,000 when Byrne received his pink slip and

would reach 167,000 by the end of the year.[46] The situation was tough, but not yet terminal. As Byrne perused the help-wanted ads, the Central Bank predicted the economy would remain "reasonably strong" in 2008 before re-accelerating in 2009.[47] Then, a few weeks later, a high-flying U.S. investment bank called Bear Stearns suddenly found itself on the brink of collapse.

CHAPTER 8

MONEY IS
JUST EVIDENCE

OR THREE CENTURIES, THE FABLED ROUND ROOM in Dublin's
Mansion House has been the site of some of Ireland's most important gatherings. British monarchs and Irish taoiseachs, a
Catholic pope and a Protestant terrorist, all have walked its halls. In January 1919, the founding fathers of the Irish Free State, including Eamon de
Valera and Michael Collins, attended the inaugural session of Ireland's parliament in the landmark building just off St. Stephen's Green. But there
have been few scenes quite like the one that played out on another brisk
January morning almost precisely 90 years later. Under slate-gray skies that
hinted of rain, television satellite trucks loitered before the stucco-and-stone
structure as hundreds of deeply unhappy people, some from as far away as
Italy and the United States, filed inside.

The shareholders of Anglo Irish Bank had assembled on January 16,
2009, to learn the fate of Ireland's third-largest financial institution. The
bank's shares were trading at just $0.28, down almost 99 percent from
their May 2007 peak of $23.61. Until the evening before, the meeting

was expected to vote on a government plan to rescue Anglo Irish with more than $2.1 billion of public money. But with the bank's prospects deteriorating faster than anyone had anticipated, government officials opted instead for nationalization. Incredibly, after almost two decades of previously unbroken success, the very emblem of the Celtic Tiger's capitalist swagger was a ward of the state.

In happier times, Sean Fitzpatrick, Anglo's chairman, had justifiably crowed: "We had ideas and we had balls. We would put in whatever hours and whatever miles it required to take those ideas and turn them into business successes."[1] Now, the several hundred shareholders, mostly white-haired retirees, including some in wheelchairs, were facing the loss of everything they had invested in the company, which was until recently the star of the Irish financial industry. For people like Patricia Grogan, 60, a caregiver for disabled children, the bank's sagging fortunes meant the loss of more than $400,000. "We've been betrayed," she said, pausing on her way into the meeting. In the public's mind, there was only one person to blame for the bank's failure: Fitzpatrick, who had resigned unexpectedly one month earlier amid disclosures that he had secretly taken out more than $175 million in personal loans from the bank and engaged in an annual shell game to hide them from auditors. The revelation accelerated depositors' flight from Anglo, imperiling its solvency and necessitating the government takeover.

As the shareholders took their seats, tiny lights on the ceiling twinkled like so many faux stars. Recognizing the kinetic mood, the bank's acting chairman, Donal O'Connor, 58, adopted a contrite tone. Fitzpatrick's secret loans had been "wrong and unacceptable," O'Connor told the simmering crowd. "I'd like to apologize for that." He blamed Fitzpatrick for a "crisis of confidence" that had convinced government officials no amount of public money could salvage Anglo. For the next several hours, shareholders trained their fury on the directors on the stage before them, at the anonymous auditors from Ernst & Young skulking in the front row, and most of all, at the man known as "Seanie," who cast a shadow over the proceedings even in absentia. Anglo Irish had been a widely held stock; most of the white-haired folks clutching anoraks and umbrellas were average retirees, not wealthy investors. Another angry shareholder linked the bank's troubles to broader Irish failings: "This is a cowboy economy run by cowboys," said Seamus Mahon. "You think American corporations are going to leave their money in this country, you've got another think coming."

How had Sean Fitzpatrick's incredible profit machine come to this? Over the course of 2008, Anglo Irish Bank had experienced an astonishing turnaround in fortune. Ireland's property market, in which prices for so long seemed capable only of advance, sounded the retreat in February 2007. No bank was more exposed to developers than Anglo, which had nearly 80 percent of its loans tied directly or indirectly to land prices. Anglo always insisted it only lent money against property that provided adequate cash flow to service the debt. But plummeting land prices and sagging demand for office space now meant that developers such as Liam Carroll and Derek Quinlan would be unable to repay their multimillion-euro loans. At the same time, the global credit crisis meant that obtaining the short-term financing Anglo and other Irish banks depended upon gradually became more difficult until, in the fall of 2008, it became impossible. Anglo's share price served as a barometer of the bank's declining fortunes. At first, from around $12 in January 2005 when Fitzpatrick handed the reins to his successor, David Drumm, it nearly doubled by mid-2007. But from then on, Anglo's value melted like a snow cone in July.

The stunned, sour mood in the Round Room bore little resemblance to the euphoria that had defined much of Drumm's tenure. Just 37 at the time, Drumm was a surprise choice to replace Fitzpatrick, elbowing aside a trio of better-known executives believed to have the inside track on the top job. He was the only contender not on the board of directors, but he had other attributes that were likely to appeal to Anglo's boss. For starters, his résumé was marked more by business achievement than by academic laurels. He had gone straight to work as an apprentice accountant after secondary school, then spent a few years in the venture capital industry before joining Anglo in 1993. When Fitzpatrick wanted to establish a U.S. base, he dispatched Drumm to scout potential locations. The younger executive built the bank's Boston-based lending operation for several years before returning to Dublin in July 2003.

As he prepared to take the helm, Drumm was conscious of pressure to measure up to his predecessor. He told one associate: "It's going great now, but I'm the poor bastard who'll have to explain some day why we're only growing at 10 percent, not at 40 percent." The newly minted boss faced skepticism on two fronts. Would he be able to retain the losing candidates in the CEO sweepstakes, or would Anglo suffer the loss of its top executive talent? And, perhaps more important, would it really be his bank? Or would Fitzpatrick, now ensconced as chairman of the board, still call the shots? It didn't take long for the first question to be answered. Two of the three disappointed contenders—Tiarnan O'Mahoney, director of operations, and John Rowan, head of the U.K. business—departed before the end of 2005. The third, Tom Browne, head of wealth management, retired in late 2007.

As for Fitzpatrick, he vowed to give his successor plenty of leeway. During his final years as CEO, he had stopped chairing credit committee meetings, where individual loans were approved or rejected, delegating that task to the head of risk management. Now, as chairman, he deliberately steered clear of most executive decisions. "How could a new chief executive come in unless he was going to be in charge?" he said. "Otherwise it wouldn't have worked. . . . It would have been a joke."[2] Outside the bank, there was profound skepticism that Anglo's hard-charging leader would really step aside. But other Anglo executives say Fitzpatrick did precisely that. "Sean had stood away. He was very chairman-like," said one former senior executive. " . . . David Drumm was chief executive and he was running the bank."

Gerry Murphy, Anglo's chairman until January 1999, says the job only required spending parts of three days each week in the office. Fitzpatrick spent time schmoozing clients on the golf course, where he liked to polish his low-double-digit handicap. And he joined the boards of other top Irish companies, including the state airline Aer Lingus, Greencore, and Smurfit Kappa. But at age 56, he was ready for the next chapter in his life, including a growing role as an investor in everything from Hungarian property to Nigerian oil wells. "He wanted more freedom to do other things. Sean didn't have to be there every day, but yet he had to be consulted," Murphy said. "He'd be good at letting people get on with it. Sean was not one that would be breathing down your neck. He would be very much, 'I'm giving you this job to do, go do it.'"[3]

Drumm took over an institution firing on all cylinders and managed to make it run even faster. Fitzpatrick had added almost €16 billion ($20 billion) to the bank's loan book in his final four years; Drumm wrote €50 billion ($73.5 billion) in new loans in the next four. Profits likewise mushroomed as Anglo rode Ireland's surging economy. Fitzpatrick had posted €396.4 million ($493 million) in after-tax earnings in his final year in the corner office. By 2007, Drumm topped €1 billion ($1.3 billion).

The mouth-watering financial results, however, didn't protect Anglo from a renewed whisper campaign. As global investors struggled in late 2007 to divine what impact losses on subprime mortgage securities would have on the world's financial institutions, rumors circulated that Anglo was allegedly approaching the European Central Bank for emergency funding. Drumm believed hedge funds that profit by betting on a decline in a stock's value were behind the campaign. In fact, Anglo wasn't threatened by losses on securitized mortgage loans or any of the other innovative financial products that were surfacing like submerged mines on balance sheets all over the United States and Europe; it stuck to traditional banking. It made loans to customers and kept the loans on its books, rather than package them for sale. "We are local lenders. When we loan it, we own it—it stays on our balance sheet," Drumm said. "We never break the chain of ownership and responsibility. That is exactly what happened with subprime. . . . If we make a mistake on a loan, it is our mistake, nobody else's. We know the deals, we are close to the customer."[4]

Doubts about Anglo's stability, however, extended well beyond hedge funds. The executive responsible for managing the Irish government's cash and borrowing, for example, was leery of the bank. Michael Somers, the head of the National Treasury Management Agency, parked government money in 100 different banks, including the three major Irish ones. Somers would deposit up to $400 million in the safest banks, but he never put more than $55 million with Anglo, despite relentless pressure from the bank's executives. "It always seemed to me that Anglo Irish Bank paid too much on deposits and charged too much when lending money out. That model may be fine when seas are calm, but as soon as it hits choppy waters it runs into trouble. . . . We were never comfortable with Anglo Irish Bank," he would say later.[5]

For those inclined to see, there were reasons to worry about Anglo's prospects in the newly volatile financial environment. Anglo told investors it was diversifying by making loans in three distinct geographic markets. But the lion's share of the bank's money was tied up, one way or another, in property. Its 2007 annual report showcased prominent examples: the purchase and refurbishment of 28 Thistle hotels in cities across the United Kingdom; a Beaux-Arts office building in Boston's financial district; and a century-old Manhattan condominium development modeled upon a Florentine palace. "The bank does not engage in speculative development lending," Drumm said.[6] Indeed, every loan was backed—at least on paper—by collateral. Often, however, that security was simply the belief that the borrower held equity in another property. And that collateral was real only so long as property prices stayed at their current bubbly level. Like Vietnam-era American generals trumpeting misleading enemy body counts, Anglo executives were comforted by carefully measured metrics that ultimately proved chimerical. In September 2007, for example, the bank assessed its loans at 65 percent of the value of their underlying assets. By April of the following year, reflecting the continuing fall in property, that figure had deteriorated to what Willie McAteer, the bank's chief risk officer, regarded as a "still very comfortable" 73 percent.[7] But with property prices continuing their inexorable decline, Anglo's margin of safety was evaporating with each passing day.

The bank also was making big bets on a mere handful of borrowers; a roster of 15 individuals each owed Anglo more than $700 million.[8] Though it portrayed its lending philosophy as conservative, the bank was running ever larger risks. On a $100 million residential building in New York, for example, Anglo might lend the developer $80 million. But Anglo would then turn around and lend $800,000 to 50 of its wealthy clients, allowing them to buy apartments in the building. The bank would be doubly exposed if something went wrong. "There were some unfortunate lending practices. . . . You're doubling up risk there in a way that's actually quite hard to understand," said the former senior Anglo executive.

The team that Fitzpatrick left in charge of Anglo had enjoyed a charmed life. Drumm was a prime example. He had joined the bank in 1993, as the worst of the European currency crisis was fading, and had known only increasing profits and loans in an always-growing economy. He and his top deputies, mostly drawn from the Dublin-based lending operation, averaged 15 years in the banking industry. But they had never really seen a crisis. "These guys would have been steeped in the Anglo culture. . . . They had never personally experienced things going wrong. Confidence can become arrogance," the former senior Anglo executive said.

On May 7, 2008, Anglo held its regular twice-yearly conference call with analysts to explain its financial results. Roughly six weeks after Bear

Stearns, once the fifth-largest U.S. investment bank, had been disposed of at a fire-sale price, global financial markets were increasingly skittish. Just the previous day, the Swiss bank UBS had staggered investors with an $11 billion first-quarter loss. Yet Drumm was serene amid the bloodletting. "We feel very, very comfortable about asset quality and what's in the loan book," he said. In fact, as Wall Street banks withdrew from the mortgage-backed securities business, traditional lenders like Anglo would have a chance to expand. "The market has actually, despite recent negativity, moved in our favor. So it puts us in very good position indeed," Drumm assured analysts.[9]

THEY WERE ALL WRONG

It was astonishing, really, how fast the façade of New Ireland crumbled. Once property prices started to slide, the Irish economy was like running a movie in reverse. Everything that had grown with property—from Anglo's profits to Bertie Ahern's political fortunes—now shriveled. Erica Cash, the "yummy drummie" shopper and property broker, was among those adjusting to a new reality. As credit dried up, no one was buying homes in Ireland, let alone Bulgaria. What had looked like a bold, but potentially lucrative, career move in 2005 suddenly seemed a one-way ticket to the dole. And sure enough, in 2008 Cash was laid off. She and her husband Glenn scoured their budget for unnecessary spending. "I could feel it start to slow down. . . . With everything that's happened, I'm just humbled. It's a completely different landscape," she said.[10] Even at Intel, where the long-term prospects still looked good, Jim O'Hara was feeling the storm's lash. He'd eventually risen to the top job at the Leixlip operation, presiding over an increase in Intel's investment to a cumulative $7 billion. Still, as the global economy wobbled, he had had to let go about 300 coworkers.

In January 2008, the Central Bank, noting a "sizeable reduction in activity in the construction sector," cut its estimate of economic growth by half a percentage point to 2.6 percent, the lowest mark since 1992, and warned of higher unemployment. Three months later, the bank again cut its growth forecast and by July, after a third reduction to near zero, predicted a "marked slowdown." Circumstances were worsening by the day.[11]

Grappling with the end of Ireland's extraordinary economic boom was a full-time job. But Ahern was distracted by the Mahon Tribunal's dogged look at his personal finances. From the moment the tribunal resumed its work after the 2007 election, the damage to Ahern had snowballed. In September, he conceded that despite his repeated claims of full cooperation with the tribunal, he had not provided all the information requested.[12] In November, one of the participants in the alleged "dig out," Padraic O'Connor of NCB Stockbrokers, refuted Ahern's story of an effort by close friends to help out during his marital separation. O'Connor instead testified that he had not known Ahern all that well and had merely made a political donation. Once-reticent opposition politicians increasingly took direct aim at the taoiseach. "I do not believe the taoiseach's story. I think his story at the tribunal was a cock-and-bull story and I think many people in this country agree with me," said Labour Party leader Eamon Gilmore during a September debate over a no-confidence motion on Ahern. By January, the public appeared to agree: 78 percent in an MRBI poll said they did not think Ahern had adequately explained the large sums of cash that had materialized in his bank accounts. Voters were evenly split on whether he should resign.[13]

If the damage had been confined to Ahern's political standing, the ongoing affair would have been costly enough. But his repeated trips to Dublin Castle to testify before an increasingly hostile tribunal were distracting the government just when the crumbling economic outlook required a single-minded focus. Ahern was on the witness stand for four days in mid-September, again right before Christmas, and again in March. "Too much government business was getting caught up in the controversy surrounding the Tribunal," he acknowledged in his autobiography.[14] The Irish political

journalist Pat Leahy found an "overwhelming sense in government circles . . . of drift."[15]

Ahern would later defend his passive approach to the economy by saying that even as the global financial system trembled, Ireland's financial regulators never sounded the alarm. Indeed, in hindsight, Irish regulators were
timid and overly deferential toward the nation's banks. When officials identified weaknesses in an individual bank's operations, the failings were regarded as isolated troubles and never rectified. Instead, under-staffed,
under-skilled regulators would engage in a leisurely correspondence with
the bank until the desultory process simply ground to a halt. Attempts to address systemic problems—such as the provision of no-money-down, 100
percent mortgages—were so mild as to be almost unnoticeable. One belated
regulatory tightening in May 2006 raised the amount of capital that banks
were required to hold against a 100 percent mortgage, from 2 percent of
the loan's value to a whopping 2.25 percent.[16] Regulators also never used
most of the powers available to them; before September 2008, for example,
no bank had ever been fined for breaching the Irish banking code. Until the
storm was upon them, Irish regulators failed to understand that the major
banks' very survival was at issue.[17] "The regulator's people never came in.
They never came in once from the time they were set up," Ahern said. The
taoiseach didn't think the credit-fueled economy of the late 2000s was a
bubble and thus saw no need for extraordinary measures to rein it in. Instead, he anticipated a gradual cooling of the construction sector, with a
manageable uptick in unemployment. "At any time had they come in and
put the doomsday [message], I think we could have done a lot of things,"
he said. " . . . But there was no sense of . . . I can tell ya, there was no sense
of that. I mean, there wasn't one meeting with the Central Bank guys, not
one meeting where they were putting the red lights on. Not one meeting.
And never did Brian Cowen or the finance officials come over to me to say
that the whole thing, the bottom was going to fall out."[18]

Between 1994 and 2006, inflation-adjusted property prices in Ireland tripled—the sharpest increase in any advanced economy in modern times.[19] That alone, to many observers, was sufficient proof that the Irish economy was desperately sick. But Ahern remained sanguine. Any time he questioned the underpinnings of the construction-crazy economy, Ahern says he was assured by private-sector contacts that the activity was supported by genuine demand. "The value that was being paid for some of the prime sites within Dublin, the price of some of the sites were astronomical. But there were bidders for the sites, numerous bidders [and] numerous banks backing those bidders and on paper the developers had people who would take what they were going to build," Ahern said. " . . . The trouble was they were all wrong: the developer was wrong, builder was wrong, bank was wrong, end user was wrong."[20]

There were, of course, dissenting voices (RTE's George Lee and economists Morgan Kelley and David McWilliams among them). It's just that no one in power listened to them. Instead, they were disparaged, dismissed, or ignored. The manic nature of what was occurring can be seen in a single, now notorious undertaking by one of Dublin's most prominent developers. In the fall of 2005, the builder Sean Dunne paid $471 million—or a record $67 million per acre—for a parcel in Dublin's Ballsbridge neighborhood. On the site were two hotels, which Dunne, a friend of Ahern's, planned to raze. In their place, he proposed a $1.2 billion complex of buildings, including a 37-story tower styled to resemble a massive diamond. Nothing like it had ever been built in Dublin (or anywhere else in Ireland, for that matter), and opposition from local residents soon scuttled the plan.

By early March, Ahern clearly had been hurt by the ongoing inquiries; the only question was whether the wound was mortal. Nearly 70 percent of voters said he should resign if it were shown that he had misled the tribunal.[21] There were new questions about the tax implications of the payments that had passed through his accounts. In February, he testified that in 1994, he had deposited into a savings account a IR £5,000 ($7,550) payment from a businessman, oddly calling it "a political donation for my personal use." Under questioning, he acknowledged that he had not declared the sum to the tax authorities until the tribunal became interested in his financial affairs in 2006.[22]

One day later, Ahern's plight grew even more serious. He had testified earlier that one of his staff members was lent IR £30,000 ($45,300) from a Fianna Fáil party account to purchase a home for the individual's elderly relatives. Now, he was asked to identify the staffer who had received the unusual loan. "Celia Larkin," he said.[23] As bad as the news that it was Ahern's partner who had received the loan of party funds was the disclosure that the 14-year-old debt had not been repaid until a few weeks earlier—when the tribunal began asking questions.

The final hammer blow fell on March 19. Both Ahern and his former secretary, Grainne Carruth, had testified that all of the deposits she had lodged in an Irish Permanent account for Ahern in 1993 and 1994 had come from his government paychecks. The tribunal, however, uncovered evidence that Carruth, who had worked for Ahern from 1987 to 1999, had actually made several large deposits of British currency.[24] The secretary, who had been earning a weekly salary of IR £67 ($101) at the time, said she had no recollection of ever handling sums reaching £6,000 sterling ($9,000) or of trading in foreign exchange. But by the end of her grilling, she'd been forced to concede "as a matter of probability" that she had. Near tears, she moaned, "I just want to go home, judge."[25]

Ahern's greatest political strength always had been his "Everyman" image and the bond of affection he shared with voters. But after exposing Carruth to the tribunal's remorseless questioning, the taoiseach no longer seemed quite so likeable. "Irreparable damage," concluded one observer, "had been done to Ahern."[26] The inevitable was not long in coming.

On April 2, he stood on the marble steps outside Government Buildings flanked by his cabinet colleagues. His northside accent as pronounced as on the day he started public life in 1977, Ahern announced he would re-sign to end the distraction his personal finances had become.[27] He took credit for an "unrivalled era of peace, prosperity and progress" in Ireland and defended his integrity, insisting he had never misused public office for personal gain. His voice thickening with emotion, he said, "I'm confident I've done no wrong and wronged no one."

Ahern's departure ended an extraordinary era in Irish politics, one that had brought the republic unprecedented economic growth as well as a his-toric power-sharing settlement in the troubled North. But his exit did little to dispel the pervasive feeling that in Ireland, where government, business, and finance intersected, all was not as it should be. On April 28, during a global victory lap, the outgoing taoiseach addressed a joint session of the U.S. Congress. Ahern took pride in being the first Irish leader who could tell the American cousins, "Ireland is at peace." Sitting in the gallery as part of the Irish delegation was Ahern's friend and invited guest, the developer Sean Dunne.

I CAN'T SAY SORRY

Inside Anglo's bunker-like office block on St. Stephen's Green, the bank's shrinking share price was a major preoccupation in 2008. The stock had peaked at $23.61 in May 2007, but months of global credit market turmoil and worries over the Irish property market had whittled it to $12.80 by the time the opening bell rang on St. Patrick's Day 2008. Bear Stearns, the fail-ing U.S. investment bank, had been rescued the previous Friday in a deal midwifed by the Federal Reserve and the U.S. Treasury. The shotgun mar-riage with J. P. Morgan averted a market cataclysm but made it abundantly clear that the global credit crisis was far from over. When trading resumed on Monday, March 17, the short sellers and rumormongers who had be-deviled Drumm for months savaged Anglo, razoring nearly 15 percent from the company's value. Incensed bank executives complained to Irish authorities, and the office of the Financial Regulator dutifully issued a statement on March 20, expressing concern "that false and misleading rumors circulating in financial markets in recent days are connected to unusual trading patterns in Irish shares."[28]

Much more than corporate pride was at stake: Fitzpatrick held 4.5 million Anglo shares, while Drumm owned 510,899 and had unexercised options of more than 1.2 million.[29] The share price plunge was bad news for Anglo brass, but it was nothing short of disastrous for a prominent investor who had quietly assembled a sizeable stake in the bank. Over the previous 18 months, billionaire Sean Quinn, Ireland's richest man, had acquired 25 percent of Anglo.[30] And he had done so using borrowed money via an obscure vehicle called "contracts for difference." The device allowed Quinn to gather a large stake in the bank without disclosing it to regulators. But if Anglo's price fell, it left him vulnerable to "margin calls," or demands that he put up more cash, from his investment bank.

Anglo's ongoing free fall thus saddled Quinn with enormous losses that he later confirmed exceeded €1 billion (almost $1.5 billion). In July 2008, he officially disclosed his holdings, saying he was converting his leveraged contracts for difference into standard shares equal to almost 15 percent of the bank. Left unsaid, however, was the fate of the undisclosed additional 10 percent of the bank Quinn still held. Quinn was a self-professed fan of both Fitzpatrick and Drumm, but he was unwilling or unable to convert the entire 25 percent holding into regular shares. Anglo executives all along had viewed Quinn's massive shareholding as a potential source of instability for the stock. Now they feared he might dump his remaining stake on the market, further depressing the share price or perhaps even triggering a run on the bank by nervous depositors. To avoid that, Anglo arranged for a so-called golden circle of ten bank clients to buy Quinn's stake with funds borrowed from Anglo itself. The bank extended loans of $663 million to the ten investors, including several major property developers, accepting as collateral the shares themselves. For the bank, it was a risky and portentous move. Each investor's personal liability was limited to 25 percent of their borrowing, meaning that three-quarters of the debt was unsecured.[31] Ultimately, Anglo would be forced to write off $453 million of this amount as unrecoverable.[32]

None of this was known publicly as investors navigated 2008's treacherous markets. By late summer, Europe and Japan were near recession, oil prices were stuck in triple digits, and financial markets were increasingly shaky. All of that was mere prelude to the onset of the worst global financial crisis since the 1930s. On September 15, U.S. authorities surprised the markets by allowing the giant investment bank Lehman Brothers to fail. Now the crisis entered a more virulent and frightening phase, as even routine interbank financial channels froze. Around the world, the confidence essential to carrying out anything other than cash-and-carry transactions was suddenly in question. It was impossible to tell which institutions held so many toxic securities that they might suddenly implode. A reminder came as soon as the next day, when AIG, the largest insurer in the United States, urgently required an $85 billion taxpayer lifeline. For institutions that depended upon borrowed money, such as Ireland's banks, the environment had suddenly become treacherous. By Friday, September 26, after U.S. regulators seized Washington Mutual in the largest bank failure in history, global financial markets were swapping rumors like a high school study hall.[33] Among Ireland's major banks, Anglo Irish was widely regarded as the weakest, the one most exposed to nose-diving property markets at home and abroad. The house that Fitzpatrick built, perhaps reflecting his avowed disdain for intellectuals, also lacked the analytical muscle its rivals took for granted; alone among the major banks, Anglo employed no staff economist.[34] The bank's shares that day swung wildly between a big gain and an equivalent loss before settling near their starting point.

Anglo's plight was even more precarious than investors realized. Beginning that Friday, three business days before the end of the bank's fiscal year, Anglo executives launched a desperate bid to dress up the books. At Anglo's request, another Irish financial institution, Irish Life & Permanent (IL&P), made five separate deposits on Friday, totaling $5 billion. In return, Anglo placed an equal amount of cash with IL&P. The bookkeeping maneuvers allowed Anglo to report higher customer deposit figures in its year-end accounts, thus hiding from investors the truth that depositors were fleeing the bank. Over the weekend, there were rumblings of additional banking dominoes about to topple. As late as Sunday, government officials, scrambling to get in front of a crisis they did not fully comprehend, believed Anglo could survive the week.[35] On Monday, September 29, a major U.K. lender, Bradford Bingley, was nationalized, and the specter of government-organized bank bailouts spread to the Netherlands and Germany. With banks capsizing at every point on the compass, Anglo executives were growing frantic. Three times that day, they contacted IL&P, pleading for fresh deposits to shore up their crumbling balance sheet. But IL&P balked, fearing that Anglo could fail before returning the funds. Anglo depositors had already withdrawn nearly $15 billion in recent weeks, with more than $7.9 billion vanishing in the previous seven days alone.[36] Privately, Anglo Irish was forecasting a "negative cash position" of $17.6 billion by October 17—in laymen's terms, the bank would be bust.[37] Only after the government announced at dawn on Tuesday that it would guarantee all Irish bank deposits did IL&P send Anglo an additional $5.9 billion. In total, IL&P deposited $10.95 billion with Anglo shortly before the end of its fiscal year and then withdrew it within a week.[38]

Hemorrhaging financial stocks on Monday dragged the Irish stock market to a 13 percent decline, its worst one-day performance since the hopeless mid-1980s. Shares of Anglo Irish, already pummeled by a year-long free fall, shed 46 percent of their remaining value. Shaken government officials met throughout the day at Leinster House to brainstorm a response to the emerging financial meltdown. That evening the chief executives of the Bank of Ireland and Allied Irish Bank asked for an emergency meeting with Finance Minister Brian Lenihan. As they awaited the minister in the main government building, Fitzpatrick was dining across town with a friend. News reached him in the restaurant that the U.S. House of Representatives had unexpectedly defeated the Bush administration's proposed $700 billion financial rescue, further weakening the fragile global environment. "At that stage, I really feared," he said later.[39]

Prime Minister Brian Cowen, Lenihan, the central bank chief, and the attorney general conferred into the wee hours of Tuesday morning, finally agreeing at 3:30 a.m. on an unprecedented two-year blanket guarantee of the debts and deposits of the top six banks. The move, conveyed to officials of the European Union in pre-dawn phone calls, exposed the Irish taxpayer to potential liabilities of $646 billion, more than twice the country's annual economic output. The government said it had acted "to safeguard the Irish financial system and to remedy a serious disturbance in the economy caused by the recent turmoil in the international financial markets." Cowen warned of "economic catastrophe" if the banks' inability to obtain routine financing persisted; Finance Minister Lenihan grumbled that the United States had erred in allowing Lehman to go bust. The government's swift move also carried a diplomatic cost: by eliminating the risk of depositors' losing money at Irish banks, the guarantee encouraged funds to move to Ireland from foreign banks, as the British prime minister promptly complained. "You'd seen the impact on corporate and individual deposits in previous days and weeks since the Lehman thing. . . . Certainly, there was a huge liquidity problem and how that would impact on the country would be viewed afterwards as a serious issue," Cowen said in an interview. "That night it was a question really of making sure that we could send a signal to the markets the next morning that we were going to stand behind our financial institutions and the bank guarantee was regarded as the way to do that."[40]

If members of the general public had been staggered by those developments, they were infuriated by what followed. That weekend, Fitzpatrick agreed to appear on the Marian Finucane talk show, Ireland's highest-rated and most influential weekend radio program. In an hour-long interview, the nation's best-known banker quickly became its most loathed. Fitzpatrick rejected Finucane's suggestion that Irish banks in general, and Anglo Irish in particular, had made "reckless" bets on an overheated property market. Though by 2008, fully one-quarter of all Irish mortgages were for 100 percent of a home's value, Fitzpatrick specifically denied that his bank had made any such loans. "Of course, banks have made mistakes and Anglo Irish Bank has made mistakes. But have we been reckless? No, we haven't," he said.[41]

The banks, Fitzpatrick argued, really were innocent victims, collateral damage in a global conflagration not of their making. Danger had emerged from an obscure "subprime" corner of the U.S. housing market to stalk and then strangle the short-term financing banks required. "The issue that faced Anglo Irish and indeed all the banks was the drying up of the global wholesale markets," he insisted. Anglo faced a real question about refinancing some short-term debt that would come due in coming months. But it still got most of its funding from customer deposits. Quoting Alan Greenspan's remark that the global crisis was an unforeseeable once-in-a-century event, Fitzpatrick turned back the interviewer's efforts to pin blame. "This was not a shameful position to be in . . . because it wasn't the creation of Ireland's banks," he said. Finally, when Finucane read on air a listener's e-mailed question asking whether he shouldn't apologize to taxpayers, Fitzpatrick paused and said, "The cause of our problems was global so I can't say 'sorry' with any type of sincerity and decency."

The air of self-justification was maddening, but it only aligned Fitzpatrick with the government in promulgating what became the official explanation for Ireland's distress: Don't blame us; blame globalization. The seizure in global credit markets precipitated by the Lehman Brothers bankruptcy severed Ireland's financial oxygen supply. What could the bankers do? Lost in this account was the uncomfortable truth that the problem with Irish banks was not simply a matter of liquidity. It was that at least some of them, notably including Anglo, were insolvent. An institution that is illiquid is fundamentally sound, but has a mismatch between short-term bills that it must pay and its assets, which are tied up in long-term investments that it can not immediately tap. Government financial aid can fix that type of problem. An insolvent institution, however, is doomed. Even if it could tap its assets, their value would be insufficient to cover its obligations. A bank with that malady can't be healed, only euthanized.

There was another way in which Irish bankers were responsible for their predicament. They had allowed themselves to become hooked on borrowing from abroad in a way that left their balance sheets profoundly vulnerable. By 2008, Irish banks owed the rest of the world an amount equal to 60 percent of the country's annual output—up from just 10 percent five years earlier, according to Patrick Honohan, the university professor who unexpectedly became governor of the Central Bank in the post-debacle cleanup. The official view that blamed the outside world for Ireland's troubles also ignored the fact that Irish government officials and regulators had slept while danger grew. The Financial Regulator, for example, was described as "slow" and "indecisive" in a stinging 2007 assessment. "When challenged by misbehaving institutions, the Financial Regulator simply backed down," wrote Brendan Burgess, chair of the Financial Services Consultative Consumer Panel.[42]

The failings were visible in Anglo's case. Somehow, regulators remained mute over an eighteen-month period while Quinn acquired an ever-larger stake in the nation's third-largest bank. "The system failed to require disclosure. They knew for a long time he was building this up; it was in the paper in January '07. It was massively wrong that he should have been allowed to build that up and massively wrong that that was not dealt with earlier and much more aggressively by the regulator," said one former Central Bank supervisor. "This should not have happened. . . . You're not supposed to buy big ownership stakes in banks without full disclosure to the regulator." Likewise, the regulator appeared, at a minimum, to have sent mixed signals to the banks during the financial crisis. IL&P, while conceding that its support for Anglo Irish had been "wrong," said regulators had personally told members of its board in May 2008 that it was "a policy objective of both the Central Bank and the Financial Regulator that Irish financial institutions would work to support each other in the face of an unprecedented threat to the stability of the Irish financial system arising from the international credit crisis." In the financial industry, this sort of nationalistic mutual assistance was known as "wearing the green jersey." And while the regulator said the circular transactions involving IL&P and Anglo were "completely unacceptable," somehow veteran banking executives managed to get a different impression.[43]

By 2008, Ireland Inc. was an economic edifice riddled with termites. Blaming its subsequent collapse on the storm outside was convenient, but it ignored the foundational rot that was truly responsible. Once property prices turned down, as they did in February 2007, the logic that had lifted Ireland to prosperity reversed course. Just as it once had made sense to buy the house today because tomorrow's prices would be higher, now the smart move was to wait. Prices would only be cheaper next week, next month, or even next year. Once that essential truth took hold, Irish banks were doomed. "This was an issue of capital, an issue of real losses on their loan portfolio. The events of September 2008, the Lehmans event, were only precipitating events. They were only the triggers that revealed this problem," Honohan said. "Maybe it would have been 2010 rather than 2008, [but] property prices had started to fall a long time before Lehmans . . . and so at some stage along the line, they [the banks] would have had started to make their loan loss provisions and it would have become increasingly evident the property developers were not able to repay."[44]

To taxpayers demanding their pound of flesh, Fitzpatrick's refusal to feign regret rankled. But it was a speech he gave that evening after leaving RTE's studios that cemented his tone-deaf image. In true Celtic Tiger style, "Seanie" had never been shy about speaking his mind. Now, appearing before a business dinner just days after sheltering behind the public purse, Fitzpatrick urged the government in its next budget to kill off the "sacred cows" of child benefits and free medical cards for the elderly. The Mercedes-driving banker's call for the government to balance its books on the backs of society's weakest lodged in the public imagination as proof of Irish bankers' disdain for the common man.

In mid-December 2008, examiners from Ireland's Financial Regulator conducting an audit of the bank's books discovered Fitzpatrick's massive undisclosed loans. He denied wrongdoing, but expressed "regret" for his handling of the issue and resigned, abruptly scuttling a 33-year career. In his December 18 letter to the board, Fitzpatrick disclosed that he had obtained from Anglo Irish sizeable personal loans "on normal commercial terms" but had omitted them from the bank's annual report. To keep auditors—and the bank's investors—from realizing both the extent of his indebtedness and his financial entanglement with the developers and builders who were the bank's major customers, Fitzpatrick engaged in a deliberate ruse for eight years. A few days before the annual audit, he would pay off his debt to Anglo Irish with funds borrowed from another major bank, Michael Fingleton's Irish Nationwide building society. Once the auditors had left, Fitzpatrick would cancel his week-old debt to Irish Nationwide with new borrowings under his revolving Anglo credit line. In essence, the chairman of Ireland's highest-profile financial institution, himself an individual emblem of the new Ireland, had been engaged in a massive, long-running shell game. "The transfer of loans between banks did not in any way breach banking or legal regulations," he insisted. "However it is clear to me, on reflection, that it was inappropriate and unacceptable from a transparency point of view."

The disclosure struck Dublin like a thunderclap. Within hours, Fitzpatrick's successor as CEO, David Drumm, had followed him out the door. And when it became known that the office of Patrick Neary, the top financial regulator, had been told of the loans 11 months earlier and had done nothing, Neary, a 40-year veteran of the Irish civil service, was pushed into early retirement. His January 2009 departure came after an internal probe blamed "a breakdown in terms of internal communications and process and in the regulatory follow-up and response of the organization" for Neary's failure to act. The sense of public outrage, already at a fever pitch, was only intensified by news that Neary was leaving with a payout of almost $880,000.

HE WASN'T ALONE

The Round Room's animosity toward Fitzpatrick in mid-January 2009 was just a sample of the increasingly furious national mood. In the weeks since his pre-Christmas resignation, Fitzpatrick, 60, had become the human face of all that was rotten in Ireland, of a cozy alliance among banks, developers, and politicians that treated the economy as its proprietary playground. In Fitzpatrick, the common man finally had found a black-hatted villain guilty of something that seemed utterly wrong. His moral blindness had potentially distorted countless individual investment decisions as well as fundamental questions of national policy. That morning's paper captured the public's boiling anger in a headline: "Sean Fitzpatrick Should Go to Jail."

What was harder to fathom, at first, was *why* he had done it. Why had he borrowed so much money? And why had he hidden the fact? After all, banking in the hectic, bubbly days of mid-decade Ireland was profitable work. Fitzpatrick's annual salary during his final year as CEO was more than $3.3 million—he earned almost $800,000 as chairman—and by the end of 2007, he held shares in the bank worth more than $80 million.[45] He lived in a gated home in Greystones, County Wicklow, a 35-minute drive south of Dublin and within spitting distance of the Irish Sea. By any measure—but especially for a country that had seen so little home-grown wealth—Fitzpatrick was a rich man. At its peak, his net worth ran to an estimated $340 million.[46]

Yet, on that January morning in the Round Room, as O'Connor spelled out his predecessor's loan history, it became evident that Fitzpatrick had craved even greater riches. As of the shareholder meeting, his unpaid loans stood at more than $122 million. But they had been even higher, peaking in 2007 at roughly $177 million, O'Connor told stunned shareholders.[47] Fitzpatrick was a promiscuous investor, pouring money into, among other things, a Danubian island development in Hungary; Dublin property; film deals; private equity ventures; and additional Anglo Irish shares. His timing was sometimes less than impeccable. In August 2007, with the Irish stock market having already tripled in four years, Fitzpatrick privately advised Martina Devlin, a columnist with the *Irish Independent,* to buy shares in all of Ireland's banks. "You can't lose," he confided, advice Devlin later said she was very glad to have ignored after the market fell by almost half over the next 12 months. Fitzpatrick was also among the well-heeled investors who lost heavily on International Securities Trading Corporation, a specialist finance provider to other banks established in 2005 by Tiarnan O'Mahoney, one of the ex-Anglo executives who had lost out in the CEO sweepstakes. After burning through $1.2 billion in investors' money, ISTC was placed into examinership, a form of court-supervised restructuring, before being sold in March 2008 for an undisclosed "nominal sum."

Following his resignation, Fitzpatrick disappeared for a vacation in South Africa and dodged the media. He was said by friends to accept that the public needed to vent its anger at someone over the financial melt-down; it was just unfortunate, he told them ruefully, that he was the tar-get. Armchair analysts trying to fathom how the banker could have so badly misfired, however, found clues in a June 21, 2007, interview with the state broadcaster RTE. As the Irish economy weakened, Fitzpatrick took to the airwaves to complain that overzealous regulators were engaging in "corporate McCarthyism." He refused the interviewer's repeated request for specifics, but grumbled that excess regulation could cost Ireland its competitive advantage. In retrospect, the interview's timing was probably no coincidence. Four months earlier, investors had begun responding to precipitous declines in home prices by stampeding out of bank stocks. So Fitzpatrick had reason to be irritable. Still, in comments that could only raise eyebrows in light of subsequent events, Fitzpatrick contrasted the pervasive corporate malfeasance of the Enron era in the United States with what he said was Ireland's comparatively clean business environment. "We haven't suffered the huge scandals that have occurred elsewhere in the corporate world. Of course, there's always going to be some bad eggs in the basket. But we have not got a history of abuse in the business world," he said confidently.[48]

His view of regulation as an annoyance to be evaded whenever possible was in keeping with a society that still seemed to wrestle with the entire concept of legitimate authority. He had symbolized the Celtic Tiger era on the way up; now he was equally emblematic as the façade crumbled. In his unwillingness to choose between incompatible desires, he reflected the national mania for having it all. Over an eight-year span, Fitzpatrick had simultaneously pursued four competing goals. He had wanted to continue receiving a large salary by working atop a major Irish corporation. He had wanted to borrow lots of money. He had wanted to borrow it from his own bank. And he did not want the press or the public knowing anything about it.

He could easily have borrowed from another bank and avoided any obligation to disclose the fact; he had done so before. Or he could have griped and accepted the disclosures required of someone running a company that raises capital from the public. Or he could have retired from Anglo and busied himself as a full-time investor and corporate statesman on other boards. He could have had almost any combination of his desires, but he could not have everything. And everything was what he wanted.

In his unbounded appetites, however, he was not much different from the politicians who promised the nirvana of a low-tax economy that also offered generous social services. Bertie Ahern and his colleagues should have chosen "Boston" or "Berlin" while times were good enough to have made choosing palatable. But they wanted the best of both, and now, with taxes heading higher and services being trimmed, they would have neither. Finally, though a furious public did not want to hear it, "Seanie" in some ways was not all that different from the shoppers who had craved overpriced handbags, vacations in Spain, new cars, and ever-bigger homes—all at once. The long boom replaced the traditional Irish inferiority complex with a robust national culture of entitlement. Sean Fitzpatrick was certainly extreme, but he was not alone. And that awkward truth likely explained the incandescent vituperation raining down on him. His secret loans were enormous, but they were symbols—of cavalier bank management and myopic government regulation—more than anything else. A hundred million dollars in loans did not bring down a $150 billion bank let alone a $235 billion economy. But they were an apt reflection of Ireland's refusal to reconcile its ambitions and its resources, its failure to master prosperity as well as a tacit national decision to trust to luck that somehow it would all work out. By 2009, Ireland's luck had run out.

Fitzpatrick was asked once, before it all fell apart, about the influence of his mother, who had schooled him in unquenchable ambition. "It's not about making money. It's the game. That's what it's all about," he said, growing animated. "Money is just evidence. All the time, it's about winning and losing and that's the way I was brought up. . . . You just want to win."[49]

THE IRELAND THAT
WE DREAMED OF

*T*HE EIGHT-STORY BUILDING ON DUBLIN'S North Quay was intended to impress. Conceived as the Irish bubble reached its zenith, the new headquarters for Anglo Irish Bank would have afforded Sean Fitzpatrick, David Drumm, and their colleagues breathtaking views of the river Liffey and the latest in environmentally friendly design, including geothermal heating and cooling systems and provisions for harvesting rainwater. Perhaps it was a bad omen that in the rush to start the project, which remains incomplete, the developer neglected to include a way for cars to enter the basement parking garage.[1]

In another new building, on the other side of the country, in Cork, the picture could not be more different. The glass-and-ocher City Gate complex, outfitted with bubbling fountains and a snazzy coffee bar, is home to several medical firms and software companies. On one floor, rows of eager, casually dressed young workers—nary a tie among them—craft computer games in a well-lit open space for Big Fish Games, an eight-year-old Seattle-based company. "We looked at a few different places in Europe and settled on Ireland.

It seemed like a very good fit. . . . We're hoping to grow this office signifi-cantly," said Michael Cordero, the company's vice president and general counsel.[2]

One of these vignettes—the half-finished concrete shell or the bustling high-tech office park—represents Ireland's post-bubble future. But while the wreckage of the recent collapse is still settling, it is not always clear which is more accurate. In the immediate aftermath of Anglo's nationalization, it seemed that modern Ireland had somehow slipped through a wormhole and returned to the gloomy days of the 1980s. The number of unemployed was soaring. Graduates were again making a beeline for the Aer Lingus ticket counter, bound for more hopeful climes. The government's finances were a ruin; unions were in revolt; and Marian apparitions—incredibly—were again drawing thousands of people to rural shrines. By March 2010, things were so bad that St. Patrick's Day was marred by a shamrock shortage.[3]

Nearly a century earlier, Yeats had written: "To be great we must seem so. . . . Seeming that goes on for a lifetime is no different from reality."[4] Had Ireland merely been posing as an economic tiger? Was it wearing the mask of a nation that had finally resolved its historic dilemmas while actu-ally remaining hidebound? By March 2010, it appeared the answer was "yes." Irish detectives had arrested Sean Fitzpatrick and interrogated him overnight at a salmon-hued police station in his hometown. The peace-maker Bertie Ahern likewise had been reduced to penning a weekly sports column for an Irish tabloid and bracing for the Mahon Tribunal's verdict on his financial affairs.

Everything about the Celtic Tiger, however, was not illusory. Much in Irish life genuinely has changed for the better. Jack Byrne came from mod-est origins to build a good life for his wife and two children. Schoolteacher Roddy Doyle is now an accomplished novelist, having just published his latest work, *The Dead Republic*. Likewise, Linda Farren has succeeded in both Manhattan's demanding legal culture and an unforgiving political arena back home. Outside of the People's Republic of China, in fact, few societies in the closing years of the twentieth century transformed themselves so quickly. The number of Irish people at work was almost 70 percent higher than it had been in 1984. "We're the first generation, for heaven's sake, that can make a living in our own country," said Prime Minister Brian Cowen.[5] Set against the long sweep of Irish history, that was no small achievement. The world's best companies, especially in the software and pharmaceuticals industries, now considered the island an important part of their global operations. Irish artists, musicians, and poets remained able cultural ambassadors. The influence of the once-omnipotent Catholic Church had receded following a trio of official inquiries that exposed the clergy's involvement in horrific sexual and physical abuse of children.[6] And, despite a handful of isolated killings involving dissident republicans, the North was at peace.

But if it is wrong to exaggerate the scale of the retrenchment amid the global financial crisis that began in 2007, it is equally ill-advised to minimize either the blow that has been absorbed or the challenges that lie ahead. The Irish recession that began officially in mid-2008 was the steepest downturn in any advanced nation, far outpacing that of the United States. The Irish housing bubble was three times as big as that of the United States. Real house prices in the United States rose roughly 50 percent in the decade preceding 2006; in Ireland, they rocketed 172 percent.[7] So when the bubble popped—Irish house prices dropped by one-third from their February 2007 peak and kept sinking—the damage was commensurately greater. "Countries experiencing the largest increases in household leverage before the crisis tended to experience the most severe recessions," concluded a January 2010 study by the Federal Reserve Bank of San Francisco.[8] As if to prove the point, Ireland's output in the fourth quarter of 2009 was nearly 17 percent below its peak production in the same period two years earlier. (Over the same period, U.S. quarterly output fell by about 7 percent.) The number of unemployed jumped quickly from 101,000 at the end of 2007 to more than

267,000 two years later.[9] In December 2009, Dick Spring, the former deputy prime minister who was now retired from politics, advised his college-educated son to remain in Australia rather than return home. "I couldn't get him a job as a laborer in Ireland at the moment. There's just nothing happening in the economy," Spring said. "There's a high sense of fear out there. People are afraid. People aren't spending money. People are afraid of losing their jobs."[10]

Fear and anger wrestled for supremacy on Ireland's emotional canvas. Byrne rebounded from his AOL layoff, landing a new full-time job about a year later. Back on sound financial terrain, he put aside a lifetime's worth of frugality and, after prolonged comparison shopping, indulged in the purchase of a BMW 520 sedan. In his middle-class neighborhood, however, he could see the gathering economic storm as clearly as thunderheads on the horizon. Like many others, he was disgusted with Ireland's governing class. One neighbor had already been warned that his job might be lost amid the financial industry's consolidation. The man's wife, unable to sleep from worry, had visibly lost weight. "This is the first time, I suppose in my life, that I've come across a recession that has me petrified. 'Cuz in the 80s, I was just a graduate and I had no money. So if I lost my job I could just go home and live with my parents," Byrne said one night, nursing a Guinness. "But now, I am seeing professional people all around me losing their jobs and at our age—people coming into their mid 50s—by the time all of this is sorted, they'll be coming onto 60 and they won't get a job."[11]

By April 2010, the government had committed $4.8 billion each to recapitalize Bank of Ireland and Allied Irish, $3.6 billion to Irish Nationwide, and a staggering $17 billion to the sinkhole that was Anglo. An additional $14 billion might yet be needed to stabilize the failed bank, according to Brian Lenihan, the finance minister, who called the scale of the required taxpayer-funded transfusion "horrifying."[12] As the country approached the second anniversary of the pre-dawn bank guarantee, public anger continued to scorch Fitzpatrick and his ilk. An RTE journalist chased him on camera along a waterfront office block, while he parried her questions and searched for an exit. He returned from a golfing trip to Spain's Costa del Sol to find that reporters from the British tabloid *The Sun* had staked a "For Sale" sign in front of his family home in a faux seizure of his assets.[13]

As the state-owned Anglo pursued repayment of his outstanding loans, Fitzpatrick sought temporary court protection from his creditors. His hopes for clearing his debts rested on the performance of investments, including a stake in a Nigerian oil well that was located off the coast of the country's volatile delta region. In Dublin, he was a near pariah, quietly asked to quit the boards of charities and foundations that had once courted him ardently. He could not walk down a street or enter a restaurant without drawing angry stares. A few friends stood by him, others fell away. He was enduring the worst time of his life, he told one, complaining privately of a "cold and lonely" existence. Government investigators were probing his role in Anglo's dealings with IL&P and the "golden circle" surrounding the Quinn share-holdings. The Institute of Chartered Accountants was investigating the handling of his Anglo borrowings. But he was confident he was in the clear on that issue, telling friends that both Anglo and Irish Nationwide had reported the loans to Irish regulators in their separate quarterly filings over eight years, or a total of 64 individual notices. And he remained proud of his role as an "architect" of the Celtic Tiger, believing he had helped create jobs and transform the country. "All of that's been stripped off me," he said. "Suddenly from being a national hero, I've been the national scapegoat for everything that was wrong and everything that was bad in Ireland."[14]

Finally, on a summer Monday, in a second-floor Dublin courtroom with faded green walls, Sean Fitzpatrick was declared bankrupt. Once he had avenged his father's humiliation at the hands of the moneyed class; now he shared it. Fitzpatrick's liabilities exceeded his dwindling assets by almost $130 million; his largest single debt remained his Anglo borrowings of $143

million. "I accept full responsibility for my own ruin, personal and professional," he had told creditors days earlier. But if Fitzpatrick's shame was complete, his ruin was less so. Thanks to his wife's half-share of his $4.7 million
pension and other assets, which were beyond creditors' reach, he would still
live comfortably.

A MINDLESS SCRAMBLE AND GHOST ESTATES

Repairing the nation's wrecked banks overshadowed all other tasks. The Irish
government in April 2009 created a vehicle to purchase the banks' worst
loans, which echoed the original formulation of the U.S. Troubled Asset Relief Program. By paying—or perhaps even overpaying—for the bad loans
clogging bank balance sheets, the National Asset Management Agency
(NAMA) could recapitalize the banks and get credit flowing again. In the
United States, however, the Treasury Department quickly had second
thoughts and opted for direct injections of capital into the banks, rather
than deal with countless soured loans. Ireland's slow start with the bank repair project appeared to vindicate the U.S. change of course. After Finance
Minister Lenihan announced plans for NAMA in April 2009, eight months
elapsed before the agency got a chief executive, Brendan McDonagh, and a
nine-member board. It took an additional three months for the first tranche
of 1,200 damaged loans to transfer from the banks. Eventually, NAMA plans
to acquire loans with an estimated face value of $110 billion in return for
$59 billion in government securities.

When McDonagh and his team began digging into the paperwork, they
found that the major Irish financial institutions were even more shambolic
than their harshest critics could have foreseen. Essential paperwork for bil-
lions of euros' worth of loans was missing or incomplete. In some cases, the
big banks lacked a clear legal claim on the assets that ostensibly secured specific debts. When two individuals had jointly borrowed money, only one

name might appear on the relevant paperwork—meaning that if the loan went bad, the bank could legally chase only one of the borrowers. Lenders sometimes believed they held first claim on a borrower's assets, only to find that because of their own sloppiness, they actually held second or third claim and thus stood little chance of recovering anything. "These are just basic things that any bank should get right when issuing large sums of money to individuals," McDonagh said.

The loans were in even worse shape than the government had anticipated. In late 2009, the government said it expected that at least partial payments were still being made on about four out of every ten loans. In April 2010 when NAMA received the first loans, the true figure proved to be 33 percent.[15] The banks, McDonagh said, were guilty of "a mindless scramble to funnel lending into one sector at considerable pace and of a reckless abandonment of basic principles of credit risk and prudent lending." In some cases, loans worth 100 percent of the estimated value of undeveloped agricultural land were made, with no security and no guarantee that permission to develop the parcel would ever be obtained. Amid the continuing downdraft in the property market, such investments by spring 2010 had lost 90 percent of their bubble-era value.

Anglo, which reported in March 2010 the largest financial loss in Irish corporate history, was the worst of the worst.[16] Of the big three banks, Anglo was the last one to transfer its first tranche because delays in verifying the documentation were so severe. Of the $110 billion in rotten loans that NAMA was taking on board, more than $49 billion was from Anglo alone—an amount equal to the combined sum from Bank of Ireland and Allied Irish and a figure that represented about one-half of Anglo's total loan book.[17] Anglo's loan quality was so poor that NAMA was paying only 50 cents on the dollar for its loans, the steepest "haircut" or discount the agency levied. One notorious loan, a $398 million transaction along with Allied Irish Bank, for developer Bernard McNamara to develop the Irish

Glass Bottle site, was written down by 87 percent.[18] The figures were an astounding indictment of Drumm and Fitzpatrick as well as of those in government who had allowed them to operate this way.

Nationally, the scale of the overborrowing and the overbuilding was so severe that NAMA acknowledged that it might bulldoze empty houses rather than allow them to rot in place. In County Leitrim, where the "ghost estates" were especially numerous, it had not escaped people's attention that Ireland had two potentially complementary problems. In cities like Dublin, there was a small army of people on waiting lists for public housing, while in rural Leitrim, there were plenty of empty houses.[19] How long would it be before some developer or politician got the bright idea to marry the people who lacked homes with the homes that lacked people? To Leitrim Councilor Enda Stenson, that prospect conjured up an image of isolated "ghettoes" rising amid emerald farmland. "There's a fear that local authorities might absorb—I'd not say other nationalities—but outsiders to come into an area that they know nothing about and are not suitable to the culture," Stenson said. Relocating an urban population, accustomed to public transport, sports facilities, and other infrastructure, to the agricultural northwest seemed a recipe for social friction. John McCartin in Newtowngore worried that urban migrants would soon occupy his village's 35 empty homes and transform the environment. "There'd be just complete social meltdown, absolute social meltdown," he said. "You would have 35 inner-city families and 15 locals."[20]

RED INK

Every nation that uses the euro must keep its government deficit and public debt within strict EU limits. By inflating the cost of social programs, such as unemployment insurance, and slashing tax revenues, the financial crisis left several countries, including Ireland, badly out of compliance with the EU rules. The sudden flood of government red ink recalled the broken budgets of the 1980s. In December 2009, Finance Minister Brian Lenihan pushed €4 billion ($5.6 billion) in cuts through parliament, his fifth budgetary intervention in 18 months and part of a long-term drive to get Ireland back in Brussels' good graces. Irish officials were proud of the tough calls they had made, including an effective cut in public-sector pay, and of how quickly they had acted. In the spring of 2010, as a virulent sovereign debt crisis threatened Europe and as Greece trembled on the brink of default, Ireland stood in contrast as a country that was taking the necessary fiscal medicine. Yet while the government's actions did stabilize the budget deficit, it remained at a level more than four times what eurozone regulations permit.[21] For all of the pain that had already been endured, Ireland's budget deficit was the largest in the eurozone—larger even than that of Greece. When questioned in February 2010 as to how Ireland would bring its finances into alignment by the EU's 2014 deadline, Cowen said: "We've more to do. We've set out our plans, €3 billion [in cuts] next year, €3 billion the following year. . . . People recognize that we've taken decisions and that we have a plan."[22] Indeed, financial markets began warming to Ireland again; the cost of insuring a notional $10 million in Irish debt against default fell to $150,000 from close to $450,000 at the time of Anglo's nationalization. Likewise, the extra interest investors demanded before they would buy Irish bonds—the spread over the yield on comparable German debt—began shrinking.[23]

But the improvement was short-lived. By June, as Europe continued to wrestle with the threat that government debt posed to its banks, default fears crept higher. The cost of insuring Irish debt rose again to $268,000, reaching its highest levels since Anglo's failure, while Irish bonds still carried the third-highest spreads in the eurozone, a sign that investors remained skeptical. The government's annual budget deficit remained the central concern. In March, on the same day that Irish police unexpectedly materialized at Sean Fitzpatrick's front door at 6:30 a.m., the European Commission gave Ireland's budget plan only a tepid endorsement. The commission said the plan was fuzzy beyond 2010 and rested upon optimistic expectations that the economy, after shrinking by more than 11 percent in 2009, would grow at an annual average rate of 4 percent in 2011, 2012, 2013, and 2014. "The budgetary outcomes could be worse than targeted in 2010 and considerably worse than targeted thereafter," the commission warned.[24] If that happened, Ireland could be trapped in a vicious circle—rising interest rates would inflate its borrowing costs and drive the overall debt higher—precisely the whirlpool it had escaped at such cost in the 1980s. In June, analysts at the investment bank J. P. Morgan concluded that despite laudable efforts, Ireland would "fall well short" of its deficit reduction goals.[25] For all of Cowen's bravado, there was no guarantee that the political support to implement the plan would survive an additional year or two or three of public outcry over the cuts' sting. "It's a little bit like when somebody's 100 pounds overweight and they make a New Year's resolution that they're going to lose ten pounds a year for ten years. And they've lost three pounds in the first few months and they're very pleased with how they're doing," said Harvard University's Kenneth Rogoff, a former IMF chief economist. "It's a long, long stretch and it's hard to keep it up."[26]

The global nature of the economic downturn was among the factors complicating the Irish recovery. Unlike in the 1980s, when Ireland could count on customers beyond its shores to pull it out of the ditch, this time things were tough all over. The world economy resumed growing in 2010, but the rebound was muted. Speaking in February, Cowen expected the domestic economy to expand in the second half of 2010. But future growth rates will be far more modest than the Irish were accustomed to during the long boom. By some estimates, in fact, it will take until sometime between 2021 and 2026 for Ireland to regain its 2007 level of output.[27]

THE LONG ROAD BACK

Ireland's ascent to riches started in the late 1980s with a formula of fiscal prudence, Social Partnership, ample foreign capital imported from the United States, generous infrastructure funding from the EU, and favorable external conditions. Having achieved genuine prosperity for the first time in their history, the Irish then surrendered to euphoria and irresponsible policies. They turned boom to bust in a way that showcased impressively the flaws in both the American and European economic models. In the absence of political will and competent regulators, a U.S.-style blind reliance upon the market and financial institutions' self-interest enables dangerous excesses to build unnoticed. Likewise, membership in a currency union where interest rates are set according to the needs of much larger economies means that to safeguard basic competitiveness and stability, policymakers must be proactive with the tools they have left. Irish officials, however, sometimes spoke of the global economy as if they were utterly powerless, as if they had no ability to affect supply and demand through fiscal policy. "We could manage adversity, but there was always a question of how well we could manage success," said Paul Haran, former secretary general of the Department of Trade, Enterprise, and Employment. "I saw us do things in the mid-naughties as a society that seemed to me that we felt that we've done it, we're there. Nobody in any business ever feels that they are there; there's always competition pushing you. Irish people seemed to take their eye off the ball. . . . We, as a people, started to believe our rhetoric. . . . We weren't building the future; we were trading off the past."[28]

The irony, of course, is that Ireland's gamble on hypercapitalism has left the economy under greater state influence than ever. The political party most closely associated with market-oriented reforms, the Progressive Democrats, collapsed two months after Lehman Brothers' demise. The banks are effectively owned by the government and must comply with specific lending mandates for small businesses and new "green economy" projects. The largest property owner in the country will be the state agency charged with disposing of the banks' mistakes. And public-sector spending once again tops 50 percent of gross domestic product.

Ireland is not going back to the misery of the 1980s. But neither can it return to the easy affluence of the Celtic Tiger. Gone is the romance of *The Quiet Man* Ireland of old. Gone, too, is the high-octane, consumption-first ethos of the Tiger. Neither was sustainable. Neither was real. And good riddance to both. The current crisis may put an end to any notion of Irish exceptionalism, but with a little luck, it will leave Ireland on a sounder footing. For a sparsely populated island of 4.5 million people boasting few natural resources, Ireland has for generations enjoyed an unusually high global profile. Outsiders were initially captivated by Éire because of an emotional narrative of deprivation and loss woven by millions of Irish men and women who fled to the United States and elsewhere. In recent years, it was muscular economic success, not romantic failure, that made Ireland globally compelling. Either way, Ireland got more attention than it might reasonably have deserved.

What lies ahead is a more modest future as a modern European country. But first there will be hard times, political donnybrooks, and elevated levels of social discontent. For a quarter century, Ireland has enthusiastically embraced globalization without debating what that embrace actually entailed. As a tiny island on Europe's periphery, Ireland really has no choice but to remain an open economy. But the details of that opening will need to be haggled over, publicly, uncomfortably, and at some length. That means, for starters, finally resolving the "Boston or Berlin" question that has been avoided for years. Eamon de Valera once spoke of an idyllic, pastoral land—"the Ireland that we dreamed of"—where people knew better than to covet material possessions. Dev's rural fantasy no longer holds sway. But his vision of successive Irish generations—from the Young Irelanders of the 1840s, to the founders of the Gaelic League a half-century later, and the Irish volunteers who rose against British rule—each advancing the national interest carries an implicit challenge for today's Irish. There is certainly plenty of unfinished business to confront on the "island of saints and scholars." Despite ample government spending during the greatest period of prosperity in the nation's history, for example, the share of Ireland's population at risk of poverty remains higher than the EU average.[29] The post-crisis debate about the type of society Ireland should be is just beginning. But the public thirst for a national makeover is already evident, symbolized in an *Irish Times* essay series called "Renewing the Republic" as well as in "Your Country, Your Call," President Mary McAleese's contest for new economic initiatives. "We need fresh radical thinking to put Ireland back on its feet," McAleese said.[30]

If the goal is to place Ireland on a path toward sustainable prosperity, merely avoiding the obvious blunders of the past decade will not be sufficient. The formula that gave rise to the Celtic Tiger needs updating. In the fall of 2009, former Intel CEO Craig Barrett jolted a government-sponsored conference by criticizing Ireland's deteriorating competitiveness. With the taoiseach and other government ministers shifting uncomfortably in the audience, Barrett said only one of the fourteen factors that convinced Intel to locate in Ireland still existed: low corporate taxes. Ireland's educational performance, infrastructure, and level of research and development spending were all second-rate.[31]

This portrait of complacency is damning, but it is not irreversible. The Irish throughout history have surmounted plenty of national traumas: Cromwell, famine, colonialism, their own boneheaded policies. In the 1950s, the country abandoned the autarkic philosophy that had suffocated the economy since independence. After reckless government spending in the 1970s derailed the subsequent boom, Ireland again corrected its errors and roared back with the Celtic Tiger. That was only the latest demonstration that a spirit of reinvention and recovery are encoded in the Irish

DNA, perhaps especially so in the case of the self-confident generation that came of age amid the Tiger. The times now call for yet another national turnaround.

There is little mystery, in any event, about what needs to be done. Since Ireland no longer controls its own currency or exchange rate, the only way to become more competitive is for prices and workers' wages to fall in nominal terms. That is already happening: in the year to May 2010, Ireland's price competitiveness improved by 9.2 percent, the most of any of the 16 European nations surveyed.[32] "People are really out there willing to work really hard for a salary that probably they would not have worked for four to five years ago. . . . I wouldn't underestimate the correction that's gone on in this marketplace in the last 18 months to two years and it's still going on," said Oliver Coughlan, Big Fish Games' vice president for European business operations. The company experienced the economic reset first-hand in early 2009, obtaining accountants, lawyers, building contractors, and office space all at bargain rates.[33]

The long boom, whatever its achievements, masked a lack of aggressiveness in areas other than the foreign-owned sector. Away from the Intels and Pfizers, Ireland's economy, even in the good years, was often more Celtic Slug than Celtic Tiger. For all the obeisance to the market over the past generation, Ireland remains hobbled by "sheltered sectors" where competition is absent and prices are high. Electricity costs are among the steepest in the EU while professionals such as lawyers and doctors are insulated from the rigors of competing on price. Top government officials are lavishly compensated. The top civil servant in a government ministry earns the equivalent of $419,000, more than twice the $191,300 salary of a U.S. cabinet secretary. Indigenous businesses, long in the shadow of their foreign-owned counterparts, continue to underperform. Especially worrisome, given the government's frequent invocation of its planned "knowledge economy," was Ireland's poor showing on the World Economic Forum's networked economy rankings. Ireland polled

24th, behind the United States and 13 other European countries. The lack-luster result was no fluke: only 0.6 percent of the country's Internet connec-tions relied on fiber, compared with the 11.3 percent OECD (Organization for Economic Co-operation and Development) average.[34]

Independent Ireland is now roughly as old as was the United States at the time of its great national trial, the Civil War. As it prepares to celebrate the centennial anniversary of the 1916 Easter Rising, Ireland needs finally to shed the anachronistic habits of mind—including the ethic of the "cute hoor"—that have kept it from fully maturing. Busting up the quasi-incestuous elite with fresh blood is also essential. In the months since Anglo's nationalization, there have been some encouraging signs. When it came time to replace the head of the Central Bank, the government eschewed the tra-ditional choice of a veteran Finance Department mandarin and instead chose Patrick Honohan, a Trinity College banking expert. Likewise, the new Financial Regulator, Matthew Elderfield, came from Australia, as did state-owned Anglo's new CEO, Michael Aynsley. The government also agreed, albeit grudgingly, to establish an inquiry into the banking industry's failure.

Yet pockets of denial linger. Government officials, including the taoiseach, and senior business executives cling to the fiction that Ireland's problems are largely the consequence of external forces they were powerless to resist. In a May 2010 speech, Cowen accepted that Irish errors had made a bad situation worse. But he added, "I believe that if the unprecedented global financial collapse had not happened, there would have been a soft landing for the Irish economy." That view put him at odds with his own Central Bank chief, most economists, and objective reality. The legacy of such self-delusion can be seen in the countryside. In Newtowngore, where the empty homes outnumber those with occupants by a margin of more than 2 to 1, planning permission has been granted for an additional 80 res-idences. Officials in the border area earlier this year were still discussing the need to plan for new houses as if nothing had changed since 2006.[35]

Even in its worst days, however, Ireland retained its appeal to foreign companies. In late 2009, McAfee, the security software company, opted to add to its Cork operation an 80-person sales team that previously had been outsourced to Israel. The U.S. company originally opened a Cork office in 2005. One of three such facilities globally, the unit specialized in adapting the company's software for individual languages and customs throughout Europe, the Middle East, and Africa. McAfee had been in Amsterdam for about a decade before moving the localization office to Cork. The Irish workers' flexibility and speed made an immediate impact, according to Paul Walsh, the company's vice president. In Amsterdam, it had taken nine months to prepare versions of one McAfee product in eight languages. A year after moving to Cork, the Irish unit was producing 16 different versions within 14 days of the product's English-language release in the United States, and at lower cost. That performance convinced McAfee to double down on its Irish bet despite the financial crisis. "We were able to build a team with tremendous expertise. All the guys we have here have come from multinational organizations," said Walsh.[36]

For those hoping for a Celtic revival, the greatest misfortune would be if the world economy rebounds so powerfully that Irish elites believe they can stick with business as usual. If the politicians and financiers aren't compelled by circumstances to adapt, they will not. The world has changed since the 1980s, with the collapse of the Berlin Wall and the rise of new competitors in Asia, eastern Europe, and Latin America. The global bar is being set higher, and Ireland must adapt.

It has done so before. In late 2009, T. K. Whitaker entertained a visiting foreigner in his neat brick home outside Dublin. Whitaker was something of a legend, having attained a public renown that was rare for customarily anonymous civil servants. His recommendation that Ireland abandon its failed protectionist policies and open itself to trade, in the study *Economic Development,* became a landmark in Irish economic history. After becoming in the 1950s the youngest person to hold the Finance Department's top post, he later served as governor of the Central Bank, helped launch the nation's leading economics institute, and was chancellor of the National University of Ireland. In 2001, he was named "Irishman of the 20th Century" by RTE.

Still driving at age 93, slowed only by a slight hearing impairment, Whitaker remained a keen observer of contemporary affairs. He had seen Ireland move in his lifetime from British rule to independence, from horse-drawn wagons to the sleek Luas light rail system, and from sectarian blood-shed to peace. More than any single individual, Whitaker was responsible for the policies that put Ireland on the path that led eventually to the Celtic Tiger. He had watched his homeland struggle from poverty and stagnation to become the toast of Europe and the world—and then he had seen those hard-won gains foolishly squandered. Yet, despite his countrymen's proclivity for such reverse alchemy, he remained defiantly optimistic, convinced that the Irish would regain the lost ground. "Down the years, it has been seen that, although we can be as wrongheaded as anybody else, we do have a capacity to recognize when we're going wrong," said Whitaker, sitting in a room warmed by a small fire. "I mean tacitly do so—we may not confess openly to our wrongdoing—but I think we learn from experience . . . and then we hopefully will re-emerge on the broad sunlit uplands."[37]

ACKNOWLEDGMENTS

*T*HE IDEA FOR THIS BOOK FIRST AROSE more than a decade ago on a drive across Northern Ireland, shortly after the Good Friday Peace Agreement of 1998. En route from Derry to Belfast, I reflected upon the tremendous changes reshaping Irish life, north and south, that I had witnessed as a London-based correspondent. I was pretty sure there was a good tale in Ireland's ongoing transformation, but I got sidetracked by a fellowship in the United States and later an opportunity to open a Beijing bureau for my newspaper. By the time I returned from China and began thinking anew about writing a book, the global economy had nearly melted down and the Irish story had become significantly more complicated.

This book is not intended to be an exhaustive academic history of the period. There are others far better equipped for that than I. In the past year, many books by talented Irish authors dealt with specific aspects of the country's recent financial collapse. I have relied on several in carrying out my own research, but most of them focus narrowly on events of the past few years. My objective was to take a longer view and chronicle what I believe is a neglected story: the full tale of how Ireland got rich for the first time in its history, then got poor, and now must finally get smart.

As I worked on this project in 2009 and 2010, I received tremendous cooperation from a number of the major figures of the era. I spoke with all of the living taoiseachs, with the exception of Albert Reynolds, who is ill. In

Washington, Myles Geiran of the Irish Embassy was a friendly sounding board and lunch companion. In Dublin, Sinead Cullinan, Elaine Healy, and Samara McCarthy at the Industrial Development Agency were extremely helpful in facilitating numerous interview requests.

In writing this book, I drew on my first-hand experiences in the late 1990s covering the rise of the Celtic Tiger and the Northern Ireland peace process. My reporting for this book included four trips to Ireland in 2009 and 2010 and interviews with more than 70 individuals. Of the principal characters, only Roddy Doyle declined to meet with me. I spoke with Sean Fitzpatrick in Boston and Dublin, though on the advice of his attorney, he declined to be quoted directly on most of what was discussed. Jack Byrne thoughtfully answered all of my questions, even when they trespassed on his privacy. Linda Farren and her husband, Brian, hosted me for several much-appreciated and very entertaining meals.

I also benefited enormously from the insights of historian Kevin Whelan, who has generously made time for my questions for almost 15 years. Likewise, several of Ireland's surprisingly large cadre of top-flight economists patiently educated me on the finer points of the nation's economic affairs. I would especially like to thank Frank Barry, Constantin Gurdgiev, Ray Kinsella, Brian Lucey, Colm McCarthy, and Kevin O'Rourke. Constantin's blog, True Economics, is an invaluable resource, as is The Irish Economy blog.

Before you can write a book, you have to sell the idea. I would like to thank my agent, Gail Ross, and her associate, Howard Yoon, for taking a chance on a first-time author. Alessandra Bastagli and Emily Carleton at Palgrave Macmillan did a nice job turning the manuscript into an actual book.

As I conducted my research, I was extremely fortunate to be offered a four-month fellowship at the Woodrow Wilson International Center for Scholars in Washington, D.C. I am deeply grateful to everyone at the center, including Lee Hamilton, Michael Van Dusen, Kent Hughes, and Lucy Jilka, for affording me a quiet place to work and the camaraderie of the center's impressive roster of scholars. I am particularly indebted to the Wilson Center's always-helpful library staff: Janet Spikes, Dagne Gizaw, and Michelle Kamalich. I do not know how I would have accomplished this project in the time available without their assistance.

My bosses at *USA Today*—Jim Henderson, Rodney Brooks, and Doug Carroll—were supportive of my writing a book. I appreciate their accommodating my absence during a challenging time for the newspaper.

Most of all, I want to thank my wife, Kathy, both for not having her first name legally changed to "long suffering" despite ample provocation and for providing her usual sound editing counsel. I also am grateful to my wonderful children, Jack, Patrick, and Declan, for tolerating my frequent absences over the past year.

And, yes, Declan, Daddy can come out and play now.

Vienna, Virginia
June 2010

NOTES

INTRODUCTION "THE BOOM TIMES ARE GETTING MORE BOOMER"

1. Lorna Siggins, "Taoiseach Denies Elitism Charge against FF Tent at Galway Races," *Irish Times*, June 25, 2005, p. 7.
2. "Champagne Flows For Big Fish in FF Tent," *Irish Independent*, August 5, 2006. The Bailey brothers' actual tax liability was €22 million. Monetary figures have been converted into dollars, here and elsewhere in the text, for the convenience of readers.
3. Cecil Woodham-Smith, *The Great Hunger* (New York: Old Town Books, 1962), p. 20.
4. J. J. Lee, *Ireland 1912–1985 Politics and Society* (Cambridge: Cambridge University Press, 1989), p. 513.
5. R. F. Foster, *Luck and the Irish: A Brief History of Change from 1970* (New York: Oxford University Press, 2008), p. 11.
6. Interview with the author, December 3, 2009.
7. Interview with the author, January 15, 2009.

CHAPTER I FRUGAL COMFORT

1. Fergus Pyle, "The Problems in Trying to Say 'Hello'," *Irish Times*, January 6, 1984, p. 7.
2. R. F. Foster, *Luck and the Irish: A Brief History of Change from 1970* (New York: Oxford University Press, 2008), p. 29.
3. Telecom Éireann (ad), "Next Year This Document Will Simply Not Exist," *Irish Times*, January 10, 1984, p. 5.
4. Dáil Éireann debates, Vol. 415, February 19, 1992.
5. Mark Callanan and Justin Keogan, *Local Government in Ireland: Inside and Out* (Dublin: Institute of Public Administration, 2003), p. 201.
6. Frank McDonald, "Very Little Left to Argue About," *Irish Times*, April 1, 1987, p. 19.
7. Dáil Éireann debates, Vol. 312, February 27, 1979.
8. Interview with the author, September 7, 2009.
9. Dáil Éireann debates, Vol. 347, January 24, 1984.
10. Diarmaid Ferriter, *The Transformation of Ireland 1900–2000* (London: Profile Books Ltd., 2004), p. 670.
11. "Taoiseach Forsees 2% Growth But Little Tax Relief in Budget," *Irish Times*, January 9, 1984, p. 9; Ken O'Brien, "Jobless Totals Rise To All-Time High of 208,041," January 10, 1984, p. 1
12. Tom Garvin, *Preventing the Future: Why Was Ireland So Poor for So Long?* (Dublin: Gill & Macmillan, 2004), p. 45.
13. Associated Press, "Ford to Close Ireland Assembly Plant," May 5, 1984.
14. Brendan Kennan, "Ford Will End Link with Irish," *The Globe and Mail*, February 13, 1984.
15. CPT statement, May, 29, 1986.
16. Alan Ahearne, Finn Kydland, and Mark Wynne, "Ireland's Great Depression," *The Economic and Social Review* 37, no. 2 (Summer/Autumn 2006): 215–243.

17. Declan Kiberd, *Inventing Ireland* (Cambridge, Mass.: Harvard University Press, 1996), p. 6.
18. Patrick Honohan and Brendan Walsh, "Catching Up with the Leaders: The Irish Hare," *Brookings Papers on Economic Activity,* April 4–5, 2002, p. 6.
19. Ferriter, *Transformation of Ireland,* p. 18.
20. Kevin Whelan, director of the Keough Naughton Center of the University of Notre Dame in Dublin, interview with the author, January 15, 2009.
21. "Bishop Warns On Access to Contraceptives by Unmarried," *Irish Times,* January 10, 1984, p. 7.
22. Mary Maher, "Contraceptive Report Denied by Desmond," *Irish Times,* January 9, 1984, p. 1.
23. Garvin, *Preventing the Future,* p. 72.
24. Tom Inglis, *Moral Monopoly: The Rise and Fall of the Catholic Church in Modern Ireland,* (Dublin: University College Dublin Press, 1998), p. 37.
25. Ali Bracken, "Vale of Tears, Veil of Silence," *Sunday Tribune,* February 1, 2009; accessed at http://www.tribune.ie/news/article/2009/feb/01/vale-of-tears-veil-of-silence/
26. Emily O'Reilly, "Death at the Grotto," *Irish Times,* January 31, 2004.
27. "Baby Found Dead on Beach," *Irish Times,* April 16, 1984, p. 9; "Garda Inquiry on Baby's Death," April 19, 1984, p. 6; Gene Kerrigan, "The Kerry Babies Case," *Magill,* May 30, 1985, p. 16.
28. Kerrigan, "The Kerry Babies Case," p. 16.
29. Kerrigan, "The Kerry Babies Case," p. 30.
30. Five detectives in the Garda's Serious Crimes Investigations Unit, known as the "murder squad," were reassigned to desk jobs following the tribunal report. Joe Joyce, "Kerry Babies Case Detectives Are 'Demoted' after Inquiry," *The Guardian,* October 24, 1985; for questioning of Hayes, see Moira Maguire, "The Changing Face of Catholic Ireland: Conservatism and Liberalism in the Ann Lovett and Kerry Babies Scandals," *Feminist Studies* 27, no. 2 (Summer 2001): 348.
31. Vincent Browne, "Editorial," *Magill,* January 1985, p. 12.
32. Kerrigan, "The Kerry Babies Case," p. 48.
33. Tom Inglis, *Truth, Power and Lies: Irish Society and the Case of the Kerry Babies* (Dublin: University College Dublin Press, 2003), p. 1.
34. Sandra L. Zimbars-Swartz, "Popular Devotion to the Virgin: The Marian Phenomena at Melleray, Republic of Ireland," *Archives des sciences sociales des religions* 67, no. 1, (1989): 126.
35. Ibid., p. 130.
36. Associated Press, "Thousands in Ireland Flock to See Statue Some Say Has Moved," August 17, 1985
37. Zimbars-Swartz, "Popular Devotion to the Virgin," 127.
38. In Melleray, one man sought the statue of Mary's intervention with Jesus to improve the weather "so that the harvest could be saved." Zimbars-Swartz, "Popular Devotion to the Virgin," p. 133.
39. Fintan O'Toole, "Seeing is Believing," *Magill,* May 16, 1985, p. 27.
40. Joe Joyce, "Warning by Church on Moving Statues," *The Guardian,* September 16, 1985.
41. O'Toole, "Seeing is Believing," p. 27.
42. Fergus Pyle, "Forum Dissension on Mixed Marriages Issue," *Irish Times,* January 2–3, 1984, p. 5.
43. Inglis, *Moral Monopoly,* p. 89.
44. Ibid., pp. 88–89.
45. Walter Schwarz, "Tide Turning in Ireland's 'Gulf Stream' Culture," *The Guardian,* August 26, 1986.
46. Joe Joyce, "Till Death Do Us Part Vote Divides State from Church," *The Guardian,* June 28, 1986.
47. Joe Joyce, "Fitzgerald Tries To Salvage Divorce Change: Irish Opinion Poll Shows Big Swing Against Removing Ban," *The Guardian,* June 26, 1986.
48. Joe Joyce, "Divorce Campaigners Scent Victory," *The Guardian,* June 27, 1986.
49. Interview with author, September 7, 2009.
50. Ferriter, *Transformation of Ireland,* p. 61 and p. 87.
51. Garvin, *Preventing the Future,* quoting Horace Plunkett and Walter McDonald, p. 51.
52. Interview with the author, September 11, 2009.
53. Ibid.

54. Ibid.
55. Ibid.
56. Ibid. Fitzpatrick's salary was IR £3,700.
57. Ibid. The bank's balance sheet was just IR £1 million.
58. Ibid.
59. Ibid.

CHAPTER 2   THE MOST IMPORTANT PUB IN IRELAND

1.   Deaglan de Breadun, "Emigration Trend Confirmed by Census," *Irish Times,* October 4, 1986, p. 1.
2.   "Bill of Rights for Emigrants Urged," *Irish Times,* October 5, 1987, p. 7.
3.   Paddy Downey, "Lynch's Emigration Poses Unexpected Kerry Problem," *Irish Times,* November 5, 1983, p. 3.
4.   J.J. Lee, *Ireland 1912–1985: Politics and Society* (Cambridge: Cambridge University Press, 1989), p. 521.
5.   Sean Cronin, "Ballyporeen Sets Election Mood for Washington Paper," *Irish Times,* February 17, 1987, p. 6.
6.   Interview with the author, September 8, 2009.
7.   Deaglan de Beadun, "Fianna Fáil Trade Their Mohairs for Hairshirts," *Irish Times,* April 1, 1987, p. 14.
8.   Dáil Éireann debates, Vol. 371, March 31, 1987, "Financial Statement, Budget 1987."
9.   In "MacSharry Cuts for Recovery," *Irish Times,* April 1, 1987, p. 1, John Cooney warned that the cuts would hit with "particular severity" health, social welfare, education and the environment. But the "cuts" actually represented a reduced increase in spending on these programs of 1 percent versus Fine Gael's planned 2.5 percent increase; for broken promises, see p. 15 of the same edition, "Builders and Unions Says Fianna Fáil Broke Promises."
10. Interview with the author, December 1, 2009.
11. Padraig Yeates, "400,000 Getting Free EEC Food," *Irish Times,* March 3, 1987, p. 6.
12. "50,000 (sic) Availed of Free EEC Food," *Irish Times,* April 1, 1987, p. 8.
13. Ray MacSharry and Padraig White, *The Making of the Celtic Tiger: The Inside Story of Ireland's Boom Economy* (Cork: Mercier Press, 2001), p. 86.
14. John Cooney, "Poll Shows Strong Support for MacSharry's Budget," *Irish Times,* April 8, 1987, p. 1.
15. Brian Donoghy, "ESB Warns of Power Cuts as Strike Day Nears," *Irish Times,* April 30, 1987, p. 1.
16. Interview with the author, September 8, 2009.
17. Bertie Ahern, *Bertie Ahern: The Autobiography* (London: Hutchinson, 2009), pp. 86–88.
18. Interview with the author, December 2, 2009.
19. Interview with the author, September 8, 2009.
20. "Five Power Stations to Be Shut By ESB Strike," *Irish Times,* May 1, 1987, p. 1.
21. This account is from Ahern's autobiography, p. 98.
22. "Galway Man Has Arm Severed," *Irish Times,* May 7, 1987, p. 1.
23. Interview with the author, December 2, 2009.
24. "Company Says Pay and Conditions Excellent," *Irish Times,* May 4, 1987, p. 8.
25. Interview with the author, Dec. 4, 2009.
26. Brian Donoghy, "Further Severe Blackouts Today," *Irish Times,* May 6, 1987, p. 1.
27. Interview with the author, Sept. 8, 2009. The discount vouchers were worth IR £150 to IR £250 per worker.
28. Tim Hastings, Brian Sheehan, and Padraig Yeates, *Saving the Future: How Social Partnership Shaped Ireland's Economic Success* (Dublin: Blackhall Publishing, 2007), p. 70.
29. Ibid., p. 8.
30. Margaret Thatcher, *The Downing Street Years* (New York: HarperCollins, 1993), p. 97.
31. Interview with the author, December 4, 2009.
32. Interview with the author, December 5, 2009.

33. Interview with the author, September 8, 2009.
34. Dáil Éireann debates, Vol. 374, October 14, 1987, "Economic Objectives."
35. Interview with the author, December 1, 2009.
36. Interview with the author, September 8, 2009.
37. Tom Garvin, *Preventing the Future: Why Was Ireland So Poor For So Long?* (Dublin: Gill and Macmillan, 2004), p. 192.
38. Mark Tynan, "Mr. Doyle Interview," *The Green Machine* (Greendale School Magazine), 1988, p. 13. Roddy Doyle papers at the National Library of Ireland.
39. Interview with the author, November 30, 2009.
40. Dermot Bolger, ed., *Invisible Dublin: A Journey through Dublin's Suburbs* (Dublin: The Raven Arts Press, 1991), p. 28.
41. Kevin Myers, "An Irishman's Diary," *Irish Times,* January 15, 1988, p. 11.
42. Fred Johnson, "Soul Makers," *Irish Times,* April 25, 1987, p. 24.
43. "Book News," *Irish Times,* March 28, 1987, p. 25.
44. Tynan, "Mr. Doyle Interview," p. 13.
45. Laura Stella, "Interview with Roddy Doyle," May 12, 1997, accessed at http://dinamico2.unibg .it/fa/fa_stel.html#Domanda12.
46. Interview with the author, December 1, 2009.
47. Roddy Doyle, *Brownbread and War* (New York: Penguin Books, 1994), p. 1.
48. Charles Hunter, "The Passion Machine: A Lust for Theatre," *Irish Times,* January 16, 1988, p. 31.
49. Doyle, *Brownbread and War,* p. 24.
50. Roddy Doyle, "Jacko's Army," *The Observer,* November 7, 1993, p. 29.
51. Department of Finance, "Budgetary and Economic Statistics," Table 59, September 2009; total employment in 1989 was 1.1 million compared with 1.08 million in 1974.
52. Interview with the author, December 3, 2009.
53. MacSharry and White, *The Making of the Celtic Tiger,* pp. 215–220. The actual figure was IR £87 million.
54. "Adams Alleges RUC Collusion With Attackers," *Irish Times,* March 17, 1988, p. 9; for details of the attack, see Fergus Pyle, Martin Cowley, and Jim Cusack, "Three Killed In Funeral Attack," *Irish Times,* March 17, 1988, p. 1; Martin Cowley, "Man Tossed Grenades and Opened Fire," *Irish Times,* March 17, 1988, p. 1; Fergus Pyle, "Headstones Gave Cover From Gunfire," *Irish Times,* March 17, 1988, p. 9.
55. Telephone interview with the author, September 28, 2009.
56. Interview with the author, September 8, 2009.

CHAPTER 3   LIFTOFF

1. Interview with the author, September 10, 2009.
2. Mary Canniffe, "U.S. Firm Has Target of 2,600 Jobs," *Irish Times,* October 4, 1989, p. 1.
3. Department of Enterprise, Trade and Employment, Forfás, *Annual Employment Survey* 1995, p. 7.
4. The unemployment rate for 1991 was 14.7 percent, down only marginally from 16.3 percent in 1988, according to the Central Statistics Office, while the number of jobless (220,100) in 1993 exceeded that of 1988.
5. Interview with the author, September 8, 2009.
6. Interview with the author, September 9, 2009.
7. The investment opportunity was so enticing that in the United States, an entirely new type of mutual fund ("short-term global income" funds) arose to take advantage of it. From effectively zero three years earlier, such funds gathered nearly $30 billion from investors by mid-1992. "International Capital Movements and Foreign Exchange Markets," Group of Ten, A Report to the Ministers and Governors by the Group of Deputies, April 1993, p. 11.
8. Telephone interview with the author, January 5, 2010.
9. Ibid., pp. 4–7.
10. Federal Open Market Committee, transcript of August 18, 1992, meeting, p. 32.

11. Kevin Muehring, "Currency Chaos: The Inside Story," *Institutional Investor* (European edition), October 1992, pp. 11–15.

12. Bertie Ahern, "An Irish Perspective," in *The European Currency Crisis,* ed. Paul Temperton (Chicago: Probus 1993,) p. 193.

13. "International Capital Movements and Foreign Exchange Markets," Group of Ten, a Report to the Ministers and Governors by the Group of Deputies, April 1993, p. 146.

14. Ahern, *Autobiography,* pp. 141–142. At the time, the U.S. dollar equivalent would have been almost $95 million.

15. Interview with the author, December 1, 2010.

16. "Ahern May Soon Consider Punt Devaluation," *Irish Voice,* October 13, 1992, p. 4.

17. Dáil Éireann debates, Vol. 423, October 7, 1992; unemployment figure from Central Statistics Office.

18. Ahern, "An Irish Perspective," p. 195.

19. Interview with the author, December 1, 2009.

20. Central Bank of Ireland, *Annual Report 1992,* Section 3 Statistical Appendix, Table A1, p. 17. In domestic currency, reserves shrunk from IR £3.83 billion to IR £2 billion.

21. Cliff Taylor, "Ahern Again Rejects Option of Devaluing the Pound," *Irish Times,* January 6, 1993, p. 1.

22. "Unions Reject Bruton's Call for Devaluation," *Irish Times,* January 27, 1993, p. 1.

23. Doyle's comments were related in an interview with Michael Somers, head of the NTMA, December 1, 2009.

24. Leonardo Bartolini, "Devaluation and Competitiveness in a Small Open Economy: Ireland 1987–1993," The International Monetary Fund (Washington, D.C.: November 1993,) p. 16.; Central Bank of Ireland, "Quarterly Bulletin 3, Autumn 1993," pp. 19–21. The "spread" or extra interest investors required to hold 10-year Irish government bonds rather than comparable German securities fell below one percentage point in mid-June compared with almost three percentage points at the end of 1992.

25. Ahern, *Autobiography,* p. 144.

26. Interview with the author, September 8, 2009.

27. Bartolini, "Devaluation and Competitiveness," p. 22.

28. Dáil Éireann debates, Vol. 425, February 10, 1993.

29. Group of Ten report, pp. 22–23.

30. Ibid., pp. 23–24 and p. 30.

31. Interview with the author, September 11, 2009. The profits increase was slightly less dramatic in Irish pounds because of the currency's appreciation during this period. Measured in punts, Anglo's profits rose from IR £644,000 to more than IR £4.3 million.

32. Telephone interview with the author, January 22, 2010.

33. "Anglo Thinks Big in Britain," *Business and Finance,* November 30, 1989.

34. For management time, see Ivor Kenny, *Leaders: Conversations with Irish Chief Executives* (Cork: Oak Tree Press, 2001), p. 83.; for decision to exit stockbroking, see Bill Murdoch, "Solomons to Close as Anglo Gets Out of Stockbroking," *Irish Times,* October 31, 1992, p. 14.

35. Kenny, *Leaders,* p. 84.

36. Ibid.

37. Annual Report of Anglo Irish Bankcorp 1991, p. 8.

38. Jackie Gallagher, "Bank Taking £1 Million Daily In Deposits," *Irish Times,* January 16, 1993, p. 12.

39. Telephone interview with the author, January 22, 2010.

40. Telephone interview with the author, January 6, 2010.

41. Telephone interview with the author, January 6, 2010.

42. Lawrence Lever, "Secret Tip-Off Left on the File," *The Mail On Sunday* (London), February 23, 1992, p. 73.

43. Telephone interview, January 22, 2010.

44. Annual Report of Anglo Irish Bankcorp 1993, p. 10.

45. Telephone interview, January 22, 2010.

46. Interview with the author, December 1, 2009.

47. Mark Tynan, "Mr. Doyle Interview," *The Green Machine* (Greendale School Magazine), 1988, p. 13. Roddy Doyle Papers at the National Library of Ireland.

48. Roddy Doyle, "Teaching," *The New Yorker*, April 2, 2007.

49. Interview with the author, November 30, 2009.

50. Anne-Marie Conway, "Bimbo's Burger Van," *Times Literary Supplement*, August 16, 1991, no. 4611, p. 22.

51. Ibid.

52. Roddy Doyle, *Paddy Clarke, Ha Ha Ha* (New York: Viking, 1994), p. 40.

53. Ibid., p. 190.

54. Karen Sbrockey, "Something of a Hero: An Interview with Roddy Doyle," *The Literary Review*, Summer 1999, p. 538.

55. Niamh O'Connor, "Snap, Van, Wallop," *Ireland on Sunday*, August 29, 1999, p. 1.

56. Boyd Tonkin, "Prize Fight," *New Statesman & Society*, October 29, 1993, p. 41.

57. "Devalued," *The Economist*, October 23, 1993; Seth's London publisher blistered the judges as "wankers" when the decision was announced; Peter Ellington, "Luck of the Irish Upstaged by Salman Rushdie," *The Age*, October 28, 1993, p. 11.

58. Lynne Truss, "Too Clever by Half," *The Times* (London), October 20, 1993.

59. Interview with the author, November 30, 2009.

60. Declan Kiberd, *The Irish Writer and the World* (New York: Cambridge University Press, 2005), p. 271.

61. Mike Hale, "The World According to Roddy; From Ireland's Mean Streets to Worldwide Literary Success, Doyle Remains A True Dubliner," *San Jose Mercury News*, February 1, 1994, p. 1D.

62. Joe Jackson, "Hitler, Stalin, Bob Dylan, Roddy Doyle . . . And Me," *Hot Press*, September 21, 1994.

CHAPTER 4   A DIFFERENT COUNTRY

1. Interview with the author, December 3, 2009.

2. W. E. Vaughan, ed., *A New History of Ireland*, Vol. 6, *Ireland under the Union, II 1870–1921* (Oxford: Oxford University Press, 1996), p. 34. R. V. Comerford, on page 47 of this volume, describes the 1881 land act, which granted tenant farmers a shared ownership in the lands they worked, as "one of the most momentous pieces of legislation in the history of modern Ireland."

3. Author's calculations derived from *1991 Census*, vol. 10, Housing, Table 10.

4. Interview with the author, September 10, 2009.

5. Department of Finance, *Budgetary and Economic Statistics*, September 2009, Table 72. In 1993, the average price of a new home in Dublin was €75,539, down from €80,749 in 1990. The Byrnes' house cost IR £125,000.

6. John Ardagh, *Ireland and the Irish* (London: Penguin Books Ltd., 1995), p. 19.

7. Department of Finance, "Budgetary and Economic Statistics," September 2009, Table 59, p. 69.

8. "240 New Services Jobs," *Business and Finance*, December 5, 1991.

9. Frank Barry and Clare O'Mahony, "Making Sense of the Data on Ireland's Inward FDI," *Journal of the Statistical and Social Inquiry Society of Ireland* 34 (2004/2005): Appendix, Table 4.

10. David J. Lynch, "Foreign Cash Fuels Irish: Grants, Tax Breaks Help Economy Boom," *USA Today*, August 19, 1997, p. 1B.

11. Telephone interview with the author, April 30, 2009.

12. Telephone interview with the author, April 30, 2009.

13. ISOCOR shares discussed in "ISOCOR," IPO Reporter, April 29, 1996, and "Playing the January Effect: Stocks Trading Below $5 And Book Value," *Standard & Poors Emerging & Special Situations*, December 15, 1997, p. 5.

14. Interview with the author, December 3, 2009.

15. Geraldine Kennedy, "Delay about Priest's Warrant Raised," *Irish Times*, October 24, 1994, p. 8.

16. Maol Muire Tynan, "Whelehan to Give Explanation to Cabinet on Warrants Delay; Labour Keeps up Pressure as Anxiety on AG Increases," *Irish Times*, November 8, 1994, p. 1.

17. Declan White, "Father Filth's Young Victims Seek RUC Help; Ulster Police Anxious to Meet Éire Police over New Complaints against Priest Convicted of Abusing Children," *The People,* October 23, 1994, p. 14; for clerical misstatements of fact, see Alison O'Connor and Paddy Agnew, "Abbot General of Norbertines Changes Statement on Meeting With Dr. Daly," *Irish Times,* October 24, 1994, p. 1.

18. Accounts of the collapse of the Reynolds government can be found in Ahern, *Autobiography,* pp. 154–166, and in John Downing, *"Most Skilful, Most Devious, Most Cunning": A Political Biography of Bertie Ahern* (Dublin: Blackwater Press, 2004), pp. 130–138.

19. Interview with the author, December 2, 2009.

20. Conor O'Clery, *The Greening of the White House* (Dublin: Gill & Macmillan, 1997), p. 147.

21. Telephone interview with the author, February 11, 2009.

22. David J. Lynch, "Flourishing Ireland Calls Its Children Home; Tide Turns as Immigration Sets a Record." *USA Today,* March 16, 1999, p. 13A.

23. David Fitzpatrick, *Irish Emigration 1801–1921* (Dundalk: Dundalgan Press Ltd., 1990), p. 7.

24. Central Statistics Office, *Census 2006 Preliminary Report,* pp. 9–10. With the exception of a minor net migration in the 1970s, census records show an outward flow in every census since 1926. The reference to the late seventeenth century is from a conversation with historian Kevin Whelan, director of the Keough Notre Dame Center in Dublin.

25. Central Statistics Office, *National Income and Expenditure: First Results for 1998,* June 30, 1999, p. 3; unemployment figures from Department of Finance, "Budgetary and Economic Statistics," September 2009, Table 62, p. 75.

26. Telephone interview with the author, February 11, 2009.

27. Telephone interview with the author, January 18, 2010.

28. Telephone interview with the author, January 28, 2010.

29. Commission of Investigation into the Dublin and Monaghan Bombings of 1974, *Final Report,* March 2007, p. 9.

30. Interview with the author, December 2, 2009.

31. Eamonn Mallie and David McKittrick, *The Fight for Peace: The Inside Story of the Irish Peace Process* (London: Reed International Books Ltd, 1997), pp. 344–368.

32. Interview with the author, December 1, 2009.

33. RTE broadcast, "IRA Announces End of Ceasefire," accessed at http://www.youtube.com/watch ?v=WXgQwftrCHI.

34. Interview with the author, December 1, 2009.

35. Barra O Cinneide, *Riverdance: The Phenomenon* (Dublin: Blackhall Publishing, 2002), p. 2.

36. Ibid., p. 76.

37. Terence Brown, *Ireland: A Social and Cultural History, 1922–2002* (London: Harper Perennial, 2004), p. 4.

38. Telephone interview with the author, February 2, 2010.

39. Declan Kiberd, *The Irish Writer and the World* (Cambridge: Cambridge University Press, 2005), p. 287.

40. Fintan O'Toole, "Life after Charlo," *Irish Times,* May 28, 1994, p. 12.

41. Lorna Siggins, "'Liberal' Media Pose a Threat to Family Life, New Association Claims," *Irish Times,* May 23, 1994, p. 5.

42. Liam Fay, "What's The Story?" *Hot Press,* April 1996, p. 20.

43. "Roddy Doyle," Letters to the editor, *Irish Times,* June 4, 1994, p. 15.

44. "Realities of Irish Life," Letters to the editor, *Irish Times,* May 25, 1994, p. 13.

45. Sam Smyth, *Thanks a Million Big Fella* (Dublin: Blackwater Press, 1997), p. 15.

46. Roddy Doyle, *Brownbread and War* (New York: Penguin, 1994), p. 205.

47. Fay, "What's the Story?" p. 19.

48. Ibid.

49. Deaglan De Breadun, "Presidents, Rain and The Media All Take a Bashing From No Activists," *Irish Times,* November 27, 1995, p. 8.

50. "Tolerance Plea by Roddy Doyle," *Irish Times,* November 22, 1995, p. 10.

51. Andy Pollack, "Church's Intervention Proved Disastrous," *Irish Times,* November 27, 1995, p. 10.

CHAPTER 5   FAMINE TO FEAST

1.   Sam Smyth, *Thanks a Million Big Fella* (Dublin: Blackwater Press, 1997), pp. 92–103.
2.   Ibid., p. 139; Pat Leahy, *Showtime: The Inside Story of Fianna Fáil in Power* (Dublin: Penguin Group), p. 69.
3.   "Ireland Shines," *The Economist*, May 17, 1997, p. 15.
4.   Interview with the author, September 8, 2009.
5.   John Downing, *"Most Skilful, Most Devious, Most Cunning": A Political Biography of Bertie Ahern* (Dublin: Blackwater Press, 2004), p. 98.
6.   Report of the Tribunal of Inquiry (Dunnes Payments), (Dublin: Government of Ireland, 1997), pp. 51–61.
7.   Downing, *"Most Skilful, Most Devious, Most Cunning,"* p. 155.
8.   Dáil Éireann debates, Vol. 480, June 26, 1997.
9.   Interview with the author, December 2, 2009.
10.   Stephen Collins, *Breaking the Mould: How the PDs Changed Ireland* (Dublin: Gill and Macmillan, 2006), pp. 189–190. Notes Collins: "McCreevy would be proved right, in spectacular fashion, in the years that followed"; revenue figures are from Department of Finance, "TSG 98/25 Capital Gains Tax," September 21, 1998, and Department of Finance, *Finance Accounts: Audited Financial Statements of the Exchequer, for the Financial Year 1st January 2001 to 31st December 2001* (Dublin: The Stationery Office, 2002), p. 11. In dollar terms, revenues from the capital gains tax rose from $134 million in 1996 to $713 million in 2000.
11.   Department of Finance, *Economic Review and Outlook 1998*, pp. 8–9.
12.   Peter Bacon and Associates, "An Economic Assessment of Recent House Price Developments— Summary," April 23, 1998, and Department of Environment, Heritage and Local Government, "Action On House Prices Following The First Bacon Report," accessed at http://www.environ.ie/en/Publications/DevelopmentandHousing/Housing/.
13.   Department of Finance, *Economic Review and Outlook 1998*, p. 11.
14.   Central Bank of Ireland, *Report of the Central Bank of Ireland for the Year Ended 31 December 1998*, p. 8.
15.   Central Bank of Ireland, *Report of the Central Bank of Ireland for the Year Ended 31 December 1999*, p. 53.
16.   Central Bank of Ireland, *Report of the Central Bank of Ireland for the Year Ended 31 December 1998*, p. 14.
17.   Central Bank of Ireland, *Report of the Central Bank of Ireland for the Year Ended 31 December 2000*, p. 11.
18.   Interview with the author, February 16, 2010.
19.   Ibid.
20.   Cormac O Grada, "Famine, Trauma and Memory," *Béaloideas* 69 (2001): 122–123.
21.   Michael De Nie, "The Famine and Irish Identity," *Irish Studies Review* 6, no. 1 (1998): 28.
22.   Ibid., p. 32.
23.   David J. Lynch, "A Nation's Hunger for the Truth: Irish Confront Legacy of the Potato Famine," *USA Today*, January 15, 1997, p. 1D.
24.   Margaret Kelleher, "Hunger and History: Monuments to the Great Irish Famine," *Textual Practice* 16, no. 2 (2002): 256.
25.   Interview with the author, February 18, 2010.
26.   O Grada, "Famine, Trauma and Memory," p. 143.
27.   Andrew Eaton fax to Roddy Doyle, October 11, 1996. Roddy Doyle Papers, MS 44,977/ 1, at the National Library of Ireland.
28.   Ibid.
29.   Michael Sharkey, "Roddy in Fight for Famine Cash," *The Mirror*, September 1, 1999, p. 20.
30.   Liam O'Flaherty, *Famine* (London: Victor Gallancz Ltd., 1937), p. 71.
31.   Michael Dwyer, "The Van and the Man," *Irish Times*, November 23, 1996, p. 1 (Weekend supplement).
32.   John Mitchel, quoted in Kevin Whelan, "The Revisionist Debate in Ireland," *Boundary 2* 31, no.1 (Spring 2004): 23.

33. Roddy Doyle, *A Star Called Henry* (New York: Penguin Group, 1999), p. 71.
34. Ibid., p. 140.
35. Whelan, "The Revisionist Debate in Ireland," p. 34.
36. Gerry Moriarty, "Trimble Says Republic Is Sectarian And Pathetic," *Irish Times,* March 11, 2002, p. 9.
37. Garrett Fitzgerald, *All in a Life* (Dublin: Gill and Macmillan, 1991), p. 377.
38. According to IMF data, Irish per capita gross domestic product in 1999 was $25,768.82 compared with $25,609.93 for the United Kingdom. Because foreign-owned companies play such a large role in the Irish economy and are able to repatriate sizeable profits to their home countries, a more precise, and intellectually defensible, comparison would rely upon gross national product. Using that measure, Irish per capita product surpasses the U.K. figure by 2002. For a comparison of the pace of growth during this period, see Central Statistics Office, *Ireland North and South: A Statistical Profile 2008,* p. 6.
39. Declan Kiberd, *The Irish Writer and the World* (New York: Cambridge University Press, 2005), p. 284.
40. Interview with the author, September 8, 2009.
41. Frank Barry and Clare O'Mahony, "Making Sense of the Data on Ireland's Inward FDI," *Journal of the Statistical and Social Inquiry Society of Ireland* 34 (2004/2005): Appendix, Table 4.
42. Central Bank of Ireland, *Report of the Central Bank of Ireland for the Year Ended 31 December 2000,* p. 106.
43. Interview with the author, September 11, 2009. Reported profits of €23.6 million in 1996 and €108.9 million are from Anglo Irish Bankcorp, Annual Report 2000, p. 2.
44. "Anglo Irish Finds Niche Boston Property Market," *International Banker,* July 12, 1999, p. 1.
45. Interview with the author, February 18, 2010.
46. Interview with the author, February 18, 2010.
47. International Monetary Fund, *Report on the Observance of Standards and Codes: Ireland, Banking Supervision* (Washington, D.C., February 20, 2001).
48. Anglo Irish Bankcorp, Annual Report 1995, p. 8.
49. Interview with the author, February 18, 2010.
50. Report of the Tribunal of Inquiry (Dunnes Payments), (Dublin: Government of Ireland, 1997), pp. 36–40, 71.
51. This discussion is drawn from the author's interview with Patrick Honohan, governor of the Central Bank of Ireland, December 1, 2009.
52. Bank for International Settlements, "Financial Stability Forum Releases Grouping of Offshore Financial Centres (OFCs) to Assist in Setting Priorities for Assessment," May 26, 2000, press release accessed at www.bis.org/press/p000526.htm; (full report is available at Financial Stability Forum, *Report of the Working Group on Offshore Centres,* April 5, 2000).
53. Emmet Oliver, "Anglo Irish Urges Action to Restore Customer Trust," *Irish Times,* April 15, 1998, p. 14.
54. "New Bankers' Ethics Code," *Irish Times,* November 29, 2000, p. 20.
55. T. W. Moody and W. E. Vaughan, eds., *A New History of Ireland,* Vol. 4, *Eighteenth-Century Ireland 1691–1800* (Oxford: Oxford University Press, 1986), p. 37.
56. Mary Kenny, *Goodbye to Catholic Ireland* (Dublin: New Island Books, 2000), p. 246.
57. Interview with the author, February 18, 2010.
58. Kathleen Barrington, "Developers' Beal Bocht Was All Talk," *Sunday Business Post,* March 22, 2009.

CHAPTER 6   HAVING IT ALL

1. Dáil Éireann debates, Vol. 541, September 18, 2001. Other EU states observed three minutes of silence at 11 a.m., but then resumed normal activities.
2. Federal Reserve Board, Federal Open Market Committee, conference call transcript, September 13, 2001, p. 4.
3. Central Bank of Ireland, *Bulletin,* Winter 2001, p. 5.
4. Ian Guider, "Central Bank Declares the Celtic Tiger Dead," *Irish Examiner,* November 8, 2001.

5.   Central Bank of Ireland, *Bulletin,* Winter 2001, p. 7.
6.   Gregory Connor, Thomas Flavin, and Brian O'Kelly, "The U.S. and Irish Credit Crises: Their Distinctive Differences and Common Features," Irish Economy Note 10, March 2010, pp. 12–13; accessed at www.irisheconomy.ie/Notes/IrishEconomyNote10.pdf. The "Taylor rule" is named for Stanford University economist John Taylor, who served as the Treasury Department's undersecretary for international affairs between 2001 and 2005.
7.   Department of Finance, *Budgetary and Economic Statistics,* September 2009, Table 58. Public service employment rose to 269,799 in 2002 from 222,013 in 1998.
8.   Tim Hastings, Brian Sheehan, and Padraig Yeates, *Saving the Future: How Social Partnership Shaped Ireland's Economic Success* (Dublin: Blackhall Publishing, 2007), pp. 131, 136–137.
9.   Pat Leahy, *Showtime: The Inside Story of Fianna Fáil in Power* (Dublin: Penguin Group, 2009).
10. International Monetary Fund, *Ireland: 2003 Article IV Consultation,* p. 9. (Generous government spending from 2000 to 2002 occurred "contrary to Fund advice.")
11. Interview with the author, February 16, 2010. McCreevy announced the change in December 1999, with effect the following year.
12. Dáil Éireann debates, Vol. 545, December 5, 2001.
13. Central Bank of Ireland, *Report of the Central Bank of Ireland for the Year Ended 31 December 2002,* p. 10.
14. Eileen Battersby, "Castletownshend Says 'No' To Housing Plan," *Irish Times,* November 30, 2000, p. 56.
15. Interview with the author, February 16, 2010.
16. Central Bank of Ireland, *Report of the Central Bank of Ireland for the Year Ended 31 December 2003,* p. 13; Gregory Connor, Thomas Flavin, and Brian O'Kelly, "The U.S. and Irish Credit Crises: Their Distinctive Differences and Common Features," p. 8.
17. "Time Capsule: Items to be Buried," *Irish Times,* July 5, 2003, p. 3.
18. John B. Keane, *The Field and Other Irish Plays* (Niwot: Roberts Rinehart Publishers, 1994), p. 104.
19. Telephone interview with the author, April 17, 2009.
20. International Monetary Fund, *Ireland: 2003 Article IV Consultation,* pp. 15–16.
21. William Slattery, "Property Price Fall of 30–50 p.c. Possible If Credit Growth Not Curbed," *Finance Magazine,* February 2000. Accessed at http://www.finance-magazine.com/display_article.php?i=3558&pi=139.
22. Ibid., p. 1.
23. Michael Grehan, "House Prices Won't Fall," *Irish Times,* October 9, 2003, p. 53.
24. Anglo Irish Bank, "Annual Report and Accounts 2004," p. 25.
25. Simon Carswell, "Names of Top 10 Borrowers in First Wave of Nama Transfers Revealed," *Irish Times,* February 18, 2010.
26. Sean Fitzpatrick, "Early Days and Busy Nights Achieve the Right Results: My Week," *Sunday Telegraph* [London], December 8, 2002, p. 6.
27. Author's calculations, derived from annual reports for Anglo Irish Bank, Allied Irish Bank, and Bank of Ireland for the years 2000 and 2004.
28. Interview with the author, December 4, 2009.
29. Telephone interview with the author, January 18, 2010.
30. Comment, *Sunday Business Post,* May 17, 2009.
31. International Monetary Fund, "Ireland: Financial System Stability Assessment Update," August 2006, p. 10.
32. Bank of Ireland Group, "Report and Accounts for the Year Ended 31 March 2005," p. 46; Anglo Irish Bank, "Annual Report and Accounts 2004," p. 25. Anglo's interbank borrowing and debt securities accounted for 40.2 percent of its lending that year versus 51 percent at the allegedly more conservative Bank of Ireland.
33. Anglo Irish Bank, "Annual Report and Accounts 2004," p. 44. These figures include medium-term notes as well as other debt securities, such as commercial paper and certificates of deposit.
34. International Monetary Fund, "Ireland: Financial System Stability Assessment Update," August 2006; p. 11 for wholesale funding, p. 18 for profitability comparison.

35. Central Bank and Financial Services Authority of Ireland, *Financial Stability Report 2004,* p. 9.

36. Karl Whelan, "Policy Lessons from Ireland's Latest Depression," prepared for McGill Summer School, July 20, 2009, pp. 11–13. Accessed at http://www.irisheconomy.ie/wp-content/uploads/2009/05/mcgill-whelan.pdf

37. Telephone interview with the author, January 18, 2010.

38. The Federal Reserve Board, "Testimony of Chairman Alan Greenspan: The Regulation of OTC Derivatives," July 24, 1998.

39. Liam O'Reilly, "Address by Chief Executive to Irish Insurance Federation Luncheon," May 24, 2004, p. 4. Accessed at http://www.financialregulator.ie/press-area/speeches/Pages/AddressbyChiefExecutivetoIrishInsuranceFederationLuncheon.aspx.

40. Interview on RTE "One to One" program, December 17, 2007; available at http://www.rte.ie/news/2007/1217/onetoone.html.

41. Interview with Denise Charlton, chief executive officer of the Immigrant Council of Ireland, February 18, 2010.

42. Office of the Refugee Applications Commissioner, *Annual Report 2001,* p. 8.

43. Roddy Doyle, *The Deportees and Other Stories* (New York: Penguin Books, 2007), p. xi.

44. Mary Burke, "Roddy Doyle: The Deportees and Other Stories," *Irish Literary Supplement,* March 22, 2009, p. 14.

45. Doyle, *The Deportees and Other Stories,* p. 25.

46. Bill Buford e-mail to Roddy Doyle, January 17, 2001, expressing "uneasiness over titles derived from other titles. What about a simple, one-word title: Chocolate." Roddy Doyle papers, MS 44,964/1, at the National Library of Ireland.

47. Doyle, *The Deportees and Other Stories,* p. 36.

48. Interview with the author, September 11, 2009.

49. Interview with the author, February 16, 2009.

50. Interview with the author, December 14, 2009.

51. Suzanne Breen and Liamy MacNally, "Ad for House Which Stated 'No Coloured' Was 'Misprint,'" *Irish Times,* March 4, 2004, p. 1.

52. Philip J. O'Connell and Frances McGinnity, *Immigrants at Work: Ethnicity and Nationality in the Irish Labor Market* (Dublin: Economic and Social Research Institute, 2008), pp. ix and xii.

53. Brian Lavery, "Voters Reject Automatic Citizenship for Babies Born in Ireland," *New York Times,* June 13, 2004, p. 7.

54. Dermot McCarthy, *Roddy Doyle: Raining on the Parade* (Dublin: The Liffey Press, 2003), p. 239.

55. "Gerard Colleran to Democracy Commission Media Seminar," May 17, 2005, p. 8; accessed at http://www.tascnet.ie/upload/Gerard%20Colleran%20paper.pdf.

56. Interview with the author, September 8, 2009.

57. Dáil Éireann debates, Vol. 481, October 7, 1997.

58. *The Second Interim Report of the Tribunal of Inquiry into Certain Planning Matters and Payments,* pp. 11–14; the actual figure of €4 million is from Dáil Éireann debates, Vol. 555, October 10, 2002.

59. *The Second Interim Report of the Tribunal of Inquiry into Certain Planning Matters and Payments,* pp. 138–140.

60. Dáil Éireann debates, Vol. 555, October, 10, 2002.

61. Ibid.

62. Mahon Tribunal transcript, Day 474, April 7, 2004, p. 164.

63. Ibid., pp. 94 and 87.

CHAPTER 7   PEOPLE LOST THE RUN OF THEMSELVES

1. Central Bank of Ireland, *Financial Stability Report 2005,* p. 20.

2. Ibid., pp. 9–10. Borrowing for purposes other than mortgages, for example, was rising at an annual rate of 25 percent.

3. Telephone interview with the author, May 18, 2009.

4. Sylvia Pownall, "Handbags at Dawn," *The Mirror* [London], November 1, 2004, p. 6. In euro terms, the Hermes bags started at €4,000.

5. Central Statistics Office, "Chapter 9: Public Finance and Banking," *Statistical Yearbook of Ireland 2009*, p. 154; figures for 2002 available in Chapter 10 of *Statistical Yearbook of Ireland 2003*, p. 174.
6. Roddy Doyle, *Rory & Ita* (New York: Penguin Group, 2002), p. 255.
7. Telephone interview with the author, May 4, 2009.
8. Diarmaid Ferriter, *The Transformation of Ireland: 1900–2000* (London: Profile Books Ltd., 2004), p. 87.
9. Interview with the author, September 9, 2009.
10. Author's calculations from International Monetary Fund data.
11. Author's calculations from data on the Web site of the Central Statistics Office, www.cso.ie. The actual euro figures were €83.7 billion in 2006 and €40.1 billion in 1998. The inflation-adjusted increase in consumption for the period was 59 percent, based upon calculations using the harmonized consumer price index figures from Department of Finance, *Budgetary and Economic Statistics*, September 2009, Table 66.
12. Interview with the author, January 15, 2009.
13. David Sharrock, "Ambassador's Jokes Get Lost in Translation as 'Avaricious' Irish Fail to See the Funny Side," *The Times* [London], September 17, 2007, p. 39.
14. Interview with the author, February 16, 2010.
15. Central Bank and Financial Services Authority of Ireland, *Annual Report 2005*, p. 14.
16. Department of Finance, *Budgetary and Economic Statistics*, September 2009, Table 52; Finland's 2007 score was 98, virtually unchanged from its 97.9 in 1999.
17. International Monetary Fund, *Ireland: Article IV Consultation*, p. 3. Note: this was the IMF analysis that was finalized as the Galway Races took place, as described in the introduction to this book.
18. "No Indication of Property Downturn, Says Ahern," *Irish Times*, April 8, 2006, p. 1.
19. Martin Wall and Stephen Collins, "Taoiseach Tells Unions He Will Support Rights Charter," *Irish Times*, July 5, 2007, p. 1. After an outcry, Ahern apologized later the same day.
20. Department of Finance, "Budget 2000—Tax Strategy Group Papers: Urban and Rural Renewal Tax Incentive Schemes," September 6, 1999, accessed at http://www.finance.gov.ie/viewdoc.asp?DocID=1165.
21. This figure comes from Elaine Byrne, the author of a forthcoming study of Irish corruption, who has studied the financing of Ireland's political parties.
22. Interview with the author, February 19, 2010.
23. Interview with the author, February 19, 2010.
24. Interview with the author, February 19, 2010.
25. Klaus Regling and Max Watson, "A Preliminary Report on the Sources of Ireland's Banking Crisis," p. 27, accessed at http://www.bankinginquiry.gov.ie/Preliminary%20Report%20into%20Ireland's%20Banking%20Crisis%2031%20May%202010.pdf.
26. Interview with the author, February 19, 2010.
27. Interview with the author, February 16, 2010.
28. Indecon, "Indecon Review of Property-Based Tax Incentive Schemes," October 17, 2005, p. i. A narrower measure of housing-related investment put its share of GDP at 13.9 percent in 2005, per Thomas Conefrey and John Fitzgerald, "Managing Housing Bubbles in Regional Economies Under EMU: Ireland and Spain," ESRI Working Paper No. 315, September 2009, p. 21.
29. Central Statistics Office of Ireland, "Table 43: Permanent Housing Units by Occupancy on Census Night," *Census 2006, Vol. 6 Housing*. Other counties eligible for the rural renewal benefit also had an enormous percentage of empty houses: 22.2 percent in Longford and 21.8 percent in Roscommon.
30. Goodbody Economic Consultants, "Review of Area-Based Tax Incentive Renewal Schemes: Final Report," November 2005, p. iii.
31. Ibid., pp. ii–iii.
32. Ibid., p. v.
33. Brian Carey, "EBS Looks Less Wholesome after Big Protest Vote," *Sunday Times* [London], April 22, 2007, p. 2.

34. Gordon Deegan, "Money Received 'Fraction' Of Figures Quoted, Says Ahern," *Irish Times*, September 22, 2006, p. 7.

35. While it is now clear that Haughey had treated the party leader's account as one in a series of private piggy banks, the tribunal said Ahern had no reason to believe the account was being used improperly. His habit of signing up to 20 blank checks at a time, however, was an "undesirable practice, and in the absence of an internal or external audit, it left the Leader's Allowance and the Leader's Allowance Account vulnerable to misuse or misappropriation." Tribunal of Inquiry, "Report of the Tribunal of Inquiry into Payments to Politicians and Related Matters Part I," December 2006, p. 111.

36. Interview with the author, September 8, 2009.

37. "Brian Dobson Interview with Bertie Ahern, Full Text," accessed at the Web site "Public Inquiry; Examining Corruption in Ireland," www.publicinquiry.eu/2006/09/27/brian-dobson-interview-with-bertie-ahern-full-text/.

38. "Fianna Fáil Soars in Poll as Opposition Suffers Decline," *Irish Times*, October 13, 2006, p. 1. Fianna Fáil was backed by 39 percent, up from 31 percent in the previous survey, while support for Fine Gael fell two percentage points to 26 percent. Ahern's approval rating was 53 percent while 64 percent felt it had been wrong for him to accept cash from friends.

39. Diarmaid Ferriter, *The Transformation of Ireland 1900–2000* (London: Profile Books Ltd., 2004), p. 680.

40. R. F. Foster, ed., *The Oxford History of Ireland* (Oxford: Oxford University Press, 1989), p. 233–234.

41. I am grateful to Kevin Whelan, Tom Inglis, and Elaine Byrne for conversations elaborating these points.

42. Gene McKenna and Tom Shiel, "No Guts, No Principles, No Spine—A Dead Man Walking," *The Irish Independent,* May 7, 2007.

43. Interview with the author, February 16, 2010.

44. Interview with the author, December 3, 2009.

45. Telephone interview with the author, April 30, 2009.

46. Central Statistics Office.

47. Central Bank of Ireland, *Quarterly Bulletin* No. 1 (January) 2008, p. 8.

CHAPTER 8   MONEY IS JUST EVIDENCE

1. Sean Fitzpatrick, "Media Should Spare Us the Polemics and Give Us Balanced Business News," *Irish Times*, September 22, 2005, p. 14.

2. Interview with the author, September 11, 2009.

3. Interview with the author, February 18, 2009.

4. "Drumm Solo Drowns Out Rumour Mill," *Sunday Times* [London], December 2, 2007, p. 7.

5. Parliamentary Debates, Committee of Public Accounts, May 14, 2009. The U.S. dollar figures in the text have been converted from the original €300 million and €40 million, respectively.

6. Anglo Irish Bank, *Annual Report and Accounts 2007,* p. 13.

7. Interim 2007 Anglo Irish Bank Corporation plc Earnings Conference Call (Final), *Fair Disclosure Wire,* May 7, 2008.

8. PriceWaterhouseCoopers, *Project Atlas—Anglo Irish Bank Corporation Plc Summary Report Extracts,* February 20, 2009, p. 26. In euro terms, the borrowers each owed €500 million.

9. Interim 2007 Anglo Irish Bank Corporation plc Earnings Conference Call (Final), *Fair Disclosure Wire,* May 7, 2008.

10. Interview with the author, May 18, 2009.

11. The information in this paragraph is taken from the economic commentaries in Central Bank of Ireland's *Quarterly Bulletins* for January, April, and July 2008.

12. Mahon Tribunal Transcript, Day 756, p. 107.

13. Stephen Collins, "Voters Divided on Whether Taoiseach Should Resign," *Irish Times*, January 25, 2008, p. 1.

14. Ahern, *Autobiography,* p. 330. The full quote is: "The credit crunch was already under way, and we were trying to grapple with that. Too much government business was getting caught up in the controversy surrounding the Tribunal."

15. Pat Leahy, *Showtime: The Inside Story of Fianna Fáil in Power* (Dublin: Penguin Group, 2009), pp. 304–305.

16. Patrick Honohan, "The Irish Banking Crisis: Regulatory and Financial Stability Policy 2003–2008," pp. 102–103, accessed at http://www.bankinginquiry.gov.ie/The%20Irish%20Banking%20Crisis%20Regulatory%20and%20Financial%20Stability%20Policy%202003–2008.pdf.

17. Honohan, "The Irish Banking Crisis," pp. 6–19.

18. Interview with the author, February 16, 2010.

19. Honohan, "The Irish Banking Crisis," p. 24.

20. Interview with the author, September 8, 2009.

21. Pat Leahy, "Tribunal Fails to Curb FF Support," *Sunday Business Post,* March 2, 2008.

22. Mahon Tribunal Transcript, Day 825, pp. 25–26.

23. Mahon Tribunal Transcript, Day 826, p. 69.

24. Mahon Tribunal Transcript, Day 839, pp. 104–107 and 131.

25. Mahon Tribunal Transcript, Day 840, p. 9.

26. Michael Clifford and Shane Coleman, *Bertie Ahern and the Drumcondra Mafia* (Dublin: Hachette Books, 2009), p. 357.

27. In an interview with the author on February 16, 2009, Ahern said: "It came to a stage for the last six months it was just endless. Monday, it was tribunal, Tuesday it was the tribunal, it was Wednesday. I was talking about the economy even when the credit squeeze started [and] the only thing I was asked about was the tribunal. . . . You couldn't get away from answering the same bloody questions day in and day out."

28. The Financial Regulator, "Financial Regulator Statement—Market Abuse," March 20, 2008, accessed at http://www.financialregulator.ie/press-area/press-releases/Pages/FinancialRegulator Statement-MarketAbuse.aspx.

29. Anglo Irish Bank Group, *Annual Report and Accounts 2007,* p. 128.

30. Brian Carey and Tom Lyons, "Anglo's Missing Pieces," *Sunday Times* [London], February 1, 2009, p. 5.

31. Anglo Irish Bank Group, *Annual Report and Accounts 2008,* p. 4. Actual figure was €451 million.

32. Anglo Irish Bank Group, *Interim Report Six Months Ended 31 March 2009,* p. 4. The actual write-off was €308 million.

33. On September 25, U.S. regulators seized Washington Mutual after panicky depositors pulled $16 billion from their accounts.

34. In a June 15, 2010, email to the author, Constantin Gurdgiev, an adjunct lecturer in finance at Trinity College, said that both Fitzpatrick and Drumm told him they regarded an in-house economist as a "luxury" and an "extravagance." Honohan, "The Irish Banking Crisis," p. 88, footnote 113, discusses one unidentified bank that is almost certainly Anglo: " . . . One bank did not have a defined stress testing framework supported by either formal processes or documentation. The bank did not employ an economist and their stress tests did not reference economic data such as GDP, interest rates or unemployment; bank representatives argue that the latter may not be as necessary in the bank's case given that they occupied the most profitable economic sector. While the bank did conduct what was referred to as 'ad-hoc stress tests' these appeared to assess the impact of actual events (e.g., the impact of the smoking ban on the pub trade) rather than severe but plausible events."

35. Honohan, "The Irish Banking Crisis," p. 123.

36. PriceWaterhouseCoopers, *Project Atlas,* p. 19. The five IL&P deposits totalled €3.45 billion. Anglo depositors withdrew €10 billion and €5.4 billion left in that last week.

37. Ibid. The stated figure was €12 billion.

38. Irish Life & Permanent, "Statement," February 13, 2009, accessed at http://www.irishlifepermanent.ie/ipm/media/pressreleases/ilpgroup/group2009/2009–02–13/ states €4 billion and €7.45 billion as the deposit figures; Anglo Irish Bank, *Annual Report And Accounts 2009,* pp. 82 and 102, state that the IL&P deposit was €7.3 billion as of the year end.

39. RTE, "Marian Finucane program," October 4, 2008, accessed at http://www.rte.ie/radio1/marianfinucane/1084847.html. Honohan, "The Irish Banking Crisis," p. 124 reports that in their September 29 meetings with the taoiseach and other officials, the heads of AIB and Bank of Ire-

land both pushed for Anglo to be nationalized. Had Anglo failed, Ireland's main banks would have run out of cash "within days" (p. 131).

40. Interview with the author, February 15, 2010.

41. RTE, "Marian Finucane program," October 4, 2008.

42. Comptroller and Auditor General, "Special Report: The Financial Regulator," May 2007, p. 79.

43. Irish Life & Permanent, "Statement," February 13, 2009, accessed at http://www.irishlife permanent.ie/ipm/media/pressreleases/ilpgroup/group2009/2009–02–13/; and, Financial Regulator, "Statement By Authority," February 13, 2009, accessed at http://www.financialregulator. ie/press-area/press-releases/Pages/StatementbyAuthority%20-%2013%20February%202009 .aspx.

44. Interview with author, December 1, 2009.

45. Fitzpatrick received €2.7 million in 2004, his last year as CEO, and €539,000 in 2008, his last year as chairman, as detailed in Anglo Irish Bank Group's annual reports for the period. He owned 4.5 million shares of the company's stock at the end of 2007.

46. Based on a private estimate of €250 million converted to dollars at the 2007 average euro value of $1.37.

47. The actual figures O'Connor cited for Fitzpatrick's loans were €83 million in early 2009 and a peak of €129 million in 2007.

48. Ian Kehoe, "Fitzpatrick Rails against 'Corporate McCarthyism'," *Sunday Business Post,* July 1, 2007.

49. RTE, "One to One: Sean Fitzpatrick," December 17, 2007, accessed at http://www.rte.ie/news/ 2007/1217/onetoone_av.html?2319247,null,230.

EPILOGUE   THE IRELAND THAT WE DREAMED OF

1. Building details from J.V. Tierney & Co. Web site at http://www.jvtierney.ie/commercial/project11.php; planning application difficulties, including omission of parking garage entrance, are discussed in *Sunday Tribune,* "Carroll Revises Anglo HQ Plan," November 22, 2009.

2. Interview with the author, February 17, 2010.

3. Renee Montagne, "Shamrocks as Elusive as a Pot of Gold," National Public Radio, March 17, 2010; Tom Shiel, "Thousands Wait For Knock Apparition," *Irish Times,* October 12, 2009.

4. Kiberd, "The Irish Writer and the World," p. 30, quotes Yeats's "The Player Queen."

5. Central Statistics Office shows 1,887,700 working in the fourth quarter versus 1,103,000 in 1984, per Department of Finance, "Budgetary and Economic Statistics," September 2009, Table 59; Cowen's quote came in an interview with the author, February 15, 2010.

6. On May 11, 1999, Taoiseach Bertie Ahern apologized on behalf of the Irish state to individuals who had been abused in church-run residential institutions and he opened a far-reaching inquiry. Beginning with the October 2005 Ferns Report, the Irish state detailed the involvement of Catholic priests and members of religious orders such as the Christian Brothers in routine and recurring sexual and physical abuse of children. In May 2009, the Ryan Report detailed a long-standing pattern of appalling mistreatment of children placed in orphanages and workhouses, including frequent beatings and "chronic" sexual abuse. Finally, in November 2009, the Murphy Report showed that four archbishops had failed to report to police well-founded complaints of abusive priests in the Dublin diocese over several decades.

7. Federal Reserve Bank of San Francisco, "Global Household Leverage, House Prices and Consumption," January 11, 2010, p. 3.; Rebecca Wilder uses price-to-rent ratios to demonstrate a 158 percent increase in Ireland versus a 76 percent gain in the United States over a slightly different time period. Her research is at http://www.newsneconomics.com/2009/05/housing-bubbles-around-world-looks.html.

8. Ibid., p. 4.

9. Central Statistics Office, "Quarterly National Accounts," March 25, 2010, p. 3.; The Economic and Social Research Institute, "Permanent TSB/ESRI House Price Index," February 22, 2010; Central Statistics Office, "Quarterly National Household Survey," online database at www.cso.ie.

10. Interview with the author, December 2, 2009.

11. Interview with the author, February 18, 2010.

12. Department of Finance, "Banks Statement by the Minister for Finance," March 30, 2010; The first €7 billion to recapitalize the banks came from the National Pension Reserve Fund, which was established in 2001 to handle the growing costs of Ireland's aging population after 2025. The actual bank support figures, in euros, were €3.5 billion apiece for Bank of Ireland and Allied Irish; €2.6 billion for Irish Nationwide; €12.3 billion for Anglo to date with an additional €10 billion potentially in the offing.

13. Sylvia Pownhall, Mark May, and Fergus O'Shea, "House About Paying Us Back Seanie?" *The Sun,* April 2, 2010, pp. 6–7.

14. Interview with the author, September 11, 2009.

15. McDonagh's testimony, including details of the poor loan documentation, can be found at Joint Committee on Finance and the Public Service, "NAMA and the NTMA: Discussion with Chief Executives," April 13, 2010.

16. Anglo Irish Bank, "Annual Report and Accounts 2009," p. 2; for the 15 months ending December 31, 2009, Anglo reported a loss of €12.7 billion.

17. NAMA's expected total of €80 billion will include €35.6 billion from Anglo, €23 billion from Allied Irish, and €12 billion from Bank of Ireland.

18. Simon Carswell, "Glass Bottle Site Given 87% Nama Haircut," *Irish Times,* April 3, 2010, p. 16. The actual loan value was €288 million.

19. Nationally, there were 56,249 households on waiting lists for social housing, according to the Department of Environment, Heritage, and Local Government's "Local Authority Assessment of Housing Needs," available at http://www.environ.ie/en/Publications/StatisticsandRegularPublications/HousingStatistics/.

20. Both Stenson and McCartin spoke in separate interviews with the author, February 19, 2010.

21. For 2010, the budget deficit was expected to be 11.6 percent versus the 3 percent upper limit for countries using the euro. But, in April, the EU said Ireland's 2009 deficit actually was 14.3 percent, not the 11.8 percent reported. The revision came after Brussels said the €4 billion spent recapitalizing Anglo should count as a current expenditure.

22. Interview with the author, February 15, 2010.

23. As of April 16, 2010, the cost of a five-year credit default swap—a kind of insurance policy—on a notional $10 million in Irish debt was $146,000. The comparable cost for the same insurance against defaults by other states follows: Greece, $417,000; the United States, $39,000; and Germany, $33,000. On June 24, as the European debt crisis simmered, the cost of credit insurance rose accordingly. For Ireland, the new figure was $268,000. Greece was up to $1,037,000; the United States was down slightly to $37,000; and Germany was up to $43,000. On April 16, the spread between the yields on German and Irish 10-year debt was about 146 basis points, compared with 279 following Anglo's January 2009 nationalization. On June 24, the spread had widened again to 278 basis points. All data is via Bloomberg.

24. European Commission, "Recommendation for a Council Opinion on the Updated Stability Programme of Ireland, 2009–2014," p. 8; Ireland also looked likely to remain well above the EU's 60 percent limit on debt-to-gdp ratio.

25. David Hensley and Joseph Lupton, "Government Debt Sustainability in the Age of Fiscal Activism," J.P. Morgan, June 11, 2010, p. 21. The Irish government projects a budget deficit of 4.9% of GDP in 2013. The J.P. Morgan forecast is for a 7.7% gap.

26. Telephone interview with the author, April 15, 2010.

27. Constantin Gurdgiev, True Economics blog, March 23 and 26, 2010, accessed at http://trueeconomics.blogspot.com.

28. Interview with the author, November 30, 2009.

29. Central Statistics Office, "Survey of Income and Living Conditions in Ireland 2008," accessed at http://www.cso.ie/newsevents/pressrelease_silc2008.htm. Between 2001 and 2007, the annual increase in gross current government expenditure ranged between 7.8 percent and 15.5 percent, according to the Department of Finance, "Budgetary and Economic Statistics," Table 2, September 2009.

30. President Mary McAleese, promotional video, www.yourcountryyourcall.com.

31. Ciaran Hancock, "Will Farmleigh Make A Difference?" *Irish Times,* September 26, 2009, p. 3.

32. European Central Bank, "Harmonised Competitiveness Indicators Based on Consumer Price Indices," May 2010.

33. Michael Cordero and Oliver Coughlan, interview with the author, February 17, 2010.

34. World Economic Forum, "Global Information Technology Report 2009–2010," p. xvii.; Ciara O'Brien, "Broadband Speeds Lag OECD," *Irish Times,* January 23, 2010, p. 9.

35. Author interview with John McCartin, February 19, 2010.

36. Paul Walsh and Tim Daly of McAfee, interview with author, February 17, 2010.

37. The reference is to a phrase from Churchill's "This was their finest hour" speech of June 18, 1940: "Hitler knows that he will have to break us in this island or lose the war. If we can stand up to him, all Europe may be free and the life of the world may move forward into broad, sunlit uplands."

BIBLIOGRAPHY

Ahern, Bertie. *Bertie Ahern: The Autobiography.* London: Hutchinson, 2009.

Ahern, Bertie. "An Irish Perspective." In *The European Currency Crisis,* edited by Paul Temperton. Chicago: Probus 1993.

Ardagh, John. *Ireland and the Irish: Portrait of a Changing Society.* London: Penguin Group, 1995.

Bolger, Dermot. *The Journey Home.* London: HarperCollins Publishers, 2003.

Bolger, Dermot, ed. *Invisible Dublin: A Journey through Dublin's Suburbs.* Dublin: The Raven Arts Press, 1991.

Brown, Terence. *Ireland: A Social and Cultural History 1922–2002.* London: Harper Perennial, 2004.

Callanan, Mark, and Justin Keogan, *Local Government in Ireland: Inside and Out.* Dublin: Institute of Public Administration, 2003.

Clifford, Michael, and Shane Coleman. *Bertie Ahern and the Drumcondra Mafia.* Dublin: Hachette Books Ireland, 2009.

Collins, Stephen. *Breaking the Mould: How the PDs Changed Ireland.* Dublin: Gill & Macmillan, 2006.

Cooper, Matt. *Who Really Runs Ireland? The Story of the Elite Who Led Ireland from Bust to Boom . . . and Back Again.* Dublin: Penguin Group, 2009.

Coulter, Colin, and Steve Coleman, eds. *The End of Irish History?* Manchester: Manchester University Press, 2003.

Downing, John. *"Most Skilful, Most Devious, Most Cunning": A Political Biography of Bertie Ahern.* Dublin: Blackwater Press, 2004.

Doyle, Roddy. *Brownbread and War.* New York: Penguin, 1994.

Doyle, Roddy. *The Commitments.* New York: Vintage Books, 1989.

Doyle, Roddy. *The Deportees and Other Stories.* New York: Penguin Group, 2007.

Doyle, Roddy. *Paddy Clarke, Ha Ha Ha.* London: Secker & Warburg, 1993.

Doyle, Roddy. *A Star Called Henry.* New York: Penguin Group, 1999.

Doyle, Roddy. *The Van.* New York: Viking, 1992.

Doyle, Roddy. *The Woman Who Walked into Doors.* New York: Viking, 1996.

Ferriter, Diarmaid. *The Transformation of Ireland 1900–2000.* London: Profile Books Ltd., 2004.

Fitzgerald, Garrett. *All in a Life.* Dublin: Gill and Macmillan, 1991.

Fitzpatrick, David. *Irish Emigration 1801–1921.* Dundalk: Dundalgan Press Ltd., 1990.

Foster, R. F. *Luck and the Irish: A Brief History of Change from 1970.* New York: Oxford University Press, 2008.

Foster, R. F. *Modern Ireland: 1600–1972.* London: Penguin Group, 1989.

Foster, R. F., ed. *The Oxford History of Ireland.* Oxford: Oxford University Press, 1989.

Garvin, Tom. *Preventing the Future: Why Was Ireland So Poor for So Long?* Dublin: Gill & MacMillan Ltd., 2004.

Gray, Alan, ed. *International Perspectives on the Irish Economy.* Dublin: Indecon Economic Consultants, 1997.

Hastings, Tim, Brian Sheehan, and Padraig Yeates. *Saving the Future: How Social Partnership Shaped Ireland's Economic Success.* Dublin: Blackhall Publishing, 2007.

Inglis, Tom. *Moral Monopoly: The Rise and Fall of the Catholic Church in Modern Ireland.* Dublin: University College Dublin Press, 1998.

Inglis, Tom. *Truth, Power, and Lies: Irish Society and the Case of the Kerry Babies.* Dublin: University College Dublin Press, 2003.

Keane, John B. *The Field and Other Irish Plays.* Niwot: Roberts Rinehart Publishers, 1994.

Kenny, Ivor. *Leaders: Conversations with Irish Chief Executives.* Cork: Oak Tree Press, 2001.

Kenny, Mary. *Goodbye to Catholic Ireland.* Dublin: New Island Books, 2000.

Kiberd, Declan. *Inventing Ireland.* Cambridge, Mass.: Harvard University Press, 1996.

Kiberd, Declan. *The Irish Writer and the World.* Cambridge: Cambridge University Press, 2005.

Leahy, Pat. *Showtime: The Inside Story of Fianna Fáil in Power.* Dublin: Penguin Group, 2009.

Lee, J. J. *Ireland 1912–1985: Politics and Society.* Cambridge: Cambridge University Press, 1995.

MacSharry, Ray, and Padraic White. *The Making of the Celtic Tiger: The Inside Story of Ireland's Boom Economy.* Cork: Mercier Press, 2001.

Mallie, Eamonn, and David McKittrick. *The Fight for Peace: The Inside Story of the Irish Peace Process.* London: Reed International Books Ltd, 1997.

McCarthy, Dermot. *Roddy Doyle: Raining on the Parade.* Dublin: The Liffey Press, 2003.

McDonald, Frank, and Kathy Sheridan. *The Builders: How a Small Group of Property Developers Fuelled the Building Boom and Transformed Ireland.* Dublin: Penguin Group, 2008.

McGahern, John. *Amongst Women.* London: Faber and Faber, 2008.

McGahern, John. *The Dark.* New York: Penguin Group, 1965.

McWilliams, David. *The Pope's Children: The Irish Economic Triumph and the Rise of Ireland's New Elite.* Hoboken: John Wiley & Sons, 2008.

Moody, T. W., and W. E. Vaughan, eds. *A New History of Ireland.* Vol. 4, *Eighteenth-Century Ireland 1691–1800.* Oxford: Oxford University Press, 1986.

Murphy, David, and Martina Devlin. *Banksters: How a Powerful Elite Squandered Ireland's Wealth.* Dublin: Hachette Books, 2009.

O Cinneide, Barra. *Riverdance: The Phenomenon.* Dublin: Blackhall Publishing, 2002.

O'Clery, Conor. *The Greening of the White House.* Dublin: Gill & Macmillan, 1997.

O'Connell, Philip J., and Frances McGinnity. *Immigrants at Work: Ethnicity and Nationality in the Irish Labor Market.* Dublin: Economic and Social Research Institute, 2008.

O'Faolain, Sean. *The Irish.* Harmondsworth: Penguin Books Ltd., 1969.

O'Flaherty, Liam. *Famine.* London: Victor Gollancz Ltd., 1937.

O'Toole, Fintan. *After the Ball.* Dublin: New Island, 2003.

Powell, Jonathan. *Great Hatred, Little Room: Making Peace in Northern Ireland.* London: Vintage Books, 2009.

Ross, Shane. *The Bankers: How the Banks Brought Ireland to its Knees.* Dublin: Penguin Group, 2009.

Smyth, Sam. *Thanks a Million Big Fella.* Dublin: Blackwater Press, 1997.

Tribunal of Inquiry. *Report of the Tribunal of Inquiry (Dunnes Payments).* Dublin: Stationery Office, 1997.

Vaughan, W. E. *A New History of Ireland.* Vol. 6, *Ireland Under the Union, II 1870–1921.* Oxford: Oxford University Press, 1996.

Woodham-Smith, Cecil. *The Great Hunger.* New York: Old Town Books, 1962.

INDEX